WOMEN AND EQUALITY IN THE WORKPLACE

A Reference Handbook

Other Titles in ABC-CLIO's
**CONTEMPORARY
WORLD ISSUES**
Series

Books in the Contemporary World Issues series address vital issues in today's society such as genetic engineering, pollution, and biodiversity. Written by professional writers, scholars, and nonacademic experts, these books are authoritative, clearly written, up-to-date, and objective. They provide a good starting point for research by high school and college students, scholars, and general readers as well as by legislators, businesspeople, activists, and others.

Each book, carefully organized and easy to use, contains an overview of the subject, a detailed chronology, biographical sketches, facts and data and/or documents and other primary-source material, a directory of organizations and agencies, annotated lists of print and nonprint resources, and an index.

Readers of books in the Contemporary World Issues series will find the information they need in order to have a better understanding of the social, political, environmental, and economic issues facing the world today.

WOMEN AND EQUALITY IN THE WORKPLACE

A Reference Handbook

Janet Zollinger Giele and Leslie F. Stebbins

A B C ✿ C L I O

Santa Barbara, California • Denver, Colorado • Oxford, England

Library of Congress Cataloging-in-Publication Data

Giele, Janet Zollinger.
    Women and equality in the workplace : a reference handbook / Janet Z. Giele and Leslie F. Stebbins.
        p. cm. — (Contemporary world issues)
Includes bibliographical references and index.
    ISBN 1-57607-937-6 (hardcover : alk. paper); 1-57607-938-4 (ebook)
    1. Women—Employment—United States. 2. Sex discrimination in employment—United States. 3. Sex discrimination against women—United States. 4. Sex discrimination in employment—Law and legislation—United States. 5. Women's rights—United States. I. Stebbins, Leslie F. (Leslie Foster) II. Title. III. Series.

HD6095.G48 2003
 331.4'133'0973—dc22

07 06 05 04 03   10 9 8 7 6 5 4 3 2 1

This book is also available on the World Wide Web as an e-book. Visit abc-clio.com for details.

ABC-CLIO, Inc.
130 Cremona Drive, P.O. Box 1911
Santa Barbara, California 93116-1911

This book is printed on acid-free paper ∞.
Manufactured in the United States of America

Contents

Preface

In 1973, Karen Nussbaum was working in a clerical job at Harvard when a male student entered the office, looked her in the eye, and said, "Isn't anybody here?" Though more than 40 percent of American women were in the labor force in the 1970s, their status and pay rendered many largely invisible. Thirty years later, more than 60 percent of American women are in the labor force, including very visible women such as Nancy Pelosi, the first female Democratic leader of the House of Representatives; Supreme Court Justice Ruth Bader Ginsburg; Carleton "Carly" Fiorina, president and CEO of Hewlett-Packard Company; and Karen Nussbaum, who went on to found 9 to 5, the Association of Working Women and later served as director of the Women's Bureau. In the past decade, Rebecca Marier became the first female valedictorian at West Point, Madeleine Albright served as the first female U.S. secretary of state, and the Family and Medical Leave Act was passed guaranteeing eligible men and women unpaid parental leave from work. During this same decade, the Tailhook scandal erupted when twenty-six female active duty officers of the U.S. Navy were found to have been sexually assaulted by at least seventy navy aviators, the pay gap between men and women stalled at 74 percent, and the bipartisan Glass Ceiling Commission reported that women and minority groups continue to be little represented in senior management positions and stated that the "glass ceiling" remains firmly in place. Much has changed, but much remains to be changed.

Although women have made substantial gains in employment, there remains a significant gap in pay, privilege, and leisure time between women and men. Gender equity in employment primarily concerns provision of equal opportunity to women for the same access, pay, benefits, and possibilities for power as men. This book provides an international and historical perspective on how the relative positions of women and men have changed since 1945. *Women and Equality in the Workplace* provides researchers and students with an overview of gender equity and employment issues and research. Chapter 1 contains an overview of the history of gender equity and employment in the United States and around the world. Women's increasing labor force participation, occupational and wage differentials, theories explaining these differentials, and future trends are analyzed in this chapter. Chapter 2 covers the legal remedies and social policies that have been put forward during the second half of the previous century to rectify inequalities in employment between men and women. Chapter 3 contains a detailed timeline from 1900 to the present, tracing the growing involvement of women in the paid labor force, the increase in women's educational attainment, the gradual narrowing of the pay gap, and the small decrease in occupational segregation. This chronology also contains key legal, political, and cultural events in the United States relating to gender equity and employment and selected international events to provide a comparative context. Chapter 4 highlights the lives of outstanding individuals through short biographies of pioneers who have broken the gender barrier in law, politics, sports, and the academic world. Chapter 5 summarizes recent U.S. legislation and case law related to equal opportunity for male and female workers and analyzes recent statistics for the United States as well as other countries on women's employment, sex differentials in earnings, the gender divide in occupations, educational levels of men and women, changes in family demographics, division of home work and child care duties by gender, prevalence of discrimination and sexual harassment, and new related issues that are emerging on the international front. Chapter 6 lists names, addresses, and descriptions of organizations and research centers working on gender equity in the United States and other countries, including relevant academic programs in the United States. Chapters 7 and 8 provide annotations to key books, videos, journals, and web sites relating to pay equity, sex segregation at work, comparable worth, the history of women's work, employment experiences of African-American and immigrant men and women, sexual harassment in the workplace, work-family policy, and child care issues.

Acknowledgments

We have enjoyed working on this project together. We thank our publisher, ABC-CLIO, for helping us discover each other, and we thank Brandeis University, particularly its leading programs in Women's Studies and its innovative Library Intensive courses, for supporting our mutual interests in women's issues and work and family policy.

Janet Giele is especially indebted to the Heller School for unwavering support of her research over many years and to the Murray Research Center at Harvard University for access to its resources and for a continuing affiliation. In addition, a number of individuals have given assistance in preparation of this book, especially Jennifer Eidelman, Donna Einhorn, and Eszter Lengyel. Most of all, however, Janet thanks her co-author, Leslie Stebbins. Without Leslie's expertise as a reference librarian and as author of an earlier book in the ABC-CLIO reference series Janet would not have undertaken this assignment nor have enjoyed it or learned so much.

Leslie Stebbins would like to especially thank Janet Giele, from whom she learned so much these past two years. As the force behind this book, Janet's experience, wisdom, generosity, and intellectual skills were invaluable. Leslie is also grateful for the support of the Brandeis University Libraries and particularly the reference librarian staff for their support of her flexible part-time schedule. She thanks the interlibrary loan staff for all their assistance. She would also like to thank Alicia Merritt and Mim Vasan at ABC-CLIO for their help along the way.

Lastly, as two professional women who are both wives and mothers, we express our gratitude to our families for their love and support and for giving us insight into the many ways in which work and family obligations can support as well as conflict with each other. As Janet's children are now adults, memories of working and child care arrangements during the 1960s and 1970s add a historical dimension to our work. On the other hand, Leslie's Anna and Will keep our insights current about the challenges for working parents of a preschool and a school-age child today. Through it all, both David Giele and Tom Blumenthal have demonstrated that fathers do share in child care and household work and that men can also be very good at cooking dinner. We thank them all.

1

Women's Progress toward Equality in Employment

All around the world, it has long been observed that women and men tend to do different kinds of work. Most troubling from the standpoint of equality between the sexes is the persistent disparity in pay and prestige that accompanies these different kinds of work. The three general factors that are most often cited as explanations for gender inequality at work are historical and institutional factors (culture), preferences of employers (often termed "discrimination"), and choices of employees (due to socialization). *Culture* refers to the prevailing values and social and economic conditions where the individual is located. *Discrimination* refers to different ways that employers treat males and females by hiring females into female-labeled occupations and by hiring males into jobs usually done by men. *Socialization* refers to the different kinds of upbringing and cultural expectations to which the sexes are exposed throughout their lives that cause them to prefer different kinds of work and to make different choices in the occupations they pursue (England, 1992: 43).

Throughout this book, the term *sex* refers to male and female persons, and *gender* refers to the masculine or feminine qualities of personality, occupation, or social roles that are typically associated with each sex. This usage follows a distinction that is generally accepted among social scientists whereby sex refers to the physical or biological distinctions between men and women that they are born with, and gender refers to the socially and culturally defined characteristics of males and females that are thought to be learned. Implicitly, the *sex* of a person is treated as a given

1

that only in rare instances is ambiguous or can be changed. The *gender* of a person, on the other hand, refers to behavior that, because it is learned, is understood to be malleable. Social roles thus have the potential for being "gendered" in a masculine or feminine direction as a continuous variable, or dichotomously as "male" or "female" (for a discussion of these two approaches, see Giele, 1988: 294; Udry, 2000). In this volume, the discussion of gender equity in employment is based on the assumption that the degree of equity is subject to variation and change depending on the surrounding cultural and historical context, the degree of discrimination, and the type of socialization, as well as the efforts of advocates and policymakers to advance equality and justice.

Before analyzing current statistics and theories on gender inequity and discrimination in employment, this chapter first examines how culture, discrimination, and socialization interact in shaping gendered expectations about work. One of the central troubling questions of this book is how and why gender inequity in employment can persist nearly universally over time and throughout the world. Comparison across countries shows that conditions of women's and men's employment differ with a given society's level of economic development. The greatest gender inequity appears in rural peasant societies such as those found in Europe before industrialization or in Russia and China before the Communist revolutions. But even in established democratic and enlightened nations such as the Scandinavian countries, the United States, and Canada, and also in the relatively new democracies such as India and Japan, there are still pervasive disparities in work, pay, and benefits that accrue to women and men. Throughout the world, women as a class are found in lower prestige jobs, are receiving lower pay and fewer benefits, and are more likely to be found in dead-end jobs without chance for promotion or upward mobility.

This chapter first considers the evidence and explanations for gender inequity in employment from a historical and global perspective. After reviewing the massive rise of women's labor force participation that came with industrialization, it then focuses on the case of the United States and current differentials between women and men in earnings, training, and occupations. The chapter concludes with a brief consideration of possible solutions for the future, including some ideas from feminist theory.

Gender Equity from an International Perspective

Women and men appear to have much more nearly equal status and power in hunting-and-gathering economies like those of the American Indians or African Bushmen, and in the advanced urban centers of most societies (Boserup, 1970). The effect of industrialization is to bring more and more women into paid employment, whether in the textile mills of nineteenth–century New England or in the new industrial enclaves in Mexico or China. Because more people—both men and women—are employed in manufacturing, stores and offices, and professional jobs than in the older rural economy, advocates for economic development have argued that modernization is the most efficient means of ridding a society of poverty and improving the lives of all.

Paradoxically, however, modernization has not always turned out to be a savior; in some instances, women's situation relative to men appears to have worsened during the initial stages of economic development. In postcolonial African countries or contemporary Latin America, for example, economic development appears to have differentially advanced the interests of men and women so that men were drawn into the modern sector and women were left behind in rural areas or were pulled off the land into the informal economy of street vendors and casual workers, where their lives became less secure (Weil, 1992; Safa, 1990). Moreover, the class and racial discrimination left over from traditional society further deepen the inequity experienced by those minority women for whom sex discrimination is yet another burden.

The Promise of Modernization

Over the past century, women who live in modern nations have generally seen an improvement in their political, economic, and social status. By 1985 they constituted at least half of all secondary school students in many industrialized nations and almost half of all college and university students as well. Women's participation in the paid labor force of many industrial countries steadily rose from about 20 percent in 1900 to more than 50 percent by 1990 (United Nations, 2000: 110). The contemporary world has come to expect that these trends will continue. Women's equality and freedom of choice have become identified with modernism and men's unquestioned privilege with traditionalism.

Clear improvements have resulted in women's educational and employment opportunities. As women's worldwide literacy rate rose from 59 to 68 percent between 1960 and 1985, their labor force participation in the developed world also rose, from 42 to 57 percent. In the decade between 1968 and 1977, the female earnings gap improved by an average of 10 percentage points (Cook, Lorwin, and Daniels, 1984; Sivard, 1985). Parental leaves and child care facilities that were almost inconceivable in the 1950s era of the "feminine mystique" had become the norm in the Scandinavian countries by 1980, and a child care act was mandated by the U.S. Congress in 1990.

But there are several tendencies that challenge the connection between modernization and women's equality:

1. *Despite reform efforts on behalf of women, industrialization does not necessarily guarantee sex equality.* Japan's highly educated female citizens are steered away from demanding professions and managerial posts. Instead, they are encouraged as young office workers to turn their talents to purely decorative and expressive functions and, after marriage, to motherhood and homemaking. The socialist state once appeared to hold great promise for gender equality, and central and eastern European nations pursued a gender policy of full employment for women. Now with the fall of these regimes and a shift to a capitalist economy, many women have been left unemployed.

2. *Increased participation in the modern paid labor force does not necessarily bring full economic equality for the sexes.* The Nordic countries with their relatively high rates of labor force participation still report an overall index of occupational segregation at 32 percent, meaning roughly one-third of men and women would need to change their occupations to eliminate segregation (Helina and Anker, 2001). In the United States, the overall index of sex segregation, as measured across nine major occupational categories, declined from 41.8 in 1972 to 33.7 in 1995. To calculate the index, the differences between percentages of the male and female population in each occupational category are summed and divided by 2. (The index for 1972 was calculated from Table 5.1 in Blau and Ferber, 1992: 121; and for 1995 from Blau, Ferber, and Winkler, 1998: 351.)

In Japan since World War II, it is still extremely difficult for women to have a career without completely foregoing marriage and family life. Nor do women in the Third World necessarily benefit in every way by joining the paid labor force. Rural women, such as those packing grapes in Chile, may become seasonal wage laborers but at the same time be exposed to chemicals and work extremely long hours standing on their feet all day. Although many of them at first appreciate the relative liberation provided by this wage labor, they must struggle the rest of the year in unpaid labor raising their own crops and then must return to the jobs provided by agro-business because no other alternatives are available. They are converted into a dependent labor class whose families have gradually sold off their small farms to the grape producers (Bee, 2000).

3. *Enlightened social policies for child care, parental leave, and equal employment opportunity do not necessarily produce gender equality in public life, the workplace, or the home.* The Nordic countries, which have the most favorable public policy in support of gender equality, report underrepresentation of women in top business and professional positions relative to men and noticeable sex-typing of male and female jobs. Central and eastern Europe, whose countries have likewise had official state policies supporting sex equality, have not been able to avoid job segregation and overburdening of women on the home front.

The Impact of Globalization

Obstacles to women's equality became apparent both in reports of the United Nations Decade for Women (1976–1985) and in the actual experience of the Third World as the development process unfolded. Mechanization of agriculture and export cash crops such as flowers or luxury foods drew women out of subsistence production and resulted in rising food imports and a food crisis in a number of African and Latin American countries. Nor did women's status improve as they entered the informal sector or marginal jobs in the cities, where their pay and security were very low (Mehra and Gammage, 1999).

In fact, the new global cities like London, New York, and Tokyo create high demand for informal services to the very wealthy and powerful global leaders who live there. Advanced capitalism creates more, rather than fewer, part-time and labor-intensive jobs in the boutiques and restaurants of the global cities. Sweatshops and informal labor relations not only help to supply the new types of apparel, crafts, food services, and domestic help required by high-income professionals and entrepreneurs; the informal and unregulated nature of these services also draws on a population of needy immigrants, women, and racial and ethnic minority groups whose need for work makes them the logical labor supply for this new demand (Sasson, 1991; Yeoh, Huang, and Willis, 2000).

The global economy is also differentiated between the urban and industrial First World countries at the core and the developing countries at the periphery, which provide raw materials and cheap labor to the core. What disturbed women-in-development scholars during the 1980s was the worsening situation of Third World women who were forced off the land by the need to earn wages and who thus joined the migratory or urban labor force. A recurrent theme of the 1990s was the growing casualization (part-time, nonstandard, and temporary work) of the labor force, particularly of women and minorities, that has come about with the general shift in economic activity to the service sector and the creation of a single global market. Contemporary development, rather than fostering equality, thus appears to deepen inequality by exploiting the most vulnerable people on the economic periphery while it serves the interest of those with wealth or education who inhabit the modern core (Sales and Gregory, 1999; Yeoh, Huang, and Willis, 2000).

The U.N. Decade for Women in the 1980s reflected these trends in the call by scholars and feminists for a better and more equitable *redistribution* of the rewards of development (Gallin, Aronoff, and Ferguson, 1989; Ward, 1990). By the end of the 1990s, however, globalization was beginning to be understood in a new way. Transnational corporations easily moved capital across national boundaries and jobs to locations with less stringent regulations of working conditions and pay. A web of interconnectedness had replaced the Cold War between the Soviet bloc and the West, and the new result was reorganization of production, labor, and services so that the traditional manufacturing jobs of men declined and the clerical and service occupations of women gained in relative size and importance (Mehra and Gammage, 1999).

In her account of Beijing Plus Five, Jo Freeman (2000) summarizes the continuity and change in concerns of the world's women between 1995 and 2000. At the Fourth World Conference of Women in Beijing in 1995, the source of many problems was identified as being "structural adjustment" policies of the

International Monetary Fund that required governments to modernize their economies in ways that many felt hurt women. By 2000, however, the major concern was "globalization" of the world economy, which seems to aggravate the poverty of women by leading to privatization of public services, liberalization of trade that hurts home industries, deregulation of national economies, and the continuing substitution of cash crops for food production.

In new global cities such as London, women became a larger portion of the labor force, 40 percent compared with 36 percent in the labor force outside London. Pay differentials between men and women decreased during the 1990s among all employees. In the United Kingdom, the gender wage gap among the top ten percent of employees decreased from a 33 percent difference in 1981 to 28.3 percent in 1995, as compared with a steeper drop among the bottom 10 percent of employees (from 32.6 to 22.5 percent) and a virtual disappearance of any difference among the lowest-paid male and female manual workers (from 37.5 to 6.27 percent). But this declining inequity at the bottom is illusory, because the full-time work and real wages of men in manufacturing have deteriorated to the extent that men are no longer much better off than women (Breugel, 1999). Blau and Kahn (2000) describe a similar situation in the United States, and Hartmann (2000) points out that the rate of progress in pay equity has slowed to the point where women's gains in weekly earnings relative to men's have virtually halted.

Factors that Promote Equality

History shows a very rough association between modernization and women's attainment of citizenship. Between 1890 and the mid-1920s, the first countries to give women the vote were the non-Catholic western democracies, various European colonies, the Soviet Union, and the United States. Next came eastern Europe, western European Catholic countries such as France and Italy, and the most developed countries of the Third World that granted woman suffrage between 1930 and 1950. Finally, since 1950, a variety of African, Muslim, and newly independent countries such as Kenya, Pakistan, and Indonesia have adopted woman suffrage (Pharr, 1981; Sivard, 1985). Since World War II, efforts to realize women's equality have had to address a whole new set of social and material conditions including the further democratization and industrialization of Japan, southeast Asia, Latin America, and central and eastern Europe. Between 1975 and 1985, the resolutions of the U. N. Decade for Women (Fraser 1987) repeatedly called for changes in the laws to ensure equality for women. The Fourth World Conference of Women, held in Beijing in 1995, reiterated these demands and further elaborated them beyond political equality to economic rights, access to health care and contraception, rights to own property, and condemnation of violence against women (Freeman, 2000).

The ideal of gender equality implies equal opportunities for women and men both in leadership and management and in productive as well as caregiving work. Equality in productive work implies equal education, job opportunities, and pay. Equality in caregiving work implies support for women's and men's family roles as parents in ways that neither confine them exclusively to the home nor overburden them with household work.

By these standards, the most developed societies appear to have made considerable progress on the caregiving side, as reflected in men's increased help with the household tasks and in greater availability of household conveniences to relieve women of household drudgery. But women in these societies are still fighting subordination in the workplace, and in all countries they are strikingly underrepresented in elective office. Women in central and eastern Europe and the USSR have in the past had the opposite problem; they were expected to be men's equals in the workplace, but they were grossly overburdened at home. Women in the Third World seem to be doubly oppressed. In their productive roles, they have been proletarianized as they are increasingly integrated into the world economy. They are also heavily burdened with family responsibilities that range from child care and cooking to obtaining water, gathering firewood, and growing their own food. As a result, women in each type of society have responded with women's movements or a version of feminism that is aimed at improving their particular situation.

Women's protest movements have had an important role around the world in advancing women's interests and gender equity at work and at home. These movements have tended to take different shapes depending on the social context. Feminism in the industrial capitalist economies like western Europe and the United States has focused on winning the same political rights for women as those enjoyed by men. In nations with a strong socialist tradition, however, such as the former Soviet Union and the eastern European countries, a focus on gender equality has usually taken a back seat to workers' movements to win labor rights from employers and owners. The Third World presents still other patterns of mobilization, in which women's movements focus on women's family roles, their rights as workers and citizens, or efforts to improve the whole community.

Feminism in Industrialized Capitalist Nations

After World War II, the industrial nations experienced an unprecedented growth in the service occupations that typically employed women. Women's labor force participation rose sharply, particularly among women in middle and older age groups (Oppenheimer, 1970). A new feminist movement combined a critique of personal life with active efforts to expand women's rights and opportunities. Sweden in particular adopted far-reaching policies for sex equality and began a review of its employment and family policies to encourage women's advancement (Liljestrom, Mellstrom, and Svensson, 1978). Feminists in the United States and Canada created both women's liberation groups and feminist political organizations in the 1960s. Their informal support groups established communication and trust among women from diverse backgrounds. Formal groups investigated women's educational and job opportunities, documented sex segregation and discrimination, and began developing an agenda for change (Carden, 1974). Even in Japan, where women were still much more likely to seek jobs than careers, a women's movement emerged in the 1960s that included both consciousness-raising groups and formal organizations working for equal opportunity laws (Pharr, 1981).

Through the 1990s, considerable progress was made. The Nordic countries with their explicit and official policy for sex equality had 70 to 80 percent of women in the labor force, and women's pay stood at 77–93 percent of men's (Sivard, 1985). Although starting from a lower base than the Nordic countries, women's labor force participation in the United States rose from 38 to 57 percent between 1960 and 1990, and pay equity in hourly earnings steadily improved from 64 to 74 percent between 1979 and 1988 (U.S. Department of Labor, 1989: 160–161; 1990: 2). The 1989 reunification of the two Germanies signaled a massive change when the socialist East with its past record of nearly all women being in the labor force joined the capitalist West, which had only slightly more than half of its women in the labor force.

Social policies in all of these countries (whether Nordic, American, or European) now appear to support a dual role for a significant percentage of women as both paid workers and family members.

Great Britain and Japan have shown more ambivalence in their attitude toward the ideal woman's role and in fact still tilt toward the traditional home-based role for women. Thus, official British policy only grudgingly supports child care centers. And in Japan, young college women find it very difficult to envision any long-term career other than that of wife and mother. Although it is difficult to say whether the British and Japanese experience will eventually replicate the Nordic and American patterns, it appears that the terms of the feminist debate are very similar in all of the industrial countries—whether to choose family, career, or a combination of the two. The implications for men mirror this debate: many happily marry a woman who works for pay, and if so, they provide some help at home.

The dominant trend since 1970 has been the emergence of three main patterns of male and female roles (Blossfeld and Drobnic, 2001; Hakim, 2000). The first pattern, though now in the minority, continues the traditional husband-breadwinner and wife-homemaker combination. In the second dual-worker pattern, both husband and wife are in paid employment, and both participate in housework and child care, although the husband tends to work more hours outside the home and the wife does much more inside the home (Hochschild, 1990). Finally, a third large group is made up of single employed adults, men and women, who maintain one-person households; this group has grown phenomenally since 1950 (Goldscheider and Waite, 1991).

The Socialist Experience
In socialist and Communist countries, the first wave of feminism stemmed from different sources and took a different course from the social democratic and capitalistic nations. The tradition of *socialist feminism* was not so much concerned with women's suffrage or higher education as with economic and political power for laboring people. Russian revolutionaries criticized women's isolated work in the middle-class household and advocated women's full involvement in work outside the home. In 1918, the new Soviet government instituted far-reaching reforms that guaranteed legal equality of husband and wife, equal education, equal employment, and the equal right to vote and hold public office.

Women in the USSR after 1918 and in the German Democratic Republic after 1950 also had some form of maternity leave and child care (Mandel, 1975: 55; Ecklein, 1982: 187). Because of heavy losses during World War II, women were very much needed in industry and the professions just to keep both German and Soviet societies running. During the 1950s in the Soviet Union, there were only 59 men to every 100 women in the middle age group (35–59). A very strong tradition of women's labor force participation emerged, combined with women's normal family duties.

Women in the eastern bloc countries, however, were the first to protest the "double burden" of employment and family responsibilities. Men's roles did not change as much with women's employment as in the West. Moreover, conveniences such as washing machines, indoor plumbing, and well-stocked supermarkets were scarce. In the 1990s as central and eastern European countries turned toward democracy and a Western-style economy, issues of gender equity have taken a different turn. The former East Germany is a good example. Where before people hoped for more household conveniences and consumer goods and less time at work and more time at home, there is now disappointment at the loss of government-supported social services such as universal child care. In addition, many women who want to work are now unemployed. In fact, in eastern Europe as a whole there has been a noticeable drop in women's economic activity rates, from 57 percent in 1980 to 53 percent in 1997. This is in marked contrast to the situation in western Europe, where women's economic activity rates rose from 47 percent to 55 percent over the same period (United Nations, 2000: Chart 5.2, p. 110).

Women's Movements in the Third World
Because political and cultural traditions of developing countries are quite diverse, they are not easily characterized with respect to feminism and women's empowerment. Muslim women in the Middle East and north Africa are traditionally secluded and their activities strictly segregated from those of men. Latin American women combine traditions derived from strong female roles of native Indian society as well as the cultural pattern of male domination or machismo derived from Spanish and Portuguese colonization. Women in east and west Africa have long had independence as food producers and traders.

Nevertheless, several forms of feminism have emerged in developing countries. These movements parallel the three forms of feminism found both in the developed nations of the West and in the socialist societies of the eastern bloc (Jacquette, 1982). Something akin to domestic feminism (based on women's private roles as mothers and caregivers) is found where women mobilize neighborhood and community resources to make their daily household chores less difficult. The analog of equal rights feminism (based on women's public roles as workers and citizens) appears as protest where gender is the basis for excluding women from democratic rights of citizenship that are becoming available to men. Finally, a form of women's mobilization somewhat similar to socialist feminism can be found where gender has historically been not as important as working-class solidarity in obtaining rights of employees to organize and bargain for better hours, pay, and job security.

Domestic or maternal women's movements in Latin America provide some of the best examples of feminism in support of women's traditional roles. These movements have emerged where there has been a breakdown in the subsistence economy that, in a number of instances, was triggered by the debt crisis of the 1980s. Women developed local communal dining, health, and child care cooperatives to meet the heavier work load that resulted from the economic crisis: a triple burden of domestic responsibility, paid work, and informal market work (cottage industry, domestic service, or street vending). In one nation after another, these women's movements have demanded help from the state (sometimes with the support of female candidates) to provide for such improvements in the infrastructure as drinking water, electricity, housing, sanitation, and transportation (Acosta-Belen and Bose, 1990; Deere, 1987; Nash, 1990; Safa 1990). Other domestic feminist movements, such as that represented by Las Madres de Plaza de Mayo, who protested against the government-sponsored abduction of their family members in Argentina, have protested human rights violations and the disappearance of loved ones in repressive regimes. Here again, women's foray into the public sphere is primarily based on their traditional roles as mothers and guardians of the home rather than on an ideology of equal rights.

Equal rights women's movements, on the other hand, are primarily oriented toward securing equal rights for women in the public sphere. In Chile, for example, a group of twelve women's organizations was able in the 1970s to draft the Demands of Women for Democracy, which included a constitutional guarantee of equality between women and men (Lago, 1987). In Brazil, a National Council on Women's Rights presented women's proposals for the new Brazilian constitution (Safa, 1990). This type of feminism appears to have more chance of developing where there is already a trend toward democracy and where men have already attained major rights of citizenship.

Socialist feminism emerges in those situations in which both women and men organize to resist oppression along class or racial lines. Such was the case, for example, in South Africa during the 1940s and 1950s in the canning and food processing industry (Berger, 1990). Unionization of the industry skipped the stage of feminism that focuses on particular gender interests and moved directly to challenging the corporate owners and the state (Acosta-Belen and Bose, 1990). Such movements seem most likely where, as in the South African case, class or racial oppression are felt by both sexes. In these cases, women and children as well as men are involved in the labor force and in efforts for reform. Benefits to workers are benefits to men and women alike and to the community and family as well.

Feminist Issues in the New Global Economy

As integration of the world economy becomes ever tighter, flows of immigrant populations are moving to where work is available, and migration has increased greatly across national borders since the 1980s. Farm laborers, household workers, computer programmers, sex workers, and doctors and nurses are among those who are in demand and are allowed to immigrate either temporarily or permanently by the countries who need them. Arlie Hochschild (2000) has described the nanny chains that bring Filipino women to the United States or to work for rich families in the Middle East. Maps depicting the state of the world's women show the flows of sex workers who originate in donor nations such as southeast Asia and are employed in western Europe and in North America (Seager, 1997). More than just a question of a "market" between supply and demand, these flows raise social and moral questions about the quality of life of the nannies who have to leave their own children to take care of others or the sex workers who are lured into exploitive conditions that are hard to escape and that may further endanger them through sexually transmitted diseases. One of the recurrent themes in the Beijing Plus Five meetings of 2000 was the variety of crimes against women that are condoned or ignored by nations that see women primarily as wives and mothers rather than as equal citizens. Advocates of the rights of women see these offenses not as "private" crimes but as violations of human rights: rape; trafficking in women; and such traditional practices as female genital mutilation, early and forced marriage, and so-called honor crimes that bring punishment or execution to a woman who is thought to have ruined her family's honor (Freeman, 2000).

Poor and uneducated men are also exploited as, for example, in slave-like conditions in northern Brazil where they are entrapped by long hours, lack of pay, and debt imposed by their employers (Rohter, 2002). One response to these conditions has been the worldwide organization of workers in the informal economy. An example is Women in the Informal Economy Globalizing and Organizing (WIEGO), which is a loose network of worker activists, advocates, and scholars who are using unionizing principles to give voice to a barely visible class of workers (see chapter 6 on organizations). Their publications deal particularly with domestics, home-based workers (such as apparel makers who do piece work in their homes), and street vendors. WIEGO is concerned with such fundamental issues as raising pay rates for piece work and working with local municipalities around the world to give street vendors permits and places to ply their trade without constantly being hounded or arrested. Together with rights to such employment come related questions of rights to a minimum wage, decent working conditions, and entitlement to social protection that is available to employees in the formal economy.

Women's Rising Labor Force Participation in the United States

The issues of inequality between women and men in the workplace were not really visible so long as women's work was largely confined to the home and therefore was unpaid. Economists refer to such unpaid labor as nonmarket or informal work (meaning that it takes place outside the boundaries of the money economy), and workers in paid and unpaid employment are treated quite differently. Entry of more women into the paid labor force, however, raises many questions about whether women and men are in fact equal in their capabilities and whether the conditions and rewards for their work should also be equal. Historically, there were many efforts to exclude women from certain types of work, such as heavy manual work like construction or high-status professions like law and medicine. It is therefore instructive to examine the factors that led to the rise in women's labor force participation and the growing acceptance of women in an ever-wider range of occupations.

Three main factors have contributed to women's growing presence in the work force from the nineteenth century up to the present. The first factor is greater demand that is seen in new work opportunities for women. The second factor is a growth in women's labor supply, meaning women's growing availability for paid work and their greater desire and preparation for paid work outside the home. The third factor is the reorganization of work sites, the family division of labor, and the individual life patterns of women and men that together enable women to take the employment that is available to them. These factors have all appeared in somewhat different guises depending on the era. Nineteenth-century industrialization was associated with employment mainly of single women before they married and had children. This pattern persisted until after World War II, when more older married women were pulled back into the labor force after their children had grown up. On the threshold of the twenty-first century, a new pattern appears to be emerging in which women as well as men are more or less continuously employed and in which women's housework and caregiving responsibilities are somewhat reduced as a result of household conveniences, help from husbands, and more use of outside services such as restaurants and child care centers. The focus here is on the changes in women's employment since 1950.

New Job Opportunities (Changes in Demand)

As late as 1940, almost half (43 percent) of the United States population lived in rural areas, and the work of women and men was intertwined with that of the family farm (Gibson and Lennon, 1999). The Second World War brought many women into the labor force to help the war effort, but, like "Rosie the Riveter," they were then demobilized from the shipyards and factories where they had been employed (see chapter 8 for a video on Rosie the Riveter). Economists were somewhat puzzled, however, that women's employment was still on the rise in the 1950s even as the suburbs were growing and the baby boom was in full swing. It had been thought that women worked primarily out of economic need; either they were single and had no male support, or their husbands did not make enough money. Yet, although fewer women were single and the incomes of married men were getting better, more women were taking paid work, especially married women. Two answers to this puzzle were provided by Jacob Mincer and Valerie Oppenheimer.

Mincer (1962) showed that over the long run, rising pay for women's work outweighed the short-run effect that high family income usually had in keeping a woman out of the labor force. This was due to the changing value of a woman's time. According to Mincer, the family made a rational decision to encourage her to work because her leisure and unpaid productive work in the home were more costly to them; the money she could earn in the labor force more than made up for the costs of buying additional home appliances, eating out more often, or hiring outside services.

Oppenheimer (1970) offered a demographic explanation for the phenomenon. She found that the demand for female workers increased just as a smaller-than-usual cohort of women born during the Depression were entering the labor market. The postwar baby boom had created a great demand for teachers, and thousands of new clerical jobs had opened up. Scarcity of labor supply met a rising demand for workers in female-labeled jobs. Moreover, there was a scarcity of young unmarried women, the traditional group of women who were most likely to be employed. As a result, the age and marriage barriers to women's employment began to soften. Women who had the needed qualifications were hired despite the fact that they were older, married, and even in some cases had children.

Roughly a decade after the baby boom abated in the mid-1960s, Richard Easterlin (1978), a demographer, began to predict that more women would eventually return to the home. He reasoned that this would be especially likely if young men's salaries returned to the relatively high levels of the postwar period. This never happened, however. Women's labor force participation has continued to rise throughout the past half century. The trend was first noticeable among married women and mothers of older children, then among mothers of school-age and younger children. In

1988, a landmark was reached when for the first time in modern history, more than half of all mothers of infants under a year old were in the paid labor force, some full-time, some part-time, and some for part of the year (Moen, 1992: 15).

Changes in Women's Availability and Desire for Employment (Labor Supply)

Even at the time of Easterlin's hypothesis about a likely fall in women's labor supply, Valerie Oppenheimer (1979) predicted that history would prove him wrong. Oppenheimer argued that women were not just in the labor force to help their families "make ends meet," but that in addition they enjoyed the independence and sense of control that they felt from being paid for their work and the added discretionary income that could help pay college tuition or raise the family's standard of living. Coincidentally, women's rising levels of education fit them for better-paying and more satisfying jobs. In addition, women were living longer and were having fewer children who were born more closely together, thus giving them more "child-free" years for work outside the home between the time their youngest child went to school and their own retirement age (Giele, 1978: 147).

Statistical trends over the ensuing decades indeed give more support to the explanation of Oppenheimer than of Easterlin. As real per capita income rose from $22,870 in 1990 (in 1996 constant dollars that take inflation into account) to $27,642 in 2000, married women's labor force participation also rose from 58.4 percent in 1990 to 61.3 percent in 2000 (U.S. Bureau of the Census, 2001: Tables 652, 575). A temporary need for more income hardly seems sufficient explanation for this seemingly one-way upward trend in women's labor force participation.

Reorganization of Work, Family, and Life Patterns

In order for the massive change in women's employment to occur, there had to be a major shift in three interlocking institutional structures—work, family, and the timing of individual life schedules. These schedules involved the way individuals timed major life events such as school completion, entry into the work force, family formation, and retirement. In fact, a shift in all of these structures did take place and has only become fully evident during the 1990s. The structure of work was affected by a decline in manufacturing and the growth of a service-based economy that brought a decrease in the jobs where men predominated. At the same time, the rise of professional, retail, and office work drew many women to fill those posts. Family change, as seen in smaller families and greater frequency of divorce, gave women time and motivation to take on gainful employment. In the process, both women and men became increasingly used to the idea that wives and mothers as well as husbands and fathers would be employed and would combine multiple roles in the workplace and in the home. These changes in work and family in turn affected the typical and expected life schedules of men and women. Rather than a linear model of doing one thing at a time and a clear division of labor between the gainful work of men and the home-based work of women, a new crossover model of multiple roles began to infuse the lives of both sexes.

Changes in the Workplace

The economic forces that continued to fuel women's rising employment in the 1980s and 1990s were partly the result of changes in the jobs available. Gone were the secure jobs with promotions and permanency that had been available to unionized workers and many male breadwinners. In their place emerged corporations that were prone to finding new locations where they could hire cheap labor and pay low taxes. Computers and mechanization also reduced the need for special skills and craft knowledge in many occupations. Many jobs became part-time, and a larger proportion than before became either temporary or contingent on rise and fall in demand (Hakim, 1996; Blossfeld and Hakim, 1997).

These conditions have put pressure on male wages and made the help of a wife in supporting a family much more common than in the past. At the same time, the creation of part-time and contingent positions, in which hiring and layoffs are expected as a result of ups and downs in the business cycle, has drawn female workers who are in search of schedules that are compatible with their family responsibilities. These new patterns have, however, sparked concern on the part of labor leaders and women's advocates, who are worried that income at the bottom of the pay scale is falling even further and that old-style labor unions have lost much of their power to domination by corporations (Aronowitz

and DiFazio, 1994; Reich, 1992). The growth of part-time and contingent work inherently undermines the collective bargaining
power of workers and of women in such jobs. Growing income
inequality between families is another result of the increase in
women's employment (Blossfeld and Drobnic, 2001).

Changes in the Family

A number of structural changes in family life have also reinforced
the changes in employment and contributed to more egalitarian
and increasingly similar patterns in men's and women's family
lives. Between 1950 and 1998, the fertility rate fell from more than
three children per American woman during her lifetime to just
over two children per woman in 1998 (Moen, 1992: 24; World Fact
Book, 1998). As a result of the rise in divorce and the increasing
numbers of children in single-parent families, these single mothers are now responsible for roughly one-quarter of all U.S. children and more than half of all black children in 2000. Rising standards of education have also given two-parent families a reason
to supplement their income with a wife's work to help pay for a
college education for their children (Oppenheimer, 1982). The
upshot has been a major shift in family norms from a division of
labor between a male breadwinner and female homemaker to a
more flexible division of labor in which the ideal is for men to do
family work as well as paid work and for women to do paid work
outside the home as well as caring work inside it.

In addition to these internal structural changes in the family,
improved household technology has also played a role in rein-
forcing the new egalitarian worker-parent ideal for both sexes.
Cheap ready-made clothes, the frozen dinner and microwave, the
automated clothes washer and dryer, thermostat-controlled heat-
ing systems, and the refrigerator and supermarket have all
greatly lessened the daily chores of sewing, cooking, laundry,
stoking the furnace, or shopping and preserving food that once
took many hours of a housewife's time. Indeed, the craft knowledge once needed to perform these tasks is now no longer necessary, and someone with little training or experience can heat up a
precooked dinner or put a load of laundry into the washing
machine.

The growth of outside services such as child care and cleaning services has also somewhat lessened reliance on the household and the homemaker as the sole provider of personal and
domestic care. Between 1970 and 1990, there was a phenomenal

growth in provision of child care outside the home so that by 1990, roughly 85 percent of all U.S. preschool children were receiving some form of care outside their homes in center-based care, family day care, or the homes of relatives (Hayes, Palmer, and Zaslow, 1990).

The most dramatic sign of the change toward a worker-parent ideal for both sexes is seen in the welfare reform legislation of 1996. The Personal Responsibility and Work Opportunity Reconciliation Act (PRWORA) of 1996 removed the public assistance to lone mothers of Aid to Families with Dependent Children (AFDC), which had been available since the 1930s. As more and more mothers in two-parent families were combining family work with paid work, the welfare mothers began to seem relatively privileged in their freedom not to work and to stay home with their children (Bergmann, 1996). The purpose of the new legislation was to set time limits—a maximum of five years—for receipt of assistance and to encourage single mothers to work to become self-supporting. Other goals were to encourage marriage and to discourage bearing children out of wedlock, objectives that the old AFDC forms of assistance were thought to undermine.

Changes in the Typical Life Course

The results of the massive changes in workplace and family have come home to the individual in the form of new expectations about the optimum timing of major life events. Instead of a distinct life path for women that is different from that of men, both sexes now expect to carry multiple work and family responsibilities most of the time. Up until the end of World War II, the clear pattern for both sexes was to finish school before getting a job, then get married, and then have children. The GI bill (Service Men's Readjustment Act of 1944) that provided college education for veterans helped to change all that. Suddenly there were married students in colleges and universities who were, in some cases, also parents and employees. Similar changes occurred throughout the industrial world, such as in Norway, Germany, and the United States (Featherman and Sørensen, 1983; Giele, 1998; Hogan, 1981). The returning veterans were the first to embody this new ideal, but as more and more married women with children continued their education into adulthood and worked outside the home, the pattern came to be widely shared not only across the gender divide but also across race and class groups. It had earlier been the poorer and less privileged women who "had" to work but who were now being joined by the broad middle class.

Variation in Employment Rates

Despite the reorganization of work, family, and life course schedules, differences by sex in labor force participation did not disappear. Instead, employment continues to vary considerably depending on the gender, education, and race of the worker as well as the age of children in the household. These individual characteristics point to a variety of differences in opportunity, wage-earning capacity, need, and cultural attitudes. At the same time, general changes in gender expectations, educational levels, and size of family are now resulting in new patterns of work over the life course of both men and women.

Employment Patterns of Men and Women

The most widely used indicator of the changing patterns of employment of women and men is their labor force participation rate, which refers to the percentage of the working-age population who are employed. Consistently throughout Europe and the United States, roughly three-quarters as many women are employed as men. In 1994 in the United States, 65 percent of working-age women were employed, compared with 79 percent of working-age men. The combined corresponding figures for fifteen European nations in 1997 were 51 percent of women employed compared with 71 percent of men. Another distinct sex difference appears in the proportion working part-time, 25 percent of women in the United States in 1994 compared with only 11 percent of men. The gap is even more dramatic in Europe (32 percent women vs. 6 percent men) where roughly one out of three employed women is working part-time compared with only one out of twenty men (Hakim, 2000).

Presence of children in the household is one of the strongest factors in lowering women's rates of employment and raising their proportion in part-time work. By contrast, men's rates show little variation by presence of young children in the household. The employment rates of married women are progressively lower, the younger their children are. In 2000, for example, 93.5 percent of men with children ages six to seventeen were working, compared with 78.7 percent of women. The comparison between men and women who had children under the age of six showed that almost all men (96.1 percent) compared with around two-thirds (64.6 percent) of all women were employed (U.S. Bureau of Labor Statistics, 2001a).

Differences by Race

The common theme for white, black, and Hispanic persons alike is that men's labor force participation rates have gradually been falling since midcentury, while the rates of women have been rising. But within each sex group, there are differences by race. Among men, Hispanics have the highest participation rates (79.8 percent in 1999), then whites (75.6), and then blacks (68.7). Among women, on the other hand, blacks are higher than whites (63.5 and 59.6, respectively), and Hispanic women have the lowest rate (55.9). Many of these differences appear to be due to educational levels. Black men have somewhat lower levels of education than other groups. The manual and manufacturing jobs that once employed men with less than a high school education are fast dwindling, and black unemployment is roughly twice as high as for whites, 8.0 percent in 1999 compared with 3.7 percent for whites (Blau, Ferber, and Winkler, 2002: 87, 275). The lower rates for Hispanic women appear to result from having larger families with more children at home and from their own preference for somewhat more domestically oriented roles.

Changing Employment Profiles over the Life Course

Along with the general rise in the proportion of women employed and the gradual decline in men's rates, there has been a subtle shift in the spacing of work over the life course. The first important change is particularly visible in the lives of men and results in the bunching of life events into three main phases—education, work, and retirement. Retirement plans were first supported by European and American governments in the late nineteenth century, as a result of improved health and longer life expectancy, to provide economic security for the aged as well as employment opportunities to younger people. The result was not only a gradual decline in the overall participation rates of men but a tendency toward ever earlier ages of retirement (Kohli 1986; Kohli, Rein, Guillemard, and Van Gunsteren, 1991). In cases where women's retirement pensions were linked to their husbands, they had an incentive to retire early also. But some women continue to reenter employment at midlife because of economic necessity (O'Rand, 1996).

For women, the main change in employment over the life course was the replacement of the M-shaped three-phase curve of labor force participation with the inverted U-shaped curve similar to men's pattern that reflects more nearly continuous employment. Thus the earlier pattern of work before childbearing, withdrawal from employment for motherhood, and subsequent return to the labor force was replaced by a shorter period out of the labor force, or the withdrawal was skipped altogether (Riley, Foner, and Waring, 1988; Giele, 1998).

Differentials in Men's and Women's Occupations and Earnings

Even as women's employment has become much more similar to men's, one persistent feature of women's work remains: its lower pay. There was dramatic improvement in women's earnings in the 1970s and 1980s, from 59 percent of men's full-time, year-round pay in 1970 to 71 percent in 1995 (Blau, Ferber, and Winkler, 1998). Nevertheless, statistical trends and detailed research continue to indicate that gender disparity is pervasive and lasting. Even as some occupations, such as editor or psychologist, have shifted from having a majority of men to a majority of women, there is concern about resegregation, male flight (men leaving jobs because those jobs are considered "women's" jobs, which happened in residential real estate sales positions), and loss of earning power and prestige (Jacobs, 1995).

Gender difference in occupations and earnings is widespread and international in scope, although countries vary in the degree of disparity and amount of improvement over time. Average hourly earnings of women are less than men's all over the world: for example, 85 percent in Sweden, 71 percent in the United States, and 65 percent in Luxembourg (Spain and Bianchi, 1996). Generally, the Scandinavian countries with their socialized government programs have the best ratios of women's to men's relative pay (85 to 90 percent); the United States and United Kingdom with their dualist public-private social programs stand at the middle of the distribution (70 to 75 percent); and the Mediterranean countries and Japan with their more patriarchal traditions of work and family roles have the lowest ratios (50 to 65 percent) (Blau, Ferber, and Winkler, 1998; Blossfeld and Drobnic, 2001).

Between 1970 and 1992 the ratio of female to male average hourly earnings in manufacturing rose about 10 percent throughout the world. For the Nordic group (Denmark, Finland, Norway, Sweden) this meant a rise from approximately 75 percent of men's earnings to roughly 85 percent. In the United States during the same period, where the increase began from a lower starting point, women's hourly wages rose from fifty-nine cents on every dollar a man earned in the early 1970s to seventy to seventy-five cents per dollar of men's earnings in the 1990s (Melkas and Anker, 1998).

Several factors account for the earnings penalty to female workers. The most important is the proportion of workers in an occupation who are female. The more concentrated women are in a job, the greater the earnings penalty. Take, for example, the occupation of teaching. In preprimary school teaching (child care), where women comprise 98 percent of the work force, women's relative pay is 59 percent of men's (based on hourly wages of males in all sectors of industry). In secondary school teaching, however, where only 56 percent of the workers are female, women's pay relative to all men's earnings in all sectors is 83 percent (OECD, 1998).

Much of the earnings gap, therefore, appears to be associated with sex-typing of occupations. Even in the Nordic countries where women's relative pay is the highest, the largest female occupational groups (in which more than 80 percent of the employees are women) are very similar to those in other countries: nurses; teachers; office workers; retail sales workers; food-related occupations like cooks and waitresses; personal care workers like hairdressers, maids, and housekeepers; and those who deal with sewing, clothing, and textiles. The largest male occupations are also familiar: architects and engineers, public officials, managers, sales supervisors, police and protective service workers, production supervisors and foremen, metal workers, and construction workers (Melkas and Anker, 1998).

Even in the same occupations, female workers are generally paid less than male workers. But the disparity is even greater in the female-labeled occupations. In the United States in 1992, female workers in the occupations with the highest percentage of females received 66 percent of the pay in hourly wages that was averaged by men across all occupational groups; the relative pay of women in all other occupational groups was 86 percent; and women overall received 73 percent of what men got. In the

Nordic countries there is also a penalty to women in female-typed occupations, but it is much smaller. In Norway, for example, women's relative pay in the top female occupations was 80 percent of men's average; women in all other occupations received 85 percent; and women overall earned on average 81 percent of what men earned (OECD, 1998).

Just as it is possible to characterize the pay differences between women and men and how they have changed, it is also possible to describe the degree to which an occupational structure has become more integrated or more nearly equal in its distribution of males and females. Similar to the pay gap between women and men that has lessened over the past thirty years, occupational disparity has also decreased. Although the proportions of U.S. women in several female-labeled occupations (e.g., social worker [63–68 percent], dietician [92–93 percent], librarian [82–84 percent], and preschool teacher [98 percent]) held fairly steady between 1970 and 1995, several male-labeled jobs showed a dramatic increase in percent female. The proportion of women architects grew by a factor of 5 (from 4 percent in 1970 to 20 percent in 1995), as did lawyers (from 5 percent to 26 percent). The share of female economists more than tripled (16 percent to 50 percent), and the ratio of female computer systems analysts and scientists more than doubled (from 14 percent to 30 percent) (Blau, Ferber, and Winkler, 1998).

The pervasive connection between women's work and lower pay makes one ask why jobs become more or less sex-typed, why certain types of occupation receive higher pay, and what workers and employers can do to increase equity between women and men. Clues to these answers emerge from a closer examination of occupations and earnings.

Gender Patterns in U.S. Occupations

The relative scarcity of women or men in an occupation is associated with two horizontal and vertical features of the occupational structure. Horizontally, jobs vary across an industry, and so does their relative attraction to each sex. Men predominate in the extractive industries such as mining, forestry and agriculture, in construction and manufacturing, in transportation, in wholesale and finance. Women predominate in retail sales, in service occupations, and in government. As the economy grew between 1964 and 1999, 70 million jobs were added, and of those, 43 million went to women and 28 million to men. This statistic shows that the tremendous growth in the women's labor force over the thirty-five-year period resulted both from new demand (creation of new jobs) and from growing labor supply (more educated women who wanted paid work). In addition, the 70 million new jobs were spread unevenly across all fields but were especially heavily distributed where women predominate: the services (43 percent increase), retail trade (20 percent increase), and government (15 percent increase). More than twice as many women as men were added in government, and 1.5 times as many in services and retail sales. In fact, women's jobs doubled in every industry or sector except manufacturing, where only 1 million jobs were added between 1964 and 1999 (U.S. Department of Labor, 2002).

The second important factor associated with a sex-typed occupation is its vertical location as represented by level of power, prestige, and authority. Fewer women than men are located at the top levels of the occupational structure. Nearly fifty years ago, the French political scientist Maurice Duverger (1955) dubbed this pattern "the higher, the fewer." A familiar example is the profession of college and university teaching. Even though the proportions of women dramatically increased in all levels of higher education between the 1970s and the 1990s, the hierarchical pattern remained and even intensified. Women were 10 percent of all professors in 1974–1975 and 16 percent twenty years later. Female associate professors went from 17 percent to 31 percent, and female assistant professors increased from 28 percent to 45 percent over the same period. Significantly, however, these increases in women were greater at the lower levels than at the top levels (Blau, Ferber, and Winkler, 1998).

It is perhaps instructive to note those professions in which women have made the largest gains in recent years and have gone from being a minority to being equally represented or a slight majority. Examples are economists (from 16 percent to 50 percent between 1970 and 1995), editors and reporters (42 percent to 53 percent), psychologists (39 percent to 59 percent), public relations specialists (27 percent to 58 percent), and secondary school teachers (50 percent to 57 percent) (Blau, Ferber, and Winkler, 1998). Unlike those fields in which there is a stable high proportion of women, such as kindergarten teachers (98 percent) or social workers (65 percent), the mixed gender occupations appear to be people-directed but with somewhat less of a requirement of intimate or personal care and more of an analytic, impersonal, or public component. The dimension of personal care that sociologist Paula England (1992) terms "nurturance" appears to be strongly associated with women's choice of professions, men's avoidance of them, and the sex labeling of occupations.

Along with the gendered association of power with males and nurturance with females, historical links are also found between occupation and race or ethnicity. Whereas white men predominate in executive and managerial positions, precision production, the crafts, and manufacturing, black men and women are found much more frequently in service occupations and as operators and laborers. They are fewer in executive and professional positions. Hispanic men and women are also more likely to be in service occupations, or work as operators and laborers; however, relatively more Hispanic men are found in farming (Blau, Ferber, and Winkler, 1998).

The Earnings Differential

The sex-typing of occupations appears to be one reason for the size of the pay gap between men and women. Women's relative pay is lowest in highly feminized occupations. Economists and demographers have explored several possibilities for why this is so. One is the greater amount of time that men spend on the job; and some traditional women's jobs, like that of kindergarten teacher, are not full-year jobs. Men's and women's earnings can be compared by using hourly, weekly, or annual wages, or the comparison can be limited to full-time, year-round workers. Depending on the basis for calculating the earnings ratios, the size of the pay gap varies dramatically, even though it has diminished over the past twenty-five years. In 1992, based on hourly wages, women's earnings were 79 percent of men's; 75 percent of weekly earnings; 71 percent of pay for full-time year-round work; and 61 percent of men's annual wages (Spain and Bianchi, 1996). Overall, based on full-time year-round work, the pay gap noticeably lessened as women's wages rose from 59 percent of men's in 1970 to 71 percent in 1995 (Blau, Ferber, and Winkler, 1998).

To understand the gender gap better, Representatives John Dingell of Michigan and Carolyn Maloney of New York asked the General Accounting Office to compile data on women in management in ten selected industries and determine how women were faring in 2000 compared with five years earlier. Using data from the Current Population Survey, the GAO found that full-time female managers earned less than their male counterparts in both 1995 and 2000, and the pay gap actually widened in seven out of ten industries. Despite gains for women over the past several decades, in 2000 only 12 percent of corporation officers were women; 60 percent of women managers had no child currently living at home; and their wages stood at 76 percent of men's. The only three industries in which female managers' earnings showed continued improvement were all in the public sector: education, hospitals and medical services, and public administration (United States General Accounting Office, 2002).

Another case study, this one of engineers, showed that women's earnings hit a glass ceiling at somewhat different levels depending on when they started their careers and how long they had worked. Morgan (1998) found virtually no wage penalty to younger women who had entered the field most recently.

These studies of managers and engineers begin to suggest factors such as type of industry or time of entry that go beyond sex alone in explaining the pay gap. Marini and Fan (1997), in a study of entry level workers and gender differences in pay, found that 30 percent of the gender gap was due to worker characteristics (such as age, sex, and race), 16 percent to level of aspirations, 14 percent to skills and credentials, and 42 percent to characteristics of the industry in which the occupations were located. These clues to the pay gap raise the question of what might be a more comprehensive explanation for the earnings penalty to women.

Explanations of the Earnings Penalty to Women

The fact that women's lower earnings can be explained in part by personal characteristics and choice and in part by employer selection and industry is an indicator that no single-factor explanation is adequate. Wage setting is instead the result of a complex process that involves both the individual woman's characteristics, actions, and choice and the employer's industry, needs, and preferences. Nevertheless, three major alternative perspectives give greater weight to one or another of these factors —employee preferences, employer discrimination, or the possibilities for social change that diminish disparities in earnings between men and women.

Preference Theory

British sociologist Catherine Hakim (2000) is one of the most out-spoken proponents of preference theory, by which she means that women's choices rather than employer discrimination are the basis for their lower earnings. Women give priority to family responsibilities over career commitment and make adjustments in their labor force participation to accommodate their families' needs. A cornerstone of Hakim's argument is that so many more women than men work at part-time jobs, 25 percent of women in the United States compared with 11 percent of men, and 32 percent of women in fifteen European Union countries compared with 6 percent of men. Women's lower earnings are thus interpreted as a natural consequence of their greater time out of the labor force for childbearing and for family responsibilities. Because their first priority is not their job, Hakim reasons that their lower educational and skill levels, shorter time on the job, and briefer work experience are not surprising. In fact, according to a 1984 survey of labor force participation over time in the United States, men spent only 1.6 percent of all their potential work years away from work, and women spent 14.7 percent of their working years out of the labor force. In 1994, those women between 29 and 33 years old who had never had a child received earnings that were 98 percent those of men in their age group (U.S. Department of Labor, 2001).

Patriarchy, Discrimination, and Segregation

A very different explanation of pay inequity comes from feminist critiques of patriarchy, by which is meant the attitudes that regularly give greater privilege and higher status to men. Heidi Hartmann (1976) was one of the first to incorporate a patriarchal theory into economic explanations of sex segregation. Pamela Stone (1995), in reviewing the sociological research, finds considerable evidence that Hartmann was right in suggesting patriarchy or "anti-matriarchy" as the engine of sex segregation. Various studies document instances when men made concerted efforts to: (1) prevent women's entry into an occupation; (2) push women out who did gain entry; (3) flee from occupations when women have entered them; (4) ghettoize women; (5) devaluate women; and (6) deprive women of authority. Sex discrimination focuses on gender distinction and labels women somewhat negatively. The process of segregation then reinforces already existing sex disparities in human capital, on-the-job experience, or self-esteem and results in the creation of internal labor markets that privilege primary workers who are predominately male and disadvantage secondary workers who are mostly female or who are members of minority ethnic or racial groups.

Innovation and Gender Crossovers

In contrast with both preference theory and segregation theory that explain women's disadvantaged status, there are also positive examples of steady improvement in women's opportunities in new and rapidly changing occupations like management, engineering, and computer programming. Stone (1995) outlines some of the conditions that are needed to encourage women's entry into and success in male occupations. Women in new fields appear to benefit from increasing numbers of women, enhanced self-esteem, and acceptance of their authority and legitimacy in the field. Stone suggests several key conditions that are usually present when such a transformation occurs. The occupation is new enough that it isn't burdened with the historical baggage of sex labeling. It has a high rate of growth, and typically the field is changing rapidly, with new technologies and procedures always around the corner. The occupation also requires high levels of education, training, and expertise that are able to outweigh any advantage given to men by virtue of their sex alone.

Education, Experience, and Human Capital Theory

Hakim's (2000) preference theory is an example of a supply-side explanation for the gender gap in pay. She argues that the attitudes and characteristics of male workers and their desire to work longer hours and be with their families less is the main reason why men receive more pay than women. This, like other supply-side explanations, fits into a human capital model for understanding differences in occupation and earnings. Just as an entrepreneur invests in land or machinery (physical capital) in order to make a product, so families and communities invest in the training of their young (human capital) so that they will grow up to earn a living and be productive citizens. A corollary of the theory is that the greater the individual's investment in education, training, or experience, the greater his or her pay. Using human capital theory, one explains women's lower earnings as being the result of a higher family commitment and a lower work commitment that results in less investment in education and less experience and time on the job than that of men. One of the best known economists to develop the human capital model is Gary Becker (1981) whose *Treatise on the Family* explores the consequences of human capital differences for the division of labor within the family. Becker's theory focuses on the comparative advantage of the marital partners and explains those instances when either the wife or the husband is the major breadwinner. The partner who has the higher earning power tends to become specialized in the breadwinning role while the partner with lower earnings potential takes on more of the household work and child care. As it is typically the man who has the higher earning power, the result is that more women end up working part-time and taking care of the unpaid work that still needs to be done in the home.

Reviewed here are three major lines of inquiry that have been stimulated by human capital theory: the effects of educational preparation, time on the job, and occupational requirements. In addition, an important underlying factor is the individual worker's own values or priorities about the type of role desired.

Educational Attainment

The relationship between educational attainment and labor force participation and earnings is very strong. Generally speaking, the more education a person has had, the greater his or her attachment to the labor force, and the greater his or her earnings. In 1990, of all women age twenty-five and over, 31 percent of those with no high school degree were in the labor force, compared with 55 percent of high school graduates and 78 percent of those with five years of college or more (Spain and Bianchi, 1996: 67). In 1998, those persons with a professional degree averaged $72,700 in annual earnings, compared with $19,700 for those with less than a high school degree. Only 1.3 percent of the professional degree holders were unemployed, compared with 7.1 percent of the high school dropouts (U.S. Bureau of Labor Statistics, 2001b).

Given these general patterns, one simple explanation of the gender gap in pay would be that women as a group have less education than men, and related to that, less attachment to the labor force and less time on the job. There is considerable support for this general explanation. Although the proportions of male and female high school graduates in 1970 and 1990 were virtually identical (52–53 percent in 1970 and 75–75.6 percent in 1990) the percentage of male college graduates was noticeably higher (13.5 percent of men vs. 7.9 percent of women in 1970; and 23.5 percent of men vs. 17.8 percent of women in 1990). When one breaks these figures down by race, one can further see a pattern of lower education among minority groups that might partly explain their lower earnings. In 1990, for example, 11 percent of black men and 11.8 percent of black women held college degrees, and 9.8 percent of Hispanic men and 8.2 percent of Hispanic women did (Spain and Bianchi, 1996: 73).

If one asks, however, whether the gender gap in pay disappears when women are compared with men of similar educational level, one is disappointed. Across all educational levels, women's median weekly earnings in 1997 were 76 percent of men's. But the results weren't that different even within the same educational level: women's earnings were 74 percent of those of men with no high school diploma, 71 percent among high school graduates, 74 percent among those with some college or an associate degree, and 75 percent among those with a college degree. Clearly the amount of education is importantly associated with amount of earnings, but it is also clear that other factors must also be affecting women's pay (Bowler, 1999).

Time on the Job

Another component of an individual's human capital is on-the-job training and experience. This appears to be one of the ways that women differ from men, even when they have the same amount of formal education. A considerably larger proportion of women work part-time than men, even those with a college degree. Hakim (1996) notes that virtually all the increase in employment in Britain from 1951 to 1995 was connected to growth of part-time jobs held by women. The proportion of women who worked full-time during this period hovered around one-third. The figures are similar for the United States; even among American women with five years of college or more, only about 40 percent were in the labor force full-time, full-year in 1990 (Spain and Bianchi, 1996: 67).

Women's careers also have more interruptions than men's because of their childbearing and homemaking responsibilities. The human capital model predicts that these women will tend to invest less in their education because they will have a shorter period of work life to recapture their investment (Blau, Ferber, and Winkler, 2002). If a woman leaves a particular employer, she has less exposure to on-the-job experience (which is another form of human capital). Moreover, her employer is likely at some point to make a judgment that investing in her training is not likely to have the same payoff as for a man, and the pattern of lower human capital investment in female workers thus begins to be reinforced and form part of everyone's expectations.

Skill Requirements of Specific Occupations

A third important theme in the human capital literature is the variation among occupations in the demands they impose and the types of skills they require. Women see some jobs as being better fitted to their situations. If the work permits flexibility, does not require travel away from home, and can be left and reentered without much penalty in obsolescence of knowledge and skill, a woman may feel that it better fits her situation than a job with the opposite characteristics. Fields such as nursing or elementary school teaching are classic examples of female-labeled professions that are thought to be women-friendly for such reasons as scheduling, stability of knowledge, and therefore lower penalties for leaving and reentering.

To find whether these explanations are correct, economists have studied turnover rates of men and women, the penalties to salary for turnover, and so on. Cohn (1996) reports, however, that the results are far from clear. About one-third of the studies show that men have more turnover; another third that women do; and a final third that there is no difference. Blau, Ferber, and Winkler (1998) also report mixed results. On the one hand, human capital theory can account for the narrowing of the gender gap in pay between 1970 and 1995. Women were getting more education, and their pay relative to men's rose more than fifteen percentage points in twenty-five years. In addition, women's flatter earnings profiles are also consistent with more work interruptions, and women more committed to working continuously have steeper growth in their earnings.

However, women earn less than men at every age, even at the beginning of their work lives, when their employment rather than time out for further schooling should give them higher income than their male counterparts. Even the committed and the more highly educated women have lower earnings than men do.

Nor do the predicted differences in earnings for people with greater or fewer interruptions turn out to be true. Women's earnings in traditionally female-labeled jobs depreciate just as much from interruptions as those in male-labeled jobs, and women with discontinuous work histories are not more often found in female occupations. The upshot is that the human capital model, although useful for explaining some broad patterns of education and earnings, still leaves a good part of the female earnings penalty unexplained. Getting to the bottom of the mystery takes one to the theory and research on discrimination.

Discrimination and Sex Segregation

The human capital approach shows that some of women's earnings penalty is due to individual characteristics such as lower education, experience, and length of tenure on the job among women as a group. But even taking education, industry location, and experience into account, a large proportion of the pay gap is left unexplained. The effort to understand this disparity has made economists and sociologists consider discrimination and the occupational structure as the other leading cause (besides human capital) of the differential in men's and women's pay. The case for a structural explanation is based on evidence from change over time and includes the concept of taste for discrimination, overcrowded occupations, and a theory of segmentation within the labor market between primary and secondary workers.

Evidence of Discrimination

Blau and Ferber (1992) report that 34 percent of the gender pay gap in the case of college graduates and 40 percent for those with a high school education or less is not explained by human capital factors or job location. If one leaves out the gender composition of the occupation, the unexplained portion of the pay differential rises to 55 percent for college graduates and 70 percent for those with less than a college degree (Blau and Ferber, 1992: 193). Just as the pay gap diminished over the past thirty years while women's education rose, thereby adding credence to human capital theory, so one might equally well credit the decline in the pay gap to a decline in occupational sex segregation. Jacobs (1989) estimates that there was about a 15 percent decline in the index of dissimilarity between occupations since 1900, when it stood at 67 percent. About half of that decline took place between 1900 and 1970 and the other half between 1970 and 1986, when it stood at 55 percent. (The index of dissimilarity can be interpreted as the percentage of women and men who would have to change their jobs in order for the distribution of women to be the same in all occupations). The decline in segregation could account for the decline in earnings disparity, as women's move into male-labeled occupations helps them gain higher wages.

The trend toward lower segregation does not explain, however, what causes segregation and the accompanying pay gap. One popular explanation is "compensating differentials," whereby men are paid for dirty and more dangerous work and women are paid less because they work in pleasant, safe, and less demanding jobs. Jacobs and Steinberg (1995) find no evidence, however, that this is the case. Women in certain jobs also experience unpleasant conditions and are not paid more; and men doing manual labor and dirty jobs are often paid less. These authors conclude that such results point to political, cultural, and institutional forces that go beyond a rational supply-demand explanation of why women's and men's wages differ.

"Taste" for Discrimination

The explanation of discrimination and segregation focuses on the demand-side factors whereas human capital focused on the supply side—the worker's characteristics. To understand the social context in which a worker experiences discrimination, theorists beginning with Becker (1971) have posited a "taste for discrimination" on the part of employers, which makes them less willing to hire female workers, and on the part of fellow employees, which makes them less willing to work with women or of customers to be served by women. When these discriminating groups have no other choice than to hire, work with, or be served by women, they expect compensation or a discount for the nonpecuniary "cost" of having to interact with female workers in a way that is distasteful to them (Blau and Ferber, 1992: 193).

The "tastes" that economists refer to are the noneconomic values, preferences, or beliefs linked to culture and normative expectations. It is particularly interesting to consider what happens to the gendered labor market when norms and beliefs begin to change. Tastes alter as an occupation begins to admit more women. Reskin and Roos (1990) did an extensive study of fourteen occupations that "tipped" from being predominantly male to having more women (and, in some cases, a majority of women). Examples included editors, typesetters, bakers, real estate agents, and banking and finance managers. The authors explained the process in terms of "gender queues" (in which employers ranked workers) and "job queues" (in which workers ranked jobs from more to less desirable). The sex labeling of an occupation depended on the point at which a match was found between who employers considered the best workers (in gender terms) and what workers considered the best jobs (in terms of pay, working conditions, etc.). Change occurred as a result of change in one or more of the key variables: (1) the size and shape of the gender queue (meaning the supply of male and female workers available); (2) the size and shape of the job queue (i.e., both the jobs available and their desirability); and (3) the ordering of priorities (tastes) on the part of both employers and workers.

In the case of residential real estate, for example, the nature of the broker's job shifted during the 1970s from full-time positions with benefits to more entrepreneurial part-time roles in which the brokers were not paid by the parent company but had to bear the risk of slow business themselves. The worker queues changed, from that of mostly male employees who were the primary breadwinners in their families and needed secure, steady work, to middle-class women in the suburbs who wanted flexible part-time work and were content to be secondary earners. "Tastes" of employees and customers also shifted, so that they began to see young married women as the ideal agents for their sensitivity to the customer's housing needs and their knowledge of the community (Thomas and Reskin, 1990).

Gender Typing and Overcrowding

A fascinating aspect of sex segregation is the coherent set of traditionally female-labeled occupations and traditionally male-typed occupations that share several underlying similarities in many countries. Anker (1998: 24–27), in a review of data on sex segregation around the world, notes that virtually everywhere, women's occupations constitute a much smaller set than men's occupations. Moreover, women are thought to share several positive characteristics (a caring nature, skill in household-related work, manual dexterity, greater honesty, and physical attractiveness) that make them better employees in female-typed occupations. They appear to be more ready to take orders, to do repetitive work, to accept lower wages, and to need less income, and they have a greater interest in working at home. At the same time, they are thought to have certain negative traits that disqualify them for male-typed occupations: less inclination to supervise others, less physical strength, less ability in science and math, less willingness to travel, and less willingness to face physical dangers. One consequence is that across the major regions of the industrialized world, of the five largest occupations for women, nearly one-third are in clerical work and another one-fifth each in services, professions, and sales.

To the extent that their characteristics on average differentiate women from men as a group, it is understandable how employers would rule out certain women as being unsuited to particular occupations. This is a phenomenon known as statistical discrimination that occurs when the average of the group is applied to the individual, often incorrectly. Stereotypes about gender, because they are so widespread, are also responsible for what are called feedback effects, whereby women and men internalize the stereotypes and shape their own behavior accordingly, thus investing less in education of girls and women or expecting the women to be less committed to a career (Blau, Ferber, and Winkler, 2002).

These gender stereotypes and the narrow range of occupations they entail for women help to maintain the overcrowding that Barbara Bergmann (1974) has given as an explanation for much of the pay discrimination experienced by racial minorities and women. The economic principle in overcrowding is straightforward. Because women are crowded into a few traditionally feminine occupations, they can easily become an oversupply and inadvertently lower their own wages. Their employers, without the discipline of having to use their workers as efficiently as possible, are likely to substitute labor-intensive production for investment in capital that promotes efficiency. A corollary of the overcrowding hypothesis is that women's recent spread over a wider range of occupations has created shortages in some of the classic women's fields and has created upward pressure on wages. This appears to be the current situation in nursing in many regions of the United States (Janofsky, 2002).

Internal Labor Markets

The most comprehensive structural explanation for discrimination and segregation in the labor market was first developed by Doeringer and Piore (1985). It attempts to account for the widespread phenomenon of internal differentiation within firms made up of a core sector of permanent workers who are fairly secure in their economic position, with pensions, benefits, and expectations of promotion within the company. Contrasted with them are a peripheral group of workers who are employed on a contingent or temporary basis; these secondary workers are more vulnerable to layoffs and are not eligible for the same benefits as the core. The explanation for these arrangements is primarily functional — that any business has its ups and downs, and that it is useful to be able to pare down to the essentials in times of slack and to be able to add staff when needed. The issue for gender equity is that the primary workers turn out to be mostly men and the secondary workers, disproportionately women.

Differentiation into a dual structure develops in relation to the perceived characteristics of the workers, whether or not they are essential to the core operations or are committed to full-time work. If not, they are likely to be relegated to the ranks of secondary workers where there is little likelihood of promotion into the primary sector.

It is easy to see how the stereotypes of women and their well-known interest in flexibility and responsibility for their families could work against their recruitment to the primary sector and channel them toward less permanent and less responsible positions. A famous example is the case brought by the Equal Employment Opportunity Commission (EEOC) against the Bell Telephone system in 1972. Male and female applicants who were the same in having no prior experience were treated quite differently. The men were sent to become linemen and had higher pay and more chance of on-the-job training and promotions. The women were assigned to become operators with lower pay, little on-the-job training, and little chance of promotion. Not surprisingly, the courts awarded a large settlement to the plaintiffs on the finding that the telephone company was guilty of sex discrimination prohibited by Title VII of the Civil Rights Act of 1964 (Equal Employment Opportunity Commission, 1972).

Such internal differentiation is widespread in many sectors and occupations: in law firms in the distinctions between partners and associates; in universities between tenured and contract professors; in hospitals between registered nurses and nurses' aides; and so on. The next chapter will summarize some of the policy proposals that have been developed to achieve equal opportunity and equitable treatment. In preparation for turning to legal and policy remedies in the next chapter, this chapter concludes with a summary of the demographic, economic, and cultural changes that have already occurred that are likely to affect equity in the future.

The Shape of the Future

What the foregoing review has shown are the key variables that affect gender equity in the workplace. Economists, sociologists, and historians have all contributed to a reconstruction of how change occurred in the past. As the economy became industrialized and the family was no longer connected with agricultural life, many more women entered the nonagricultural paid labor force. The degree of dissimilarity between women's and men's jobs declined by about 15 percent after 1900, and the ratio of women's pay rose over the course of the century from 50–60 percent to around 75 percent of men's pay in most industrial economies of the world.

Much of that decline in inequity was due to improvement in the education of workers, the expansion of jobs that were attractive to women as well as men, and changes in public attitudes and policies. Future changes will likely rest on continuing evolution in the same overall framework. This structure includes the larger societal context in which work and family roles are set, the size and shape of the population that makes up the labor supply, the nature of the economy and occupations available that constitutes labor demand, and the changing values or tastes of employers and workers that affect the gender queues and job queues and that result in a more or less segmented occupational system, with more or less equal access for women and men. Summarized here are some clues drawn from research that suggest how gender equity may evolve in the future.

Major Role Patterns

Before discussing the various factors likely to speed gender equity in the future, it is useful to consider the probable range of likely outcomes. Several observers suggest that there will always be several types of households. Some will have no children and be committed primarily to work (dual-career families). The households that have many children will likely make a clear distinction between the wife's and husband's roles (breadwinner-homemaker families). In between these two poles will be all those households where both husband and wife are in the work force, but one of them is the primary earner and the other a secondary earner ("compromise" or dual-earner families). Hakim (1996) estimates that as many as 20 percent of all women have no desire for children and are committed primarily to career. At the other end of the continuum are perhaps 10 percent of women who want four children or more. In between is a vast group who want to combine work and parenting. Jacobs and Gerson (2002) likewise emphasize that households come in various forms, ranging from those with the highly educated "overworked Americans" identified by Juliet Schor (1991) to many other types who have about as much time for work and leisure as they want. The important point for policy purposes is not to generalize from an aggregate that represents an average across groups but that may not be true of any sizable category of individuals. Recognizing the variety of role preferences among men and women is important for the correct interpretation of current data and for a realistic definition of policy goals.

Importance of Societal Context

Comparative studies of occupational segregation and gender differences in pay show that the culture and institutions of each country are important in shaping the relative size of the three major household patterns and role types. Societies with a more socialist or corporatist philosophy see childbearing and child rearing as family activities that should receive strong support from the state, and they impose a smaller penalty for part-time work (Gornick and Meyers, 2003). "Dualist" societies like the United States and United Kingdom that rely primarily on the private sector for such support give less help to women and families in their child rearing functions and impose greater penalties for parental leave and part-time work (Rosenfeld and Kalleberg, 1990). In a comparison of European countries in their attitudes toward childbearing and its consequences for women's work and income, Wetzels (2001) shows that policies toward parental leave affect whether a highly educated woman is more likely to follow a career or become a homemaker. In Sweden and the United Kingdom, parental leaves and legislation on child care permit women to pursue the equal role-sharing model. In Germany, however, taxation and leave policies are likely to push families toward the breadwinner-homemaker model.

Changes in Labor Supply

Improvement of education for women, minorities, poor people, and many other previously excluded groups generally changes the labor supply in a way that promotes equity between groups. Thus, to the extent that women continue to pursue higher degrees and that more women complete college, it is likely that they will seek to enter an ever wider range of occupations. The one possible brake on this development might be specialized or vocational on-the-job training that is more open to one sex than the other, as was found by Blossfeld (1987) in the Federal Republic of Germany. Government training programs, child care, and parental leaves that result in retention of workers can lessen somewhat the unequal family burden usually carried by women and can permit them to invest more time on the job and in their own human capital (Blau and Ferber, 1992: 178–187).

Changes in Occupational Structure

Demand-side changes also enhance the chances of equity by lowering barriers to male-dominated fields, by organizing the workplace through union activity, and by such policies as affirmative action to hire previously excluded groups. Blossfeld and Drobnic (2001), in a large cross-national study of occupations and earnings, predict that an increasing symmetry in occupational requirements will lessen the comparative advantage of men and lead to a more symmetrical allocation of time to paid work between husband and wives, as would be predicted by Becker's (1981) theory. As the standard of women's pay rises in the nonfemale labeled occupations, the supply of women to the traditional female jobs may become so threatened as to restructure the pay and the job itself, as is currently happening in nursing. Scholars like Hochschild (2000) point to a "care drain" in which foreign workers are being imported from Third World countries for child care and domestic service.

Callahan (2001) and Stone (2000) in addition call attention to the shortage of nursing home workers in a time of rapid growth in the population of frail elders, and Stone calls for a "care movement" to demand higher pay and more attractive working conditions for care workers. In other service occupations, living wage campaigns for maintenance workers and efforts to organize office workers, such as those that have been successful at Yale and Harvard, also suggest that it is possible to raise pay scales for traditionally low-paying women's occupations.

Finally, affirmative action is a policy that can raise the opportunities and pay of groups that have been confined to secondary jobs. DiPrete (1987) documents the overall positive effect of equal opportunity legislation on the fifteen largest agencies of the U.S. government from 1962 to 1977. Lower-level employees were able to move into entry level administrative posts. This result particularly benefited women and minorities.

Changes in Tastes and Values

A change in taste for discrimination can be used to explain an improvement in pay equity over and above what can be explained by supply and demand alone. Eisenhart (1996), in a clear-eyed assessment of the reasons why highly educated women do not go on to more challenging careers, finds that traditional socialization, family and friends' values, and the "chilly" classroom (which does not encourage girls' achievement) all contribute to girls' unwillingness to place their own interests in the forefront. These attitudes are further reinforced by the college peer culture and by blatant sex discrimination in some male-dominated fields. Hakim (1996) notes that public policies for equity in the workplace cannot address the "freeze out" of women from those fields in which social and psychological processes already inhibit them from competing effectively for senior positions and management posts. By contrast, there is a long tradition of high value placed on black women's education and professional accomplishment and of equality between black women and men (Werum, 1996). Arguments by such analysts as Jackson (1998) that women are "destined for equality" in modern society seem all too simple against the complexity of such psychological and cultural barriers.

In the end, however, the likely future changes that will come in supply, demand, and general tolerance for new gender roles will allow traditional expectations to be applied more flexibly. Feedback effects from actual life experience will cause tastes and values about what is masculine and feminine to vary over the lifetime of the individual and according to particular economic and societal conditions rather than being set for all times and all places.

Summary

This review of gender equity in the workplace makes clear that inequality in employment of women and men is a worldwide phenomenon. Some differences in treatment of men and women are based on sex differences rooted in fundamental biological traits. Others, however, are due to culture and socialization and are reflected in the wide variation in gender roles. Although gender equality appears to be relatively greater in the simplest and the most modern societies, with patriarchy being strongest in peasant agricultural societies, it is nevertheless true that throughout the world women as a class hold lower status and less well-paid jobs. But this picture should not obscure the progress that has been made over the past century. More than half of the world's women are now in the paid labor force, and more than two-thirds are literate. Public provision for child care and paid parental leaves have existed in the Scandinavian countries for several decades and are a model for reformers in many other countries as well.

The area in which there is still uncertainty is in the future impact of globalization. On the one hand, United Nations world conferences on women have called for and documented the improved rights of women, and there is wider public recognition of the issues of equal pay and equal educational opportunity. On the other hand, the new global cities reveal immense inequality between the standard of living of managers and professionals in transnational corporations and the immigrant women and ethnic minorities, who still experience long hours and sweatshop conditions in the service jobs that they hold.

The chief engine of gender equity in the workplace appears to be women's rising participation in the paid labor force. Female employment began to rise with industrialization and was particularly fueled by the service and information economy that grew up after World War II. Demand increased for jobs traditionally done by women such as teaching, nursing, and clerical work. The supply of women who could work was also rising; fewer children, more household conveniences, and more education made women more available for work outside the home. The earlier profile of female workers as young and single women who would leave employment when they had children, also began to change, and by the 1980s employment among women with children had become more common than full-time homemaking.

Even as more women took jobs, however, they differed from men in the occupations they entered, their frequency of part-time work, and their pay. Four-fifths of all employed women could be found in just five major occupational groups, whereas men's jobs spanned a much wider range. Even among college-educated women, nearly 40 percent currently work part-time or part-year as compared with less than 10 percent of men. Average pay of women, based on hourly wages, is still only three-quarters of men's pay, although this figure represents a considerable improvement over the approximately 60 percent figure of the 1970s.

Explanations for the wage penalty to women are generally of two major types. The human capital explanation focuses on the characteristics of women workers and points to their lower average education, higher part-time rates, and narrow choice of occupations as the reasons for lower rewards. Nevertheless, even when men and women with the same characteristics are compared, women still receive 10–20 percent less in pay. The explanation (based on discrimination and the internal or dual labor markets) points to the demand side of employment and suggests that women and men are treated differently by employers. Employers' tastes for discrimination determine whether they prefer a man or a woman in a certain type of job. Opportunities, responsibility, training, and chances for promotion are all largely determined by type of job. It is more common for men to be assigned to permanent primary sector jobs with more opportunities and for women to be assigned to the secondary dead-end jobs.

Possibilities for achieving equity occur in some of the newer information-related and managerial jobs in which women have been successful, such as those found in finance or the computer field. Evidently the newness of a field keeps it from being labeled as traditionally male or female, and women are then more likely to be evaluated on the basis of their actual abilities rather than on stereotypes about what women can do. In addition to new opportunities provided by the labor market, women themselves have gained new skills and entered male-dominated fields. Activists have also organized to obtain legal remedies against inequity and discrimination. The next chapter documents some of the most important legal milestones in the quest for sex equity in employment, education, and access to work-related benefits.

References

Acosta-Belen, Edna, and Christine E. Bose. 1990. "From Structural Subordination to Empowerment: Women and Development in Third World Contexts." *Gender and Society* 4 (no. 3, September): 299–320.

Anker, Richard. 1998. *Gender and Jobs: Sex Segregation of Occupations in the World.* Geneva: International Labour Office.

Aronowitz, Stanley, and William DiFazio, eds. 1994. *The Jobless Future: Sci-Tech and the Dogma of Work.* Minneapolis: University of Minnesota Press.

Becker, Gary S. 1971. *The Economics of Discrimination.* 2nd ed. Chicago: University of Chicago Press.

———. 1981. *A Treatise on the Family.* Cambridge, MA: Harvard University Press.

Bee, Anna. 2000. "Globalization, Grapes, and Gender: Women's Work in Traditional and Agro-Export Production in Northern Chile." *The Geographical Journal* 166 (no. 3, September): 255–265.

Berger, Iris. 1990. "Gender, Race, and Political Empowerment: South African Canning Workers, 1940–1960." *Gender and Society* 4 (no. 3, September): 398–420.

Bergmann, Barbara R. 1974. "Occupational Segregation, Wages, and Profits When Employers Discriminate by Race or Sex." *Eastern Economic Journal* 1 (nos. 1–2 , April–July): 103–110.

———. 1996. *Saving Our Children from Poverty: What the United States Can Learn from France.* New York: Russell Sage Foundation.

Blau, Francine D., and Lawrence M. Kahn. 2000. "Gender Differences in Pay." *Journal of Economic Perspectives* 14 (no. 4, fall): 75–99.

Blau, Francine D., and Marianne A. Ferber. 1992. *The Economics of Women, Men, and Work.* 2nd ed. Englewood Cliffs, NJ: Prentice-Hall.

Blau, Francine D., Marianne A. Ferber, and Anne E. Winkler. 1998. *The Economics of Women, Men, and Work.* 3rd ed. Saddle River, NJ: Prentice-Hall.

————. 2002. *The Economics of Women, Men, and Work.* 4th ed. Saddle River, NJ: Prentice-Hall.

Blossfeld, Hans-Peter. 1987. "Labor Market Entry and the Sexual Segregation of Careers in the Federal Republic of Germany." *American Journal of Sociology* 93: 89–118.

Blossfeld, Hans-Peter, and Sonja Drobnic, eds. 2001. *Careers of Couples in Contemporary Societies: From Male Breadwinner to Dual-Earner Families.* New York: Oxford University Press.

Blossfeld, Hans-Peter, and Catherine Hakim, eds. 1997. *Between Equalization and Marginalization: Women Working Part-time in Europe and the United States of America.* New York: Oxford University Press.

Boserup, Ester. 1970. *Woman's Role in Economic Development.* London: Allen & Unwin.

Bowler, Mary. 1999. "Women's Earnings: An Overview." *Monthly Labor Review* (December): 13–21.

Breugel, Irene. 1999. "Globalization, Feminization, and Pay Inequalities." Pp. 73–93 in *Women, Work, and Inequality: The Challenge of Equal Pay in a Deregulated Labour Market.* Edited by Jeanne Gregory, Rosemary Sales, and Arione Hegewisch. New York: St. Martin's Press.

Callahan, James J. 2001. "Policy Perspectives on Workforce Issues and Older People Solutions for Persistent Problems." *Generations: The Journal of the Western Gerontological Society* 25 (part 1): 12–16.

Carden, Maren Lockwood. 1974. *The New Feminist Movement.* New York: Russell Sage Foundation.

Cohn, Samuel. 1996. "Human Capital Theory." Pp. 107–110 in *Women and Work: A Handbook.* Edited by Paula J. Dubeck and Kathryn Borman. New York: Garland Publishing.

Cook, Alice H., Val R. Lorwin, and Arlene Kaplan Daniels, eds. 1984. *Women and Trade Unions in Eleven Industrialized Countries.* Philadelphia: Temple University Press.

Deere, Carmen Diana. 1987. "The Latin American Agrarian Reform Experience." Pp. 165–190 in *Rural Women and State Policy: Feminist Perspectives on Latin American Agricultural Development.* Edited by Carmen Diana Deere and Magdalena Leon. Boulder, CO: Westview Press.

DiPrete, Thomas A. 1987. "The Professionalization of Administration and Equal Employment Opportunity in the U.S. Federal Government." *American Journal of Sociology* 93 (July): 119–140.

Doeringer, Peter B., and Michael J. Piore. 1985. *Internal Labor Markets and Manpower Analysis.* Armonk, NY: M. E. Sharpe.

Duverger, Maurice. 1955. *The Political Role of Women.* Paris: UNESCO.

Easterlin, Richard A. 1978. "What Will 1984 Be Like? Socioeconomic Implications of Recent Twists in Age Structure." *Demography* 15: 397–432.

Ecklein, Joan. 1982. "Women in the German Democratic Republic: Impact of Culture on Social Policy." Pp. 151–197 in *Women in the Middle Years.* Edited by Janet Zollinger Giele. New York: Wiley.

Eisenhart, Mary. 1996. "Contemporary College Women's Career Plans." Pp. 232–235 in *Women and Work: A Handbook.* Edited by Paula J. Dubeck and Kathryn Borman. New York: Garland Publishing.

England, Paula. 1992. *Comparable Worth: Theories and Evidence.* New York: Aldine de Gruyter.

Equal Employment Opportunity Commission. 1972. "A Unique Competence: A Study of Equal Employment Opportunity in the Bell System." *Congressional Record* 17 (February): E1243-E1268.

Featherman, David L., and Annemette Sørensen. 1983. "Societal Transformation in Norway and Change in the Life Course Transition into Adulthood." *Acta Sociologica* 26: 105–126.

Fraser, Arvonne S. 1987. *The U.N. Decade for Women: Documents and Dialogue.* Boulder, CO: Westview Press.

Freeman, Jo. 2000. "UN Reviews Women's Progress Five Years after Beijing." *Off Our Backs* 30 (no. 9, October): 1, 6 ff.

Gallin, Rita S., Marilyn Aronoff, and Anne Ferguson, eds. 1989. "Introduction: Women and International Development: Creating an Agenda." *The Women and International Development Annual* 1: 1–22. Boulder, CO: Westview Press.

Gibson, Campbell, and Emily Lennon. 1999. "Historical Census Statistics on the Foreign-Born Population of the United States: 1850–1990." Census Population Div. Working Paper No. 29, Table 18.

Giele, Janet Zollinger. 1978. *Women and the Future: Changing Sex Roles in Modern America.* New York: Free Press.

———. 1988. "Gender and Sex Roles." Pp. 291–323 in *Handbook of Sociology.* Edited by Neil J. Smelser. Beverly Hills, CA: Sage.

———. 1998. "Innovation in the Typical Life Course." Pp. 231–263 in *Methods of Life Course Research: Qualitative and Quantitative Approaches.* Edited by Janet Z. Giele and Glen H. Elder, Jr. Thousand Oaks, CA: Sage.

Goldscheider, Frances K., and Linda J. Waite. 1991. *New Families, No Families? The Transformation of the American Home.* Berkeley: University of California Press.

Gornick, Janet C., and Marcia K. Meyers. 2003. "Welfare Regimes in Relation to Paid Work and Care." *Changing Life Patterns in Western Industrial Societies,* vol. 8 of *Advances in Life Course Research.* Edited by Janet Z. Giele and Elke Holst. London: Elsevier Science.

Hakim, Catherine. 1996. *Key Issues in Women's Work: Female Heterogeneity and the Polarisation of Women's Employment.* Atlantic Highlands, NJ: Athlone.

———. 2000. *Work-Lifestyle Choices in the 21st Century: Preference Theory.* New York: Oxford University Press.

Hartmann, Heidi. 1976. "Capitalism, Patriarchy, and Job Segregation by Sex." *Signs* 1: 137–170.

———. 2000. Testimony, June 8, 2000. U.S. Senate Committee on Health, Education, Labor, and Pensions. Senate Hearing 106–631, June 8, 2000.

Hayes, Cheryl D., John L. Palmer, and Martha J. Zaslow, eds. 1990. *Who Cares for America's Children? Child Care Policy for the 1990s.* Washington, DC: National Academy Press.

Hochschild, Arlie Russell. 1990. *The Second Shift: Working Parents and the Revolution at Home.* New York: Avon.

———. 2000. "The Nanny Chain." *The American Prospect* (January 3): 32–36.

Hogan, Dennis P. 1981. *Transitions and Social Change: The Early Lives of American Men.* New York: Academic Press.

Jackson, Robert Max. 1998. *Destined for Equality: The Inevitable Rise of Women's Status.* Cambridge, MA: Harvard University Press.

Jacobs, Jerry A. 1989. "Long-Term Trends in Occupational Segregation by Sex." *American Journal of Sociology* 95 (no. 1, July): 160–173.

Jacobs, Jerry A., ed. 1995. *Gender Inequality at Work.* Thousand Oaks, CA: Sage.

Jacobs, Jerry A., and Kathleen Gerson. 2002. "The Time Divide: Work, Family, and Social Policy." Philadelphia, University of Pennsylvania. Unpublished manuscript.

Jacobs, Jerry A., and Ronnie J. Steinberg. 1995. "Further Evidence on Compensating Differentials and the Gender Gap in Wages." Pp. 93–124 in *Gender Inequality at Work.* Edited by Jerry A. Jacobs. Thousand Oaks, CA: Sage.

Jacquette, Jane S. 1982. "Women and Modernization Theory: A Decade of Feminist Criticism." *World Politics* 34 (no. 2, January): 267–284.

Janofsky, Michael. 2002. "Shortage of Nurses Spurs Bidding War in Hospital Industry." *New York Times*, May 28: A1.

Kohli, Martin. 1986. "The World We Forgot: A Historical Review of the Life Course." Pp. 271–303 in *Later Life: The Social Psychology of Aging*. Edited by V. W. Marshall. Beverly Hills, CA: Sage.

Kohli, Martin, Martin Rein, Anne-Marie Guillemard, and H. Van Gunsteren, eds. 1991. *Time for Retirement: Comparative Studies of Early Exit from the Labor Force*. Cambridge, England: Cambridge University Press.

Lago, Maria Soledad. 1987. "Rural Women and the Neo-Liberal Model in Chile." Pp. 21–34 in *Rural Women and State Policy: Feminist Perspectives in Latin American Agricultural Development*. Edited by Carmen Diana Deere and Magdalena Leon. Boulder, CO: Westview Press.

Liljestrom, Rita, Gunilla Furst Mellstrom, and Gillan Liljestrom Svensson. 1978. *Roles in Transition: Report of an Investigation Made for the Advisory Council on Equality between Men and Women*. Stockholm: LiberForlag.

Mandel, William M. 1975. *Soviet Women*. New York: Anchor.

Marini, Margaret Mooney, and Pi-Ling Fan. 1997. "The Gender Gap in Earnings at Career Entry." *American Sociological Review* 62 (August): 588–604.

Mehra, Rekha, and Sarah Gammage. 1999. "Trends, Countertrends, and Gaps in Women's Employment." *World Development* 27 (no. 3, March): 533–550.

Melkas, Helinä, and Richard Anker. 1998. *Gender Equality and Occupational Segregation in Nordic Labour Markets*. Geneva: International Labour Organization.

———. "Occupational Segregation by Sex in Nordic Countries: An Empirical Investigation," pp. 189–213 in *Women, Gender, and Work: What Is Equality and How Do We Get There?* Edited by Martha Fetherolf Loutfi. Geneva: International Labour Organization.

Mincer, Jacob. 1962. "Labor Force Participation of Married Women: A Study of Labor Supply." Pp. 63–105 in *Aspects of Labor Economics: A Conference of the Universities—National Bureau Committee for Economic Research*. Princeton, NJ: Princeton University Press.

Moen, Phyllis. 1992. *Women's Two Roles: A Contemporary Dilemma*. New York: Auburn House.

Morgan, Laurie A. 1998. "Glass-Ceiling Effect or Cohort Effect? A Longitudinal Study of the Gender Earnings Gap for Engineers, 1982 to 1989." *American Sociological Review* 63 (August): 479–483.

Nash, June. 1990. "Latin American Women in the World Capitalist Crisis." *Gender and Society* 4 (no. 3, September): 338–353.

OECD (Organisation for Economic Cooperation and Development). 1998. *The Future of Female-Dominated Occupations.* Paris: OECD Publications.

Oppenheimer, Valerie Kincade. 1970. *The Female Labor Force in the United States: Demographic and Economic Factors Governing its Growth and Changing Composition.* Westport, CT: Greenwood.

———. 1979. "Structural Sources of Economic Pressure for Wives to Work: An Analytical Framework." *Journal of Family History* 4 (no. 2): 177–197.

———. 1982. *Work and the Family: A Study in Social Demography.* New York: Academic Press.

O'Rand, Angela M. 1996. "Women and Retirement in the U.S." Pp. 25–27 in *Women and Work: A Handbook.* Edited by Paula J. Dubeck and Kathryn Borman. New York: Garland.

Pharr, Susan J. 1981. *Political Women in Japan: The Search for a Place in Political Life.* Berkeley: University of California Press.

Reich, Robert B. 1992. *The Work of Nations: Preparing Ourselves for 21st Century Capitalism.* New York: Vintage.

Reskin, Barbara F., and Patricia A. Roos, eds. 1990. *Job Queues, Gender Queues: Explaining Women's Inroads into Male Occupations.* Philadelphia: Temple University Press.

Riley, Matilda White, Anne Foner, and Joan Waring. 1988. "Sociology of Age." Pp. 243–290 in *Handbook of Sociology.* Edited by Neil J. Smelser. Newbury Park, CA: Sage.

Rohter, Larry. 2002. "Brazil's Prized Exports Rely on Slaves and Scorched Land." *New York Times,* March 25: A1, A6.

Rosenfeld, Rachel A., and Arne L. Kalleberg. 1990. "A Cross-National Comparison of the Gender Gap in Income." *American Journal of Sociology* 96 (no. 1, July): 69–106.

Safa, Helen Icken. 1990. "Women's Social Movements in Latin America." *Gender and Society* 4 (no. 3, September): 354–369.

Sales, Rosemary, and Jeanne Gregory. 1999. "Immigration, Ethnicity, and Exclusion: Implications of European Integration." Pp. 97–114 in *Women,*

Work and Inequality: The Challenge of Equal Pay in a Deregulated Labour Market. Edited by Jeanne Gregory, Rosemary Sales, and Ariane Hegewisch. New York : St. Martin's Press.

Sasson, Saskia. 1991. *The Global City: New York, London, Tokyo.* Princeton, NJ: Princeton University Press.

Schor, Juliet. 1991. *The Overworked American: The Unexpected Decline of Leisure.* New York. Basic.

Seager, Joni. 1997. *The State of Women in the World Atlas.* 2nd ed. New York: Penguin.

Sivard, Ruth. 1985. *Women . . . A World Survey.* Washington, DC: World Priorities.

Spain, Daphne, and Suzanne M. Bianchi. 1996. *Balancing Act: Motherhood, Marriage, and Employment among American Women.* New York: Russell Sage Foundation.

Stone, Deborah. 2000. "Why We Need a Care Movement." *The Nation,* March 13: 13–15.

Stone, Pamela A. 1995. "Assessing Gender at Work: Evidence and Issues." Pp. 408–423 in *Gender Inequality at Work.* Edited by Jerry A. Jacobs. Thousand Oaks, CA: Sage Publications.

Thomas, Barbara J., and Barbara F. Reskin. 1990. "A Woman's Place Is Selling Homes: Occupational Change and the Feminization of Real Estate Sales." Pp. 205–223 in *Job Queues, Gender Queues: Explaining Women's Inroads into Male Occupations.* Edited by Barbara F. Reskin and Patricia A. Roos. Philadelphia: Temple University Press.

Udry, J. Richard. 2000. "Feminist Critics Uncover Determinism, Positivism, and Antiquated Theory." *American Sociological Review* 66 (4): 611–618.

United Nations. 2000. *The World's Women 2000: Trends and Statistics.* New York: United Nations. ST/ESA/STAT/Social Statistics and Indicators, series K, no. 16.

United States Bureau of the Census. 2001. *Statistical Abstract of the United States: 2001.* Washington, DC: U.S. Dept. of Commerce, Economics and Statistics Administration, U.S. Census Bureau.

United States Bureau of Labor Statistics. 2001a. Labor Force Statistics from the Current Population Survey. Table 5, "Employment status of the population by sex, marital status, and presence and age of own children under 12, 1999–2000 annual averages." http://stts.bls.gov/news. release/famee.t05.htm (accessed May 31, 2001).

————. 2001b. "Education Pays." *Working in the 21st Century.* Washington, DC: Bureau of Labor Statistics.

United States Department of Labor. 1989. *Employment and Earnings.* Washington, DC: Bureau of Labor Statistics.

————. 1990. *Facts on Working Women.* Washington, DC: Women's Bureau. October.

————. 2001. "Earnings Differences between Women and Men." Women's Bureau: Facts on Working Women. http://www.dol.gov/dol/wb/public/wb_pubs/wagegap2000.htm (accessed November 20, 2001).

————. 2002. "Women's Jobs 1964–1999: More Than 30 Years of Progress." Women's Bureau. http://www.dol.gov/wb/stats/main.htm (accessed May 17, 2002).

United States General Accounting Office. 2002. "A New Look through the Glass Ceiling: Where Are the Women?" Washington, DC: Author.

Ward, Kathryn. 1990. *Women Workers and Global Restructuring.* Ithaca, NY: ILR.

Weil, Gordon. 1992. "Caught in the Crisis: Women in the Economies of Sub-Saharan Africa." Pp. 47–68 in *Women's Work and Women's Lives: The Continuing Struggle Worldwide.* Edited by Hilda Kahne and Janet Z. Giele. Boulder, CO: Westview Press.

Werum, Regina A. 1996. "Gender Ideology in Early Twentieth-Century Black Educational Reform." Pp. 230–231 in *Women and Work: A Handbook.* Edited by Paula J. Dubeck and Kathryn Borman. New York: Garland.

Wetzels, Cécile. 2001. *Squeezing Birth into Working Life: Household Panel Data Analyses Comparing Germany, Great Britain, Sweden, and the Netherlands.* Burlington, VT: Ashgate.

World Fact Book. 1998. Washington, DC: Central Intelligence Agency.

Yeoh, Brenda S. A., Shirlena Huang, and Katie Willis. 2000. "Global Cities, Transnational Flows and Gender Dimensions, the View from Singapore." *Journal of Social and Economic Geography* 91 (no. 2, May): 147–158.

2

Legal Remedies and Social Policies

C hanges in the actual work of women and men have ultimately had an impact on the laws and social policy related to pay and equal opportunity. Changes have gradually taken place all over the world. Economic modernization brought more women into the work force. It began to be recognized that girls as well as boys should have the opportunity for advanced and professional education. The movement for sex equality begun in the nineteenth century had focused on women's political equality and the right to vote, and by the middle of the twentieth century, women's political rights had been widely established. The new frontier concerned women's economic rights. A new women's movement arose following World War II and this time focused on a wide range of concerns ranging from family planning to property rights, but chief among them was equity in employment.

Symbolic of the emerging new consensus on women's rights was a collection of various conventions adopted by the United Nations and the International Labor Organization. Most important among them was the United Nations Charter itself, which set out as one of its purposes in Article 1 "promoting and encouraging respect for human rights and for fundamental freedoms for all without distinction as to . . . sex." Article 13 directs the General Assembly to "initiate studies and make recommendations for the purpose of . . . assisting in the realization of human rights and fundamental freedoms for all without distinction as to . . . sex. . . ." (quoted in Halberstam and Defeis, 1987: 18). The U.N. Charter was established in 1945 and has since been ratified by 159 nations, including the United States.

53

A second important agreement stemming from the United Nations is the International Covenant on Economic, Social, and Cultural Rights, which is a charter of basic rights that was adopted by the U.N. General Assembly in 1966. Two provisions are especially important for women's rights: first, that the participating countries guarantee that all rights will be exercised without discrimination as to sex; and second, that workers receive equal remuneration for work of equal value, with particular guarantees that women not work in conditions inferior to those of men and that they receive equal pay for equal work. This convention went into force in 1976 and has been signed by 101 countries, but ten years later, it had been ratified by only 83 (the United States signed but Congress did not ratify) (Halberstam and Defeis, 1987: 21).

Parallel to the United Nations agreements were several similar conventions adopted by the International Labor Organization (ILO). The Convention Covering Equal Remuneration for Men and Women Workers for Work of Equal Value was adopted in 1951, came into force in 1953, and by 1986 had been ratified by 107 countries. Two other ILO conventions are especially relevant to gender equity. The Convention Concerning Discrimination in Respect of Employment and Occupation bans employment discrimination; it was established in 1960 and by 1986 had been ratified by 107 countries. The Convention Concerning Employment Policy is particularly concerned with freedom of choice in employment and opportunity for work to which the person is well suited, regardless of sex. This convention was instituted in 1966 and twenty years later had been ratified by seventy countries (Halberstam and Defeis, 1987: 24–26).

Thus, UN and ILO conventions established legal standards of sex equality in employment that *preceded* such reforms in many of the signatory nations. In the United States, the adoption of domestic antidiscrimination and equal employment policy came a decade or more later, stimulated in part by a civil rights movement and a new feminist movement.

The way employment issues have been handled has varied according to the country. Japan, which in 1947 was just emerging from a traditional and heavily patriarchal and mostly rural society, in its constitution shortly after World War II established for the first time that women could divorce and inherit on an equal basis with men (Giele, 1995; Pharr, 1981). The Labor Protection Laws of 1947 were replaced in 1986 by an Equal Employment Opportunity Act. Nevertheless, most women are still pink-collar employees, and husbands generally do not yet help at home (White, 1996). France, which had large numbers of women in the work force even prior to World War I, set up preschools (*écoles maternelles*) and provided child supports first to working-class women and then to others (Pedersen, 1993; Bergmann, 1996). Sweden, in a sweeping critique of sex inequality in the 1970s, provided generous preschool programs. In 1974, it became the first country to provide parental leaves so that mothers as well as fathers could have time for both work and parenting (Cubbins, 1996; Liljestrom, Mellstrom, and Svensson, 1978). In Australia in the 1970s, tribunals evaluated all jobs and reset the pay scales to apply principles of comparable worth to women's and men's jobs, with the result that there is currently less sex difference in pay (17 percent) in Australia than in any other major country in the world (Blau, Ferber, and Winkler, 1998; Sullivan and Herne, 1996).

Soviet bloc countries also experimented with provision of child care and created expectations that most women would work, even while having children. In the former U.S.S.R., for example, between 1970 and 1985, 51 percent of the work force was women (Lapidus, 1992). In East Germany, more than 90 percent of women of working age were in the paid labor force before reunification in 1989 (Rudolph, 1992). In China, collectivization under Mao during the 1950s and 1960s brought the establishment of communal kitchens in rural communes and efforts to make women equal workers in agriculture alongside men. Article 48 of the People's Republic of China guaranteed equal rights to women and outlawed arranged marriage, betrothal of children, concubinage, selling of women, and female infanticide. At the same time, it guaranteed women the right to divorce and remarry. China's one-child policy resulted in smaller families and more women in the work force. Although there are three times as many men as women in college in China, the legal status of women is near equality (Ball, 1996). Capitalism and the return of more autonomy to the private sector have encouraged massive numbers of women and men to migrate to urban areas to find jobs. By 1990, 53 percent of the urban work force was female, although discrimination against women in education and employment was still evident (Zuo and Tang, 1994).

Although there are a number of similarities in the issues that all nations face with respect to sex discrimination in employment, this chapter will focus primarily on the history of these questions in the United States. American legal remedies and social policies deal with three main aspects of gender equity in the workplace: (1) equality in employment; (2) equality in educational opportunity; and (3) equal treatment of women and men with respect to integration of work and family responsibilities. A theme running throughout each part of the American story is the importance of the women's movement in raising the issues and persuading legislators, the courts, and the general public that change was called for.

Equal Opportunity in Employment

The story of growing sex equity in employment traces a zigzag line that has veered between two different emphases within feminism. The difference perspective treats women as distinct from men in their biology, psychology, and social roles in the family. The sameness perspective treats women as comparable to men in strength, intellectual power, and capacity to fill any occupation that men perform. These two themes go back to the nineteenth century and were embodied in the two arms of the suffrage movement. The woman's temperance movement sought the vote to rid the country of the ravages of alcohol and emphasized women's superior moral sense and greater concern for families and children. The woman's suffrage movement sought the vote as a right of all citizens under the Constitution. Women's equal right to vote was finally established by a constitutional amendment, but only after the two kinds of feminists were able to join forces and combine both arguments to advance their goal (Giele, 1995).

After the adoption of the Nineteenth Amendment in 1920, the women's movement entered the doldrums. For the next forty years, only sporadic skirmishes kept alive the issue of women's status in the workplace. Between 1920 and 1960, however, a gradual shift took place from an emphasis on protection of women to an emphasis on equal rights (Freeman, 1990). In the 1960s, all of this sub rosa development blossomed into a broad range of legal remedies that emanated from all three branches of government and concerned a wide spectrum of issues ranging from equal pay and occupational requirements to protection against sexual harassment and less favorable working conditions.

From Protectionism to Equal Opportunity

The laws regarding women's position in the work force were predominantly protectionist until the passage of the Civil Rights Act of 1957 and the Equal Pay Act of 1963. The protectionist philosophy was first clearly stated in 1908 in *Muller v. Oregon* in what came to be known as the "Brandeis brief." The case concerned the hours of work that could be demanded of workers, and Louis D. Brandeis (who later became a justice of the U.S. Supreme Court), drawing on a background paper prepared by leading feminists including his sister-in-law, Josephine Goldmark, and Florence Kelly of Hull House (a famous settlement in Chicago founded by Jane Addams), argued that women, because of their physical and social traits, should be protected from overly long working hours. The decision was seen as a victory for progressives who were fighting the *Lochner v. New York* decision of 1905, which had held that any regulation of working hours for men, women, or children was an abridgement of the free right of contract.

The progressive decision in *Muller* was not viewed as benign by all feminists. The National Woman's Party (NWP), led by Alice Paul, believed that protection of women was dangerous because it reinforced an ideology that women were not equal to meeting the same demands as men. The NWP took the position that women's rights should be the same as men's and, in 1923, it proposed an Equal Rights Amendment (ERA) that "equality of rights under the law shall not be denied or abridged by the United States or any State on account of sex." From the 1920s through the 1950s, the National Woman's Party battled opponents led by the Women's Bureau who espoused the protectionist view, including such well-respected and mainstream organizations as the National Consumer's League, the YWCA, and the League of Women Voters, as well as various labor unions.

The upshot, initially proposed by the National Committee to Defeat the Un-Equal Rights Amendment (NCDURA), was a version of the Equal Pay Act first proposed to Congress in 1946. This bill led to the establishment of a National Commission on the Status of Women to study discrimination against women, which in turn created a precedent for the President's Commission on the Status of Women appointed by President Kennedy in 1961. The President's Commission, headed by Eleanor Roosevelt and consisting of various luminaries such as anthropologist Margaret Mead, documented the many instances when women could not serve on juries, were excluded from certain jobs, and were denied benefits equal to those of men. The very existence of the commission and its findings helped to spur passage of the Equal Pay Act of 1963 and Title VII of the Civil Rights Act of 1964, which prohibited discrimination on the basis of sex. Esther Peterson, an activist for AFL-CIO who had been active in the NCDURA, was appointed head of the Women's Bureau by President Kennedy in 1961 and helped to bring about the eventual passage of the Equal Pay Act in 1963 (Freeman, 1990).

The example of the President's Commission led to the creation of state commissions on the status of women by governors in all but one state. These state commissions began to hold annual conferences, and their third annual meeting in 1966 resulted in the formation of the National Organization for Women. NOW was shortly to reactivate the campaign for an ERA, which was voted out of Congress in 1972 and went to the states for ratification. The ERA was never adopted because it failed by three states to reach the required number needed to ratify a constitutional amendment within the time limit that had been set by Congress (Freeman, 1990).

Legal Progress toward Equal Employment Opportunity

Leading up to the breakthroughs of the 1960s, there had been a series of court decisions that gradually eroded the protectionist position and established women's equal rights with respect to jury service, occupational requirements, working conditions, and working hours. Legal analysts Lindgren and Taub (1993) point out that the difference-oriented approach to treatment of women and men had two strands. The first strand of the protectionist position treated women as weaker, smaller, and more vulnerable. A series of court decisions cemented this philosophy in *Muller v. Oregon* (1908), which limited women's working hours, *West Coast Hotel v. Parrish* (1937), which upheld a minimum wage for women and children (but not for men), and *Goesaert v. Cleary* (1948), which excluded women from certain occupations, such as bartending. The second strand of the protectionist tradition came from the idea that women deserve special compensation or consideration for bearing different burdens from men and for their maternal functions. This reasoning was expressed in *Breedlove v.*

Suttles (1937), which exempted women from poll taxes "in view of burdens necessarily borne by them for the preservation of the race . . ." (quoted in Lindgren and Taub, 1993: 44), and *Hoyt v. Florida* (1961), which excused women from jury service for similar reasons. *United States v. St. Clair* (1968) upheld women's exemption from the military draft.

Even against this backdrop, the climate had been changing slightly in the direction of equal treatment of women and men under the law. Both the Fair Labor Standards Act (FLSA) of 1938 and the Civil Rights Act of 1957 established landmark precedents in this regard. The FLSA legislated the minimum wage for both men and women. The Civil Rights Act of 1957, though primarily addressed to race discrimination, also implied sex equality in voting rights and the right to serve on juries. Moreover, certain court decisions reinforced the equality theme. *Rosenfeld v. Southern Pacific* (1971) struck down the prohibition of night work and long hours that had been upheld ever since *Muller*. The weightlifting requirement associated with a railroad clerk's job was shown to be irrelevant to the job in *Weeks v. Southern Bell* (1969). Through such decisions the principle of equal treatment enunciated in the Equal Pay Act of 1963 and the Civil Rights Act of 1964 was becoming ever more firmly established.

Alongside this rich array of legal remedies in employment was a changing backdrop with respect to women's lives apart from work. *Roe v. Wade* in 1973 established women's right to abortion. The Education Amendments of 1972 set in motion a variety of new initiatives to improve women's access to higher education. Finally, there was widespread optimism that the ERA would eventually establish a floor of protection against all other kinds of sex discrimination. By 1982, however, ten years after it had been voted out of Congress, the amendment again failed.

Enforcement of the Equal Pay Act and of Title VII

Using the Equal Pay Act and Title VII of the Civil Rights Act along with several executive orders, the advocates for sex equality had an array of legal tools with which to pursue and punish sex discrimination in employment. (Executive Order 11246 of 1965 banned discrimination in employment on the basis of sex and was amended by Executive Order 11375, which banned sex discrimination by any federal contractor.) Several mechanisms for enforcement were also available. The Equal Employment Opportunity Commission, the Office of Federal Contract Compliance, the U.S. Civil Service Commission, and in all some seventeen federal agencies were active in the early 1970s to enforce the rules against sex discrimination. Near the end of the decade, Giele (1978) reported that a total of 130,000 cases were awaiting action, with delays of up to three years until resolution. Between 1964 and 1971, the U.S. Department of Labor found that underpayments to nearly 71,000 workers (mostly women) totaled $26 million (Castro, 2001).

Particularly interesting during the 1970s and 1980s was the evolution of judicial interpretations of the laws against sex discrimination. When the Equal Pay Act came into being, there was ambiguity in what was meant by "equal work." In a series of court decisions beginning with *Shultz v. Wheaton Glass* (1970), the courts made clear that mere difference in name did not make jobs different enough to avoid a charge of sex discrimination if the work entailed was substantially similar. Nor in the case of *Corning Glass Works v. Brennan* (1974) did the refusal of men to work for wages as low as women's constitute sufficient grounds to justify pay differences (Castro, 2001).

It also took a series of court cases on a variety of other aspects of equal employment opportunity besides equal pay to test and further specify the implications of Title VII of the Civil Rights Act. During this time, the courts sorted out which arguments were supported by the due process clause of the Fifth Amendment, the equal protection clause of the Fourteenth Amendment, and Title VII of the Civil Rights Act. Gradually the Supreme Court developed a standard of intermediate scrutiny for sex discrimination cases that contrasted with its standard of strict scrutiny for cases of race discrimination. In general, when the case involved a distinction based on tradition, stereotype, or social role, the courts struck down practices based on a classification by sex (Lindgren and Taub, 1993). Thus, *Reed v. Reed* (1971) found that a woman could not be denied a role as executor of an estate simply because she was a woman. *Frontiero v. Richardson* (1973) upheld the right of a female military officer to claim her spouse as a dependent.

But in a series of cases in which the issue was women's right to receive disability benefits connected with pregnancy, the court took a more difference-oriented position and used a lower standard of scrutiny to deny pregnancy-related benefits. Thus,

Geduldig v. Aiello (1974) upheld a California disability insurance program that excluded women, and *General Electric v. Gilbert* (1976) allowed the exclusion of pregnancy from disability benefits on grounds that such exclusion was not a violation of Title VII and its prohibition of discrimination "on the basis of sex." The court reasoned, according to Lindgren and Taub (1993: 113), that "where there are 'real differences,' there can be no question of inequality: Inequality presupposes comparability; and a finding of uniqueness denies that comparisons are possible." The effect of these pregnancy cases was dramatically reversed by passage of the Pregnancy Discrimination Act in 1978. The focus shifted from the nature of the disability (pregnancy) to the effect of disability (which men also shared) on absence from work. The principle of including pregnancy in coverage for disability benefits was tested and upheld in *California Federal Savings and Loan v. Guerra* (1987). Earlier, in *Craig v. Boren* (1976), an Oklahoma case about the discrepancy between the drinking age of eighteen for women and twenty-one for men, the court further clarified the intermediate standard of scrutiny by arguing that classification on the basis of sex was defensible only if it served an important state interest (which the arrest statistics for drunk driving in Oklahoma did not show). The net effect of the 1978 Pregnancy Discrimination Act and *Craig v. Boren* was thus to reinforce a growing emphasis on the equality perspective.

In addition to these court actions, several kinds of proactive strategies were put forward to prevent or remedy unequal pay and job segregation between the sexes. During the 1970s, various women's advocacy groups took an active part in uncovering potential violations of federal contracts and bringing them to the attention of authorities. Thus the Women's Equity Action League (WEAL), headed by Bernice Sandler, was a gadfly for enforcement, especially in the education arena (Freeman, 1975; Giele, 1978).

One of the great successes of this era was the Equal Employment Opportunity Commission (EEOC) case against the American Telephone and Telegraph company (AT&T) in 1973, which resulted in an out-of-court settlement between EEOC, the Office of Federal Contract Compliance (OFCC), and AT&T that awarded $15 million in back pay to women employees who had suffered job discrimination (Giele, 1978). But the most sustained strategies for improvement came through programs for affirmative action and comparable worth that sought both to remedy past sex discrimination and prevent unequal treatment in the future.

Affirmative Action in Employment

Executive Order 11478 (1969) enjoined affirmative action in federal agencies to be administered by the U.S. Civil Service Commission. Revised Order 4 (1971) set out guidelines for the Office of Federal Contract Compliance in enforcing Executive Order 11375 (1968) that banned sex discrimination by federal contractors. Throughout the 1970s and 1980s there was major tension in the courts and with the Reagan and Bush administrations over the interpretation of Title VII. Conservative court justices, like the administration, understood the intent of Title VII to be the prohibition of deliberate and intended discrimination. The liberals thought Title VII was also relevant in cases in which existing practices had a disparate impact on the sexes, even when not intended. Eventually, the broader interpretation prevailed, and the law came to be understood as prohibiting any practice not relevant to job performance that had a disparate impact on one race or one sex, even if that consequence was unintended. The reasoning was first spelled out in *Griggs v. Duke Power Co.* (1971), a case involving race discrimination at a power plant that required a high school education and certain test scores. The requirements were not relevant to the job but had a disparate impact on blacks, who were less likely to have completed high school and to perform well on the tests and who therefore had less chance of being employed.

Affirmative action programs build on several ideas embedded in these cases. The first step is an analysis to discern the sex and race composition of the qualified labor pool and to compare it with the sex and race composition in the occupation of interest. The second step is to examine the barriers or employment practices that may bias the selection process against the underrepresented minority. A third step is proactive, to increase the actual numbers of the underrepresented minority in the hiring pool and among those who are hired. Thus the United Steelworkers and the Kaiser Aluminum and Chemical Corporation deliberately sought to get more black workers into craft jobs. Although the program sparked charges of reverse discrimination by more senior white workers who were passed over for promotion, its legality was upheld in *United Steelworkers v. Weber* (1979).

The purpose of goals and timetables in affirmative action is to try to move the race or sex distribution of the employed population closer to the ratio in the supply population. Thus, the Glass Ceiling Commission of the first Bush administration was acting

in the spirit of affirmative action when the Office of Federal Contract Compliance, in cooperation with the Department of Labor,
interviewed ten major employers who were federal contractors to
make them aware of ways they might increase the numbers of
women and minorities in their managerial ranks. At the time,
only 16.9 percent of their managers were women, compared with
37.2 percent of all their workers who were women (Berger, 1992).

Comparable Worth

Comparable worth, like affirmative action, is one of the main
strategies for increasing sex equity in employment. Unlike affirmative action, which works toward moving minority groups out
of low-paying occupations, the purpose of comparable worth is to
raise the value of those very same low-paying occupations and
thereby increase the pay. The method of comparable worth is to
evaluate all jobs in a given firm on the basis of job content. Several
job evaluation plans such as the Hay System rate jobs in terms of
skill, effort, responsibility, and working conditions (Treiman and
Hartmann, 1981). Jobs with similar scores are then compared in
terms of their salaries, and in those cases in which there is a
noticeable discrepancy in pay between jobs with similar ratings,
discrimination is suspected and there is a case for raising the pay.

In San Jose, California, in 1980, for example, when a rating
system was used to rank all municipal jobs, it was discovered that
the mayor's secretary earned only a little more than half the pay
(53 percent) of a senior air conditioning mechanic, and a nurse
earned $9,120 less than a fire truck mechanic (Blum, 1991). Using
such findings, the local union of the American Federation of State,
County, and Municipal Employees (AFSCME) tried to negotiate
with the city council to raise wages in the higher-rated occupations with the lower salaries, occupations typically held by
women. After a brief strike, they eventually won a settlement of
$1.45 million that included a large cost-of-living increase as well
as an average 10 percent increase in salaries of the clerical workers and professionals (librarians, nurses, and recreation coordina-
tors) whose jobs had been found to be undervalued (Blum, 1991).

The comparable worth movement began in the late 1970s as
a result of analysis by scholars and efforts by unionized government employees among whom women and minorities were
heavily represented. In a study sponsored by the National Academy of Sciences in the late 1970s, a panel of economists and social
scientists analyzed the merits of a comparable worth approach for

identifying discrimination and increasing pay equity. Their report concluded that even when differences in skill and job content were taken into account, a sizable pay differential remained between jobs dominated by men and women. Recognizing that the Equal Pay Act could not effectively address these discrepancies because the jobs were never "equal" in the sense of being exactly alike, they advocated some sort of job evaluation to address discrimination on the basis of sex or race that came under the provisions of Title VII. They also recognized that such job evaluation schemes did contain three inherent difficulties: (1) job evaluation is often colored by existing pay rates; (2) job evaluation criteria vary according to the type of job being evaluated, thereby making it difficult to find a scheme with sufficient breadth to cover high- as well as low-paying jobs; and (3) there is no definitive test of fairness, and jobs are evaluated differently by employers and employees and by women and men (Treiman and Hartmann, 1981).

Bolstered by the victories of municipal employees in San Jose and of state employees in *Gunther v. Washington* in 1981, the comparable worth movement gained momentum during the 1980s. There was an outpouring of scholarship on the subject, and union leaders and feminists began to see it as a major strategy for overcoming the effects of sex segregation in the workplace.

In 1985, however, the Ninth Circuit Court of Appeals in *AFSCME v. Washington* rendered a decision against the principle of comparable worth that essentially stalled the movement and greatly limited its scope. In his decision, Judge Anthony Kennedy (now Justice Kennedy) held that pay differentials are not necessarily caused by discrimination but are the result of a number of interacting forces, among them labor supply and demand, the preferences of workers, and collective bargaining agreements (Lindgren and Taub, 1993). Therefore, to impose a requirement on the state of Washington that it adopt a plan for implementing comparable worth would be to try to interfere with the free market and to hold the state responsible for disparate impact that it neither intended or originated.

Since the *AFSCME* decision, scholars have continued to write about comparable worth and to assess the reasons for its stalling in the 1980s and the possibilities for its resurgence in the future. A sober assessment comes from the work of several economists who doubt that bureaucratic imposition of comparable worth is any more effective than wage setting mechanisms based on the working of the labor market. Thus Blau, Ferber, and Winkler

(1998) suggest that raising wages in low-wage jobs ultimately results in a loss of jobs as the price of the work goes higher. This analysis is upheld in a National Bureau of Economics study of the impact of equal opportunity laws on employment of women and racial minorities (Neumark and Stock, 2001). Nelson and Bridges (1999), however, argue that the courts, in rejecting the arguments for comparable worth, allowed discrimination to continue and that true reliance on external market rates would actually raise women's wages within firms if they were used for setting women's pay as they are for men's (England, 2000).

A more positive assessment of comparable worth comes from analysts who see the court decisions and the promotion of comparable worth itself as a reflection of shifts in power and the political climate. Conservative judicial reasoning could eventually change as a result of composition of the courts; interpretation of comparable worth as an interference in the free market might then be transformed into an argument that discrimination interferes with the laws of the market. In addition, as Goldin (1990) notes, women's voices and interests will likely continue to grow. She attributes the early successes of the comparable worth movement to the rise in the number of unionized women employees among government workers. (Among teachers alone, the proportion who were union members doubled between 1975 and 1980, from one-quarter to one-half.) This strength of women and minorities in the unions of state, county, and local government employees helped to advance comparable worth in the setting of pay scales for government workers. To the extent that such organizing continues on college campuses today or takes the form of Living Wage Campaigns for service employees and unionization of clerical workers in academia, the potential for raising pay scales in the disadvantaged part of the segregated labor force is still alive.

Sexual Harassment

In addition to achieving pay equity as a key dimension of gender equity in the workplace, another important aspect is the atmosphere and working conditions, such that a worker, whether male or female, is able to do his or her job without the annoyance or barrier of being treated as a sexual object. Although sexual harassment is now broadly recognized as a form of sex discrimination in the workplace to be dealt with under the provisions of Title VII, this was not always the case.

In fact, the concept and the term *sexual harassment* were not invented until 1974 when a clerical employee at Cornell University and several of her colleagues began to name the problem (Brownmiller and Alexander, 1992). During the late 1970s, Catharine MacKinnon (1979) developed a legal analysis of the problem and the conceptualization of two kinds of sexual harassment: one that implicitly or explicitly demanded a quid pro quo exchange of sexual favors as a condition of employment; the other that created a hostile atmosphere that interfered with an employee's work. Also at this time, Eleanor Holmes Norton, head of the EEOC during the Carter administration, listed a one-page set of guidelines that further defined the phenomenon of sexual harassment and the ways in which it violated the prohibition against sex discrimination contained in Title VII (Brownmiller and Alexander, 1992).

Then a series of court cases developed the legal analysis of sexual harassment and produced decisions that gave solidity to the distinction between behavior that makes sexual favors a condition of employment and behavior that creates a hostile climate that affects employment decisions or unnecessarily interferes with the employee's work. In the case of *Tomkins v. Public Service Electric Gas Company* (1977), the Third Circuit Court of Appeals prohibited the tangible benefit form of sexual harassment and called it a violation of Title VII. Adrienne Tomkins was invited to lunch by her supervisor to discuss her work and was asked to go out with him several times. When she declined, she was demoted. In *Bundy v. Jackson* (1981) the District of Columbia Court of Appeals held that the District of Columbia Department of Corrections violated Title VII by creating a hostile climate of sexual teasing and propositions by supervisors that made it difficult for Sandra Bundy to perform her job as a vocational rehabilitation specialist for criminal offenders. When the Supreme Court heard its first case on sexual harassment in 1986 in *Meritor Savings Bank v. Vinson*, the groundwork had been laid for treating unwanted sexual advances and a hostile climate as violations of Title VII. Mechelle Vinson had complied with pressure for her sexual favors from the beginning of her employment at the bank in 1974, but unwillingly, and she was fired after she started dating a steady boyfriend in 1977 and took an indefinite sick leave in September 1978. The Court found that even though she had given the sexual favors, her claim fell under Title VII protection against a hostile environment.

Although sexual harassment was thus beginning to be recognized by the courts, it was not widely known or understood by the general public. Yet the Merit Systems Protection Board, which protects the merit-based system of federal employment, in surveys of 20,000 federal workers in 1980 and again in 1988, had found that 42 percent of the women and 15 percent of the men had been subject to unwanted sexual attention in the previous two years. In September 1990, the U.S. Department of Defense found in a survey of 20,000 military personnel that 64 percent of the women reported sexual harassment. Still, there was shock and disbelief on the part of the all-male judiciary committee at the testimony of Anita Hill in 1991. Hill accused Clarence Thomas, later confirmed as a Supreme Court justice, of inappropriate sexual remarks and invitations when he was her supervisor and head of the EEOC in the early 1980s. Earlier that same year, the Tailhook Association, a group of active and retired naval flying officers, had held its annual convention in a Las Vegas hotel, resulting in a drunken revel where eighty-three women and seven men were sexually assaulted.

Although these dramatic events raised awareness, Baker and Stover (1996) report the sum total of relief for sexual harassment to be very limited. In a survey done by the Illinois Department of Human Rights over a two-year period, only 29 percent of the claims were settled in favor of the complainants. To win, the charge had to be that sexual harassment was severe, with management failing to take action and with witnesses and documents to support the claim. When settlements did result, they were quite meager, an average of $3,234 for these Illinois cases. Given this sober assessment, it appears that legal action alone is a rather unwieldy tool for dealing with the problem. Thus, training programs and efforts to raise awareness and prevent harassment before it begins have become the main remedy of choice.

Social Policy for Women in Blue-Collar Work

Although it is clear that over the course of three decades, sex discrimination in employment has been identified and curtailed, and sex equity in pay and job opportunities has increased, it is still worth considering whether women in blue-collar occupations are getting as much help as they need to deal with the harsh realities of their particular circumstances. This issue seems worth consideration, given that much of the affirmative action efforts and comparable worth strategy has been aimed at pink-collar employees in clerical work and semiprofessional positions. In addition, the largest advances in union organizing have occurred among this same category of female employees.

What, then, of blue-collar women? Roughly three-quarters of them are in semiskilled jobs, and only 12 percent are in the higher-paid skilled occupations such as plumber or electrician. Moreover, they work in factory and service occupations where males have dominated the unions, and unions in the manufacturing sector have declined to less than 20 percent of the current work force.

In addition, the working conditions in blue-collar occupations are often difficult, requiring speed, physical exertion, shift work, and sometimes an exposure to toxic materials. The threat of unemployment is also higher (Padavic, 1996). Finally, because women represent only 16 percent of the nation's 30 million blue-collar workers, they may be in situations dominated by the opposite sex, a condition that is much more likely to be associated with sexual harassment (Clark, 1991).

Under these adverse conditions, one of the most hopeful signs is the continued union organizing and the expansion of unions into fields that employ many women. The Coalition of Labor Union Women became active in the 1980s (Roth, 2003). Before that, in the 1970s Karen Nussbaum organized 9 to 5 when she was a clerical worker at Harvard. She rose through organized labor to become head of the Women's Bureau during the Clinton administration. Perhaps the situation of working-class women will be aided in the future by the type of unionization effort that has made inroads among middle-class female teachers and clerical workers (Cornfield, 1996). Perhaps women will reach across class lines in feminist solidarity because they understand their common needs to earn a living, support families, and find time for their children and other responsibilities at home.

Equal Opportunity in Education

To achieve gender equity in employment, boys and girls and men and women need equal opportunity in education. Education provides a foundation for employment in three ways. First, learning in school and on the job forms individuals' human capital (knowledge and skills) that qualify them for their eventual occupations. Second, the social expectations, rewards, and sanctions that go with education have the power to influence a person's self-concept and self-confidence and to shape future goals. Finally, educational institutions themselves are major employers and provide job opportunities in settings ranging from preschools to high schools and universities. Whether women and men are treated equably as employees in education has implications not only for their capacity to serve as positive role models, but also for demonstrating that actual job opportunities in education can be equitable.

Role of the Women's Movement

The effort to uncover and fight sex discrimination in education has drawn heavily on the work of feminists. Bernice Sandler, a counseling psychologist, though qualified, was not considered for any of several openings at the University of Maryland in 1969. Suspecting that the main problem was that she was a woman, she set out to track incidents of sex discrimination in academia. Working through the Women's Equity Action League (WEAL) and the Association of American Colleges, her Project on the Status and Education of Women helped lay the groundwork for the major piece of legislation, Title IX (1972), which has increased equal educational opportunity for women. These efforts were joined by advocates and activists from NOW and the Committee on the Status of Women of the American Association of University Professors (AAUP) (Freeman, 1975).

The problem for feminists in the 1960s in fighting sex discrimination in education was that Title VII of the Civil Rights Act of 1964 excluded education from its purview. Sandler, WEAL, NOW, and others therefore lacked the obvious tools to challenge sex discrimination in hiring and promotions in academia. They hit on a brilliant alternative strategy, however, which was to use Executive Order 11375, which *did* prohibit sex discrimination by any federal contractor. Suits could be brought to the attention of the Office of Federal Contract Compliance and one could thereby threaten that all federal funds be withheld from any institution that was charged with and found guilty of sex discrimination. Very soon after this strategy was developed, the Department of Health, Education, and Welfare brought suit against several high-profile universities such as Harvard University and Brown University, which had very few women in professorial positions, to charge them with sex discrimination. This strategy, which was invented for enforcement of Executive Order 11375 through threat of withdrawal of federal funds, became a central strategy for enforcement of Title IX (Freeman, 1975).

Any account of gender equity in American education in the past three decades must begin with the provisions of Title IX and must then consider the way its implementation has evolved, especially with respect to hiring college faculty, the creation and continuation of single-sex programs, and its application to sports and athletics.

Provisions of Title IX

The Higher Education Act of 1972, of which Title IX is a part, is one of the amendments to the Civil Rights Act of 1964. Its express purpose is to ban sex discrimination in public education and in any educational program that receives federal funding. The act states: "No person in the United States shall, on the basis of sex, be excluded from participation in, be denied the benefits of, or be subjected to discrimination under any education program or activity receiving Federal financial assistance" (Title IX of the Education Amendments of 1972, 20 U.S.C. Section 1681).

The wording of the prohibition against sex discrimination is very broad and therefore touches every conceivable activity or program related to education, either by inclusion or by exception: for example, admissions, counseling, curriculum, financial aid, hiring and promotion of faculty, housing, research, sexual harassment, extracurricular activities, and athletics.

It is important to understand that the theory and language of Title IX were not accidental but were prefigured by the work of Sandler and WEAL and other feminist organizations such as NOW. In 1971, Representative Martha Griffiths of Michigan began holding hearings of the House Education Committee to document the many and varied forms of sex discrimination in education as well as employment. In addition, Sandler and WEAL helped build the agenda of the Department of Health, Education, and Welfare (the forerunner of the Department of Health and Human Services) for identifying and prosecuting cases of discrimination to threaten loss of government funding (Freeman, 1975).

Another aspect of implementing Title IX was to raise awareness about the many guises in which sex discrimination could appear. Throughout the 1970s, the Project on the Status and Education of Women elaborated and illustrated the problem through their periodic newsletters. Their findings were summarized in two papers that have become classics: one on discriminatory teaching practices in the "chilly classroom"; the other on the "chilly climate" outside the classroom that puts girls and women at a relative disadvantage vis-à-vis their male peers (Hall and Sandler, 1982; 1984). Many of their illustrations rang true to the experiences of the 1970s and 1980s, and some do even now. Their illustrations included teasing of college women when they enter a men's lounge or sitting area; panty raids; belittling of women's comments in class or failing to take note of them; the huge attention paid to male athletic teams and the condescending attitude toward or lack of interest in women's teams; expectations that women will make the coffee and bring the food to social events; and the like. These examples sound familiar twenty years later, but their impact was powerful and surprising at a time when such behaviors were thought to be normal or trivial and hardly worth public attention. With the implementation power of Title IX backing the feminists, however, educational institutions began to take notice and review their hiring and promotion practices and their allocation of resources to men's and women's programs.

The documentation of sexism and discrimination had an impact on female students as well. The lesson was not to blame themselves for being harassed or abused, nor to lower their goals or withdraw from the field. Sandler and others, by making public a pattern of discrimination that needed to be changed, were helping to create a new climate of opinion and expectation. They were laying the groundwork for identifying problems in the current system.

Accomplishments in Academia

Over the course of the three decades following its enactment, the mere existence of Title IX provided legitimation to feminist efforts to raise the number of faculty and administrators in higher education and to change the climate of expectation from focusing on "token" women to considering women's presence in positions of authority as normal. Especially during the 1970s, huge gains were made. With the conservative Reagan administration, however, enforcement slowed. Then it picked up again after the Civil Rights Restoration Act of 1988 (Lindgren and Taub, 1993).

At elite institutions like Harvard where female full professors were a rarity, some women alumnae protested by withholding their financial contributions until more female professors were hired. By 2002, enough progress had been made that the Committee for the Equality of Women at Harvard allowed its contributions (which had been held in escrow) to be used for the Radcliffe Alumnae Professorship, which "is designed to recruit women and men to tenured faculty positions" in the Harvard Faculty of Arts and Sciences ("Alumnae Show Strong Support for Professorship," 2002).

The number of women as presidents and provosts of leading universities also rose dramatically during the 1990s, with women at the helm of Brown, Duke, Princeton, and the universities of Michigan and Wisconsin. Credit for these changes belonged not only to activists, but also to committed organizations including the American Council on Education, the American Association of University Professors, the Higher Educational Resources Service (HERS, which prepares individuals for administrative positions), and such foundations as Ford and Carnegie. According to O'Toole (1996), in the late 1980s only 10 percent of the chief executive officers of the roughly 3,000 colleges and universities in the United States were women, and this represented a doubling of the previous decade's number.

By the 1990s, there was a widespread sense that many of the problems of women in higher administration were a thing of the past. The percentage of female faculty members had risen from 24 percent in 1974 to 35 percent in 1995, and the percentage of female faculty with tenure increased from 41 to 51 percent (Stith-Willis, 1999). But in 1999, a carefully conducted five-year study by faculty women at the Massachusetts Institute of Technology showed that problems still existed. Measured in terms of job titles, salaries, or square feet of office and laboratory space, these highly qualified female professors at MIT were still paying a penalty because they were women. The president of MIT took the study seriously, remedies were instituted, and numerous other science faculties at elite universities followed suit (Loder, 2000; Wilson, 1999).

Affirmative Action in Education

A strategic issue in the campaign for sex equality in education has been the concept of affirmative action. As far back as the 1960s, when feminists were learning how to tackle discrimination in education through enforcement and contract compliance under EO (Executive Order) 11375, they also learned how to use Revised Order 4, which set out goals and timetables for achieving equity.

Although affirmative action is nothing other than a good faith effort to remedy past discrimination through setting positive goals and timetables and attempting to achieve them in the future, the concept of affirmative action got a bad name as soon as its opponents equated it with preferential hiring or quotas. In the past, quotas had especially been associated with the setting of tacit upper limits on the number of Jews who would be admitted to a selective college or university. The quota issue, or "preferential hiring," thus turned the concept of affirmative action on its head and raised the specter of keeping out qualified men or whites in order to let in more women or people of color (Freeman, 1975). One of the best known cases is that of Alan Bakke, who in the late 1970s claimed that as a white male, he had been kept out of the University of California Medical School at Davis in order to save a place for a minority person who was less qualified than he. The California Supreme Court ruled that the burden of proof was on the University of California to show that Bakke would not have been admitted even in the absence of a special minority admissions program.

The issue of affirmative action is still salient in higher education, particularly in California and Texas. In 1996, various women's rights and civil rights groups organized "Freedom Summer" to campaign against California's Proposition 209, a state referendum to ban discrimination against or "preferential treatment to, any individual or group on the basis of race, sex, color, ethnicity, or national origin in the operation of public employment, public education, or public contracting." The proposition passed in November 1997 and was widely interpreted as a setback to affirmative action by such groups as the Feminist Majority Foundation (2002). In Texas in 1996, in the case of *Texas v. Hopwood*, court rulings forced the state to drop its affirmative action policy at the University of Texas Law School as well as at all other public colleges, universities, and law schools. According to *Feminist Daily News* (2001), the immediate effect on law school admissions of minorities was devastating, with just over one-tenth of the entering class in 2000 at the University of Texas Law School being either black or Mexican American compared with 40 percent of the population of the whole state. To address this imbalance, Texas adopted a policy of guaranteed undergraduate admission to any public university for those who graduate in the top ten percent of their high school class. This course of action promises to improve minority admissions, as many minority applicants come from racially homogeneous schools. Affirmative action with respect to sex is also sometimes blamed by those not hired when they suspect they might have had a better chance if they had been a woman or a minority. But as the economists Blau, Ferber, and Winkler (2002) have noted, blaming affirmative action can be the result of turbulence in the labor market and resentment that there are not enough jobs to go around. By extension, opposition to affirmative action in education may stem in part from having many more candidates for admission than the number of openings available, especially at the most sought-after universities.

Single-Sex and Coeducational Programs

Single-sex programs in education give rise to an important class of exceptions in the legislation and implementation of Title IX. Programs are exempt from coverage of Title IX if they have been offered only to males or females since their founding. Single-sex schools are permitted in the case of preschools, elementary and secondary schools, and private colleges and universities. But single-sex programs are prohibited in vocational schools, public undergraduate higher education, professional schools, and graduate schools. That said, there is still a great deal of room for interpretation of the law. Historically, the trend has been away from single-sex education to coeducation. By the 1990s there were only three all-male undergraduate colleges in the country, with a total of less than 5,000 students. By contrast, there were still more than 150 all-female colleges serving some 84,000 students (Blau, Ferber, and Winkler, 1998). Clearly, there continues to be a market for all-female education that appears in some instances to be more successful in encouraging women to take leadership positions and to study math, science, and economics (Sadker and Sadker, 1995; Tidball, 1980). The higher success rates of the alumnae of elite women's colleges may also in part be due to their more advantageous social positions from the start (Giele and Gilfus, 1990).

Two types of legal precedents are involved in permitting or prohibiting sex segregation in education. The first type concerns "separate but equal" programs. Such ventures must show that the single-sex provision serves a government interest in equal protection of individuals of that sex and that it makes up for past discrimination. Thus, in *Vorcheimer v. School District of Philadelphia* (1976), a girl who wanted to attend the publicly funded Central High School for boys was denied her petition because she could attend Girls' High School, which was said to be as good. In *Mis-*

sissippi University for Women v. Hogan (1982), the Supreme Court found for Hogan: male nurse Hogan was granted entrance to the nursing program at MUW because the Court found that no government interest in equal protection was served by a segregated program in nursing. In *Garrett v. Board of Education of the School District of Detroit* (1991), the board was prohibited from setting up three publicly funded all-male academies for inner-city minority boys. The court held that such programs would allocate resources to boys without fairly providing an equivalent for girls (Lindgren and Taub, 1993).

The second type of case uses the standard of strict scrutiny that finds "separate-but-equal" arguments suspect. A good example is seen in the case that culminated in the Supreme Court decision against the Virginia Military Institute (VMI). Justice Ruth Bader Ginsburg wrote the opinion in *United States v. Virginia* (1996) that found this all-male publicly funded program inherently unequal to the parallel program that VMI had established for women at a nearby college. Nor could VMI justify a legitimate state interest in keeping the sexes separate (Greenhouse, 1996). Several precedents for integration had already been established, and women had shown their capability of meeting the requirements satisfactorily. In 1972, women had been admitted to the Reserve Officer Training Corps (ROTC), of which the first class graduated in 1976. Women were accepted into Officers' Candidate School in 1976. Also in 1976, Congress opened the service academies to women. In 1996, even though women were still barred from direct combat roles, women represented 11 percent of the armed forces at various command levels (Hancock, 1996).

As a result of the 1996 VMI decision, the Citadel, a similar institution in South Carolina, was also opened to women, thus overturning the 1970 decision in *Williams v. McNair* that had justified sex segregation between the Citadel and Winthrop College for Women, a publicly funded institution parallel to the Citadel, on the grounds that the Citadel and Winthrop were separate but equal (Greenhouse, 1996; Lindgren and Taub, 1993).

Athletics and Competitive Sports in Schools and Colleges

Just as Title IX has had enormous impact on admissions, curriculum, financial aid, and hiring, the law has also changed the profile of athletic programs by increasing participation of girls along with boys in school-sponsored sports. During the twenty years following passage of the law, the numbers of girls active in school sports teams rose from less than 300,000 to more than 2 million (Morse, 1992). Women's tennis and girls' basketball became important spectator sports, and the numbers of American women winning Olympic gold medals rose dramatically (Blau, Ferber, and Winkler, 1998).

Widening opportunities to women in athletics, as in education as a whole, are considered by many to be an important precursor to women's advancement in the workplace (Morse, 1992). Thus, in an article about Shannon O'Brien, the winner of the 2002 Massachusetts Democratic gubernatorial primary, the *New York Times* reported that she is seen as something of a "tough cookie" who is free of the problems that plague other female candidates. Pictures showing her playing rugby and soccer at Yale are mentioned as helping to create that image (Belluck, 2002).

The Higher Education Act's provisions for sex equity in sports programs contain two important exceptions to the principle of total integration between the sexes in educational programs. The first exception allows separate but equal programs for boys and girls, a provision that after *Brown v. Board of Education* (1954) was no longer permitted in education of different racial groups. The second exception is the provision for different treatment of the sexes wherever contact sports are involved.

As a result of these two exceptions in the law, virtually all the legal issues and cases in the matter of sex equity in sports have revolved around two questions: first, whether separate and different programs for males and females are really equal; and second, whether the sport in question is a contact sport. Over time, one can discern a gradual evolution in the interpretation and implementation of the law. Early cases focused on whether parallel teams were available for the boys or girls who sought remedy, or whether a boys' team could exclude a girl because the sport was or was not a contact sport. In *Carnes v. Tennessee Secondary School Athletics Association* (1976) a girl was allowed to join an all-boys' baseball team because baseball was deemed not to be a contact sport. In *Clark v. Arizona Interscholastic Association* (1982), a male volleyball player was excluded from the girls' team even though there was no boys' team. This exclusion was upheld, first on the grounds that the single-sex team served a positive government interest in providing encouragement to girls to succeed at sports in a supportive atmosphere; and second on the grounds that it helped to remedy past discrimination. For different reasons, however, in *O'Connor v. Board of Education of School District 23* (1982), Karen O'Connor was not allowed to join a boys' basketball team that was much more competitive because a separate girls' team already existed, and there was a legitimate state interest in protecting girls' ability to participate in interscholastic sports and not have their activities overshadowed by the boys.

In contrast with the separate-but-equal tradition in sex segregation of sports, there is the important alternative precedent of equal protection that was enunciated in *Brown v. Board of Education*. In *Commonwealth by Packel v. Pennsylvania Interscholastic Athletic Association* (1975), the decision of the court, which preceded *O'Connor*, was different in concluding that interschool sports could not exclude a girl merely because of her sex, especially when the girls' group was known to carry a stigma and not be so demanding as the boys' group.

Assessment of the Implementation and Effects of Title IX

In a thoroughgoing critique of the benefits and results of Title IX over the past three decades, the American Association of University Women (AAUW) (2000) has reviewed enforcement and categorized the issues in terms of content and overall trends. The report covers the chief categories of complaint: from sexual harassment, admissions, financial aid, testing, discipline, and participation in nontraditional fields, to sex discrimination against employees.

Who brings the complaints differs by type of issue. In cases of sexual harassment in elementary and high schools, more than 80 percent of the cases are brought by females, whereas in colleges and universities, the figure is more than 70 percent. In matters of admissions, evaluation, and discipline at the college level, however, more than 60 percent of the complaints are brought by men.

Types of complaint by female employees in educational institutions differ by whether the setting is the primary/secondary schools or higher education. The most common complaint in higher education is sexual harassment (63 percent), and the most common in elementary and high school is retaliation for reporting grievances related to sex discrimination (64 percent). Promotion and tenure and hiring and firing account for less than 30 percent of the complaints for all levels of educational settings.

To recommend ways to standardize and speed up the complaint and investigation process, the AAUW report concludes with a suggested action agenda for continued and improved implementation of Title IX. Not only must Congress provide sufficient funds for the Office of Civil Rights to pursue enforcement through timely investigation of complaints. In addition, educational institutions need to become more aware of the law, collect better data, and take positive steps to train faculty, staff, and students to remedy and prevent sex discrimination in education.

In a *Ms.* review of the effects and potential of Title IX, Denise Kiernan (2001) notes that sports have received the lion's share of Title IX attention, with sexual harassment a close second. The next big issue hovering on the horizon is career and vocational education. Girls are still not getting exposure to shop, carpentry, and auto mechanics, fields in which the jobs pay more than typical pink-collar occupations. Even the new programs that come out of the School-to-Work Opportunities Act of 1994 are still segregated by sex. Kiernan concludes that after thirty years of experience with Title IX, the situation is "part celebration, part wake-up call."

Integration of Work and Family Obligations

Both equal employment and equal educational opportunities for women and men presuppose that their physical, mental, and social capacities are very similar and that any abridgement of the rights of either sex is discriminatory. This reasoning, however, comes up against a wall as soon as responsibilities for children and families are brought into the equation. It then becomes clear that the social expectations of the two sexes are very different. Men have traditionally been expected to be the primary breadwinners and women the primary homemakers and caretakers.

Particularly since 1970, the traditional assumptions have been seriously challenged as many more married women with children have entered the labor force and as numbers of single mothers have increased. The question is how to devise laws and social policies that support the employment of both women and men while at the same time promoting the care and supervision of children, the maintenance of family life, and the prevention of poverty in families in which a single parent has responsibilities for both work and caregiving. The history of social policies to address these issues is fraught with deep ambivalence that stems from fundamentally different views on women's roles. Those who continue to believe that women have the primary responsibility for children and families are hesitant about providing universal child care and paid family leave, although they are usually willing to make an exception if a woman is already poor. Despite this ambivalence, however, there appears to be a long-term trend toward greater acceptance of working mothers and greater willingness to provide the social supports that are required. In general, American programs are much less generous in state support of working families than are those in European countries (Christopher, 2002; Meyers and Gornick, 2001). The difference can be traced to the American history of targeting work programs to the poor rather than to everybody and to being unsure whether a mother's employment is healthy or harmful for her family and children.

Child Care Policy

Gender equity in employment is virtually impossible without a universal and affordable child care system. Otherwise, mothers will be expected to leave the work force while their children are of preschool age and to take part-time rather than full-time jobs so that they can be available to meet the needs of their families. Such demands reduce a woman's chances of building her human capital in jobs that require more time and commitment (Blau, Ferber, and Winkler, 2002). Or, if mothers work with no provision for child care, their children are at risk of poor development, poor performance in school later on, and lower productivity as adult citizens.

Formal child care for children of preschool age has grown rapidly since 1950, when there were only 3,525 nursery schools and child care centers in the entire United States, one-third of which were in California and New York (Michel, 1999). By the late 1990s, 75 percent of children were in some form of child care arrangement, whether in centers, family day care, or another home (Cohen, 2001). Despite this rise, the use of child care is still lower and plagued with more difficulty in the United States than in Europe, where most countries have more than three-quarters (and some as many as 90 percent) of their children aged three to five in formal child care arrangements (Stebbins, 2001).

Widespread public support for child care in the United States has been a long time in coming because at the beginning it was associated in the public mind with the dire family needs of the Great Depression or with the labor shortage and need for women workers of World War II. Once those crises disappeared, there seemed to be no widespread demand for child care. Public consciousness was not engaged until more women workers, more divorced parents and single-parent families, and more need for child care created a new consensus that permanent government support for child care was needed. The story is closely intertwined with the question of gender equity in employment and the changing roles of women and men in breadwinning and caring for children.

In her detailed history of child care, Sonya Michel (1999) shows the deep conflict in American feelings about whether mothers should work and leave their young children in the care of someone else. During the 1930s and 1940s a quiet tug of war took place between New Deal advocates of Aid to Dependent Children, Children's Bureau officials, social workers, and child psychologists (who generally believed it was better that mothers stay at home with their children) and the women professionals, Women's Bureau, Works Progress Administration, and those engaged in mobilization for the war effort (who believed that excellent child care could be provided that was good both for children and for their working parents).

The conservative camp preferred such measures as Aid to Dependent Children (ADC) that provided poor single (primarily widowed) mothers with financial assistance; they thought of child care as only a fall-back measure in extreme cases where the family was unfit, the parent was disabled, or the child was orphaned. Child care advocates, on the other hand, pointed to the excellent and beautiful child care centers built with government subsidies by the Kaiser shipyards on the West Coast during the war. Their bright, open layouts and attractive play yards even won architectural design awards. They also served hot meals for tired mothers to take home when they picked up their children (Michel, 1999).

After the war was over, however, there was little hope of government support for child care in peace time. During the 1950s, child care advocates like Eleanor Guggenheimer in New York began to build a movement for child care. Organizations like the National Council of Jewish Women saw the growing crisis of more mothers at work with neither child care available nor the means to pay for it and published their findings with sometimes shocking vignettes (Giele, 1995). Without a war emergency or a temporary labor shortage, it was difficult to find a rationale that would command wider public support. One particular argument, however, kept surfacing, and that was one in which child care was seen as a support for working-class and low-income mothers who "needed" to work. The only problem with this approach was that it created a legacy that would be hard to change later on, namely, the idea that child care was for people with special needs (means-tested or "targeted") rather than for everybody ("universal").

Child care policy thus has had what Michel has termed "a divided constituency": those who believe that publicly supported child care should be just for the neediest; and those who believe it should be available to all regardless of income or whether a mother participates in the labor force. The more targeted approach was embodied in the Family Support Act of 1988, which made child care an entitlement for women who were enrolled in various kinds of programs to get them into a job. The more universal approach emerged in the Better Child Care legislation first proposed in the late 1980s and finally adopted in 1990 in the form of the Child Care Block Grants (CCBG). The block grants were meant to increase the supply and improve the quality of available child care programs.

The trend toward a more universal approach was the result of increasing use of child care by middle-class families and reliance by them as well as by poor and working-class families on government tax credits as subsidies. The National Child Care Survey of 1991 showed that fully 50 percent of nonworking mothers were sending their three- to five-year-old children to nursery school, as compared with 60 percent of working mothers (Hofferth, 1999). During the preceding decade, Congress had actually been spending more on child care for subsidies to middle- and upper-income people than for poor and low-income families.

Tax subsidies, together with the Child Care Block Grants of 1990, have gradually created a broader foundation for the expansion of child care. The block grants to the states pay for services that improve quality and supply to low-income families. The At-Risk program targets those who are at greatest risk of needing welfare, and it supplements Head Start, which already helps lower-income children. Blau, Ferber, and Winkler (2002: 375) list four types of federally supported tax subsidies for child care. Through the Dependent Care Tax Credit, employed parents can receive a tax credit of up to 30 percent of actual expenses (up to

$2,400 for one child and $4,800 for the care of two or more) if their adjusted income is under $10,000. Those whose income is over $28,000 per year are able to claim up to 20 percent of actual expenses on their taxes. (But this credit is nonrefundable, so they will not see it if they do not pay taxes.)

Early in 2003, two other mechanisms for supporting children, the Child Tax Credit and the Earned Income Tax Credit (EITC), came under increasing scrutiny as part of Republican efforts to cut costs and lower taxes. It was proposed to abolish the Child Tax Credit introduced in 1998, which gives families with incomes up to $100,000 a nonrefundable tax credit of $500 for every child under seventeen. At the same time the Internal Revenue Service was tightening its enforcement of eligibility limits for the EITC, a refundable tax credit to low-income families that in 2000 could be as high as $3,888 for two children. As a result of sharp political protest, it appeared by the summer of 2003 that the Child Tax Credit would continue and that Congress would uphold its bipartisan support of the EITC, but details of eligibility and benefit amounts had yet to be spelled out (Firestone, 2003).

Finally, tax subsidies are available for those who use flexible spending accounts. These devices reduce tax liability for employees who have such accounts and use them. In addition to these forms of state support for child care, private programs are available from many employers, either in on-site child care, information and referral systems, or provision of family leave.

Not surprisingly, the number of children aged three to five in child care has risen dramatically since the 1980s, from 38 percent in 1990 to 65 percent in 1997. As child care has become part of the entitlement of mothers moving from welfare to work, federal spending on child care has also risen substantially, to a total of $17.2 billion in 2001. Of that amount, Head Start accounted for slightly more than one-third ($6.2 billion); the Child Care Block Grants for more than one-quarter ($4.6 billion); and the remaining portion covered several smaller programs including the Dependent Care Tax Credit ($2.2 billion), the Community Learning Centers ($1.8 billion), and food and social services programs ($2.4 billion) (Cohen, 2001).

Among advocates, experts, and consumers of child care, there is wide agreement that the big issues for the future are how to improve availability, affordability, and quality. Using data from the National Child Care Surveys of 1989–1991, David Blau (2001) has analyzed the effects of mothers' working hours and pay rates and price of care on such choices as type of care or quality of the program that is used. He finds that a lower price for care would increase the demand for paid center-based care by about 20 percent and would lower the demand for parental and unpaid care. A lower price of care would also likely raise the employment level of women. If mothers' wages were doubled on average from $7.50 to $15.00 per hour, the use of child care would increase by about 15 percent.

Although most current public policy focuses on care of young children, after-school care of school-age children is also of concern to working parents and the community. The 1991 National Child Care Survey found that of children aged six to twelve, only about 8 percent were in some form of after-school care, and 3.5 million were latchkey children unsupervised by adults during the after-school hours (Stebbins, 2001). Those who direct or teach in after-school programs often report that older children gradually lose interest and that it is difficult to provide a range of interesting activities that appeals to the teenagers as much as to younger children. Advocates for youth may then have to get involved to survey the needs of teenagers in the community and find a combination of entertainment, exercise, hobbies, and supervision of homework that is as good as what the family or just a parent can provide.

Work and Family Policy

Just as change in the family and the economy has increased the pressure to develop child care programs, so also the same forces have led to new customs and new policies concerning the relationship of work time to family time. Beginning in the 1970s, scholars, feminists, employers, and workers proposed a variety of schedules and other means to increase flexibility in the allocation of time to the family and workplace. By 1993 the United States had passed the Family and Medical Leave Act (FMLA). Yet at the same time, the average working hours of Americans were the highest in the world, higher than in 1980, and the labor market was split between those who had more work than they wanted or needed and those who were unemployed or underemployed (Schor, 2002).

Any assessment of the current work and family situation must consider these contradictory trends. This chapter examines four aspects of work and family programs as they have evolved in the United Sates since World War II: first, the impact of the changing economy and its relation to family life; second, the emergence of a feminist perspective; third, the development of alternative work and family arrangements; and finally, various proposals for the future.

The Changing Economy in Relation to Family Life

In rural society, work life and family life are closely intertwined. Men, women, and children are all workers on the family land, in the workshop, or in the store. There is no commuting, because work life and family life are virtually one and the same. Women are producers as well as caretakers. Men are caretakers as well as producers, as is necessary in animal husbandry, growing of crops, and the teaching and supervision of children as workers. These age-old patterns, however, were drastically changed in the developed world with the spread of the industrial revolution and the gradual movement of the population to urban places. Beginning in the middle of the nineteenth century, and reinforced by the "cult of true womanhood" that celebrated female domesticity, the two worlds of work and family became ever more sex-typed, with men presumed to be the primary breadwinners and women the primary homemakers (Sennett, 1970; Welter, 1976). The workplace became physically separated from the home, and work for pay outside the home (market work) became sharply distinguished from the unpaid work of food preparation, laundry, housekeeping, and care of children and other dependents that took place inside the home (nonmarket work). The separation between work time and family time was marked by specific working hours and the factory whistle (Hareven and Langenbach, 1978; Smelser, 1959). The fact that market work was paid and nonmarket work was unpaid set up an implicit ranking whereby paid work took precedence and had higher status than unpaid work.

Although most poor women and women of color had always worked in addition to caring for their families (Jones, 1998), the American middle class idealized women as primarily caregivers and homemakers. Even during the high unemployment of the 1930s and the labor shortage of World War II, women's work was widely regarded as a temporary necessity and possibly a threat if it took jobs from men (Hartmann, 1982; Ware, 1982). These beliefs were briefly intensified during the 1950s when, as Betty Friedan (1963) described in *The Feminine Mystique*, families built their houses in the suburbs, produced a baby boom, and romanticized the feminine role by attributing special maternal qualities to women at home while simultaneously devaluing their potential for achievement in the public realm.

Despite the feminine mystique, however, the family and the economy continued to change in the direction of ever more advanced technology and use of information. The numbers of jobs in farming and manufacturing shrank, and those in the service sector expanded. More and more married women and mothers returned to the workplace because of labor shortages in the female-labeled professions such as teaching, nursing, and office work (Oppenheimer, 1970). The labor force participation of mothers of children under 18 rose from only 8 percent in 1950 to 63 percent in 1990 (Moen, 1992). In addition, almost one-third of all births occurred outside of marriage in 1993 compared to one-tenth in 1970, and in 1990 some 24 percent of all families were single-parent households, compared with only 8 percent in 1950 (Stebbins, 2001). Clearly the old patterns dictated by a rural economy, factory shifts, and a breadwinner-homemaker family no longer fit the everyday life of the modern United States.

The Emergence of a Feminist Perspective

What was to be done? One important trend, described earlier, was the growing demand for child care programs that responded to the dual needs of young children and working mothers. Work and family proposals responded to another pair of needs, those of employers and families. A new paradigm was needed to replace the old work and family model. During the 1970s, feminist scholars and advocates began to imagine a different scenario in which *both* men and women did *both* breadwinning and caretaking. A landmark statement of this possibility appeared in Rosabeth Moss Kanter's (1977) essay *Work and Family in the United States,* in which she showed that earlier theorizing and writing had stereotyped men's and women's roles as well as the nature of work and family life. In fact, productive (instrumental) and caregiving (expressive) activities have always been present both in the workplace and in family life. Giele (1978; 1980), in conceptualizing sex-role "crossover," suggested that in many instances the public contribution of feminism was to call attention to emotional needs and human feelings in the public sphere and to help rationalize and limit reliance on emotion in the private sphere. Arlie Hochschild (1975; 1983), in her careful descriptions of male and female professors in academia and flight attendants in the airline industry, also brought to light women's close interweaving of reason and feeling in the workplace.

What the women's movement added to these new analytic frameworks was a public policy dimension. Rather than seeing caregiving as the obligation of women in the private domain with the costs to be borne by the private family, feminists began to argue that healthy families were necessary not only to growth and socialization of healthy children but also to economic growth and productivity. Economist Carolyn Shaw Bell (1972) termed this family function "consumer maintenance," by which she meant the unpaid and unseen contribution that families (especially women) make every day to feeding, clothing, protecting, and nurturing (or "maintaining") the population of workers and consumers. The distinctive feature of Bell's statement was her focus, not on children, which is quite familiar, but on the private family needs of adult workers that must be met if they are to be able to contribute to the public good.

Alternative Work and Family Arrangements

Coinciding with the emergence of a feminist and more policy-oriented view of work and family issues has been the development of practical new ideas about location of work, scheduling of the work day and work week, leaves of absence, job sharing and part-time work, as well as employer subsidies such as flexible benefit accounts.

From an employer's point of view, the advantages of these several programs are the cost savings that result from being able to retain valued and skilled employees while avoiding the turnover that imposes additional costs in recruiting and training new hires. A national survey of workers with access to such work and family programs reports higher satisfaction and greater loyalty (Bond, Galinsky, and Swanberg, 1997). The downside for employers is to find substitutes for workers who may not be present on a particular day or may be on leave. Filling that person's job imposes the additional cost of having extra people available or of reorganizing managerial procedures to deploy a flexible and far-flung work force efficiently. For these reasons, large employers have been the leaders in developing flexible work arrangements, because they can spread the costs more easily than a small employer, for whom the absence of one key employee has a much greater impact (Blau, Ferber, and Winkler, 2002).

Of all the solutions to the conflicting demands of work and family, the most traditional option is part-time work, which can mean working less than a full day, less than five days per week, or less than a full year. Part-time work requires no corporate initiative but is the option chosen by a sizable number of women in most Western industrial countries. In 1997, 25 percent of all U.S. working women were employed part-time, compared with 11 percent of working men; this compared with an average of 32 percent part-time among working women in twelve European Union countries and 45 percent in the United Kingdom. The comparable rates for part-time work among employed men were 6 percent for the European Union and 9 percent for the United Kingdom (Hakim, 2000: 58). From the worker's standpoint, the advantages of part-time work are its flexibility and the fact that no particular program need be put in place for the individual to initiate such a schedule. But typical disadvantages are lack of entitlement to benefits such as health care, little opportunity for promotion and higher pay, and lack of job security. Employers benefit from the flexibility of part-time work by being able to adjust the amount of hours to the work available, being able to retain valuable workers and dismiss the less valuable more easily, and by lower costs of benefits (which are typically limited to those employer contributions mandated by law, the Social Security tax and unemployment tax) (Stebbins, 2001).

Since the height of the new women's movement in the 1970s, a variety of different proposals have surfaced for improving the conditions surrounding part-time work (Kahne, 1985). "Job-sharing" is the concept of two part-time people sharing a full-time job, an idea that has been used by couples in academia, publishing, travel agencies, and real estate firms. By 1998, at least one-third of large firms were offering this option, although utilization was far lower (Blau, Ferber, and Winkler, 2002). Another concept is the so-called "mommy track," a rather pejorative term for the idea put forward by Felice N. Schwartz (1989) in the *Harvard Business Review*. The idea was that women essentially end up choosing between a high-powered managerial track whereby they decide to be childless, or have less close involvement in care of their children; or else settle for a lesser job, perhaps only temporarily, that offers greater flexibility for parenting. Although most feminists strenuously resist this suggestion, as evidenced by the letters to the editor responding to Schwartz's article, both Hewlett (2002) and Stone (2000) report that the phenomenon is real, that a number of women in very responsible professional and managerial positions do in fact cut back their schedules and follow a less demanding work life in order to meet the needs of their families.

With provision for flextime, an employee can work full-time but at hours that depart from the typical 9-to–5, five days per week schedule. The variation may involve only the starting or ending times of the day, or it can take the form of bunching work into several very long days and being off work the rest of the week, such as would permit two parents to share child care if both of them had flextime. Certain occupations lend themselves better to such flexibility than others, depending on the flow of work and the degree to which it is subject to scheduling, and the availability of others to handle immediate demands as they arise. In 1997, 29 percent of male workers and 26 percent of female workers had flexible schedules. It is instructive that 42 percent of managers have such arrangements available, as compared with 23 percent of administrative support staff, and only 20 percent of the blue-collar work force (Blau, Ferber, and Winkler, 2002). Flextime presumes autonomy and motivation on the part of the employee to get the work done without having to rely on external controls or having to be present (put in "face-time") to signal that one is doing a good job.

Finally, the most inclusive category for manipulation of the times of work is that of nonstandard work schedules. Economists Blau, Ferber, and Winkler (2002) attribute the rapid growth of nonstandard work, which now includes 40 percent of the working population, to the growth of the twenty-four-hour economy. Such around-the-clock work as that of cashiers, nurses, retail clerks, and home health aides involves shift work and work on nights and weekends. Globalization and high-speed Internet communications are also undoubtedly a factor in expanding the "24/7" economy. Although nonstandard work can offer some flexibility for care of dependents, there are potentially serious consequences for families, both for the relationships within couples who have too little time together, and for parents who need time to care for young children (Presser, 1998). Biorhythms are possibly also disrupted by working at night and trying to sleep during the day.

Flexibility of location is another way of rearranging the ecology of work and family life to permit greater communication and movement back and forth. Self-employment is one solution that many women have found to provide themselves with control over their own schedules. Opening one's own business, setting up a law practice, being a research consultant, working free-lance—all these are ways to get out from under the rigid sched-ules of an employer who is unsympathetic to family needs or is otherwise unable to provide such flexibility.

Another solution, sometimes related to self-employment but not necessarily, is working at home or telecommuting. The grow-ing use of computers, e-mail, faxes, and phones makes it possible to conduct a great deal of desk work without having to be physi-cally present in an office or other public place of work. Such arrangements seem to work best with highly motivated and self-directed workers who are capable of setting their own goals and monitoring their own progress. The advantages of telecommut-ing are an increased ability to balance work and family life, greater productivity, and less work-related stress. The main dis-advantages appear to be either interference from the demands of children and family or the potential for overwork and insufficient separation between work and leisure. Also, although working at home may protect the person from interruptions, it may at the same time bring isolation from coworkers and colleagues, thereby limiting some of the positive benefits of social networks and learning from others (Stebbins, 2001).

Of the new formal solutions mandated by government and adopted by employers, family leave is rapidly becoming the most prominent work and family policy to be mandated by govern-ment and the public alike. The positive development of family leave legislation followed advances made with the Pregnancy Discrimination Act (PDA) of 1978, which redefined pregnancy as a disability that kept women from their work just as men's health disabilities interfered with their work (Vogel, 1993). Failure to provide benefits and job protection for pregnant workers was thus defined as discrimination, and the PDA was passed as an amendment to Title VII of the Civil Rights Act of 1964.

The Family and Medical Leave Act (FMLA) of 1993 requires employers of more than fifty workers to provide unpaid leave for up to twelve weeks in any twelve-month period for the birth of a child or for an adoption; to care for a child, spouse, or parent with a serious health condition; or for the worker's own serious health condition that makes it impossible to perform a job. The same job or an equivalent one must be held open for the worker, and the employer must continue providing health benefits. The worker on leave cannot collect unemployment or other government compensation during this time (Lindgren and Taub, 1993). Employees in both private and public sectors are eligible if they have worked for the same employer for at least one year or 1,250 hours.

Implementation of the FMLA resulted in a rise between 1991 and 1997 in the number of workers covered, up from 39 percent of female and 27 percent of male workers in 1991 to 95 percent of full-time employees in medium and large establishments in 1997. Use of the entitlement to a leave did not raise employers' costs of re-placement or training as had been predicted by opponents of the legislation. What did result was a more modest proportion of total workers eligible than might have been hoped for, either because they had worked only part-time or part-year. On balance, the law appears to have had a positive effect in helping women keep their jobs, encouraging men to share in parenting, and giving infants more time with a parent (Blau, Ferber, and Winkler, 2002).

One of the most often noted deficits of the FMLA is the fact that it has no provision for paying a worker on family or medical leave, and this fact disproportionately affects the poorest work-ers, who cannot afford to take unpaid leave. President Clinton proposed that unemployment insurance (UI) be made available for this purpose, a proposal that worried some, who argued that such a use threatened to deplete funds that were meant for cov-ering the unemployed. Proponents of using UI, on the other hand, contended that the costs would not be all that great and were well worth it, given that they ultimately promoted employ-ment of those who might otherwise quit work or leave their chil-dren in suboptimal care because they had to work (Blau, Ferber, and Winkler, 2002).

Innovation in figuring out ways to provide paid care has now begun at the state level. California was the first state to in-stitute paid leave in 2002. The new law requires employers to give workers paid time off to care for new babies or sick family mem-bers, and similar legislation is currently being considered by at least twenty-seven other states. The California plan sets up a fund to which employees contribute that operates like social and un-employment insurance (Keefe, 2002).

Finally, in addition to the work and family programs that in-volve either flexible scheduling, flexible location, or leaves, a fur-ther possible way of supporting work and family integration is through flexible benefit plans. There are two major types, cafete-ria plans that permit an employee to choose among various alter-native benefits provided by the employer, and flexible spending accounts based on pretax deductions from the employee's pay to cover health care, child care, retirement funds, or other entitlements to which both the employer and the employee make contributions. Blau, Ferber, and Winkler (2002) report that in 1997, 13 percent of employees in middle- and large-sized firms were offered cafeteria plans, and 32 percent had access to flexible spending accounts. Comparable numbers for small firms were much lower, 4 percent for the cafeteria plans and 12 percent for the flexible spending accounts.

Possibilities for the Future

Although enormous progress has been made in the expansion of work and family programs since the civil rights legislation of the 1960s, many of the leading proponents point to the need for still more fundamental change in public consciousness, typical life course patterns, culture of the workplace, and child and family policy.

England and Folbre (1999) argue that children are the future workers of the society and therefore represent a public good. Children's care and development is therefore the responsibility of the whole society, not that of their parents alone. Society, employers, and workers thus need to take a longer view of each employee's life cycle. Harrington (1999) broadens the argument to include the value of all kinds of care work. She argues that society should recognize and support not only care of children but other dependent members of the society and should accord care workers equal rights and status. Such work, she argues, is in the public interest.

Bailyn (1993) envisions the possibility of allowing a period in the lives of young parents when they will be given permission for more time to look after their children's needs, even as they are continuing to be productive workers. They should not be expected to put in overtime just at that moment of highest home demands. Another possibility is that one spouse's work will be more intense at one period and the other's at a different period so that they can take turns assuming more or less responsibility. Han and Moen (1999) also view couples as sharing a division of labor in which the life course of one partner affects the other. The challenge in a market economy, which focuses on workers as individuals, is how to take these family needs into account and give them support while also maximizing the productivity of each worker.

A third issue is how to change the culture of the workplace to redefine achievement in terms of authentic productivity rather than of appearances, as measured mechanically by how many hours one is present in the workplace ("face-time"). Incentives for efficiency can result in time saved that can be made available for other activities besides work. Many women working part-time, for example, report that they get more done in the time they spend at work than the full-time people who don't have to be so efficient. Rapoport and Bailyn (1996) outline the characteristics of a workplace culture in which such innovation is possible. If such arrangements could become more widespread (Barnett, 1999), they would presumably break some of the stranglehold of career on individual lives that makes men turn into breadwinners without time for family or that makes ambitious women forego motherhood because it is so difficult to combine with a career (Goldin, 1997; Hakim, 2000; Hewlett, 2002).

Lastly, social policy experts look for a way to change American political culture to be more supportive of policies that will promote child and family well being. Research on brain development in young children, the destructive effects of poverty, and the importance of child care by parents or other nurturing adults raises the question of how to promote healthy development and prevent irreversible damage to children's psyches. These issues also implicitly raise questions about how the parents of these children are faring and whether they have sufficient income and time available to meet the children's needs. Journalist Ann Crittenden (2001), who has investigated these questions, has come to the conclusion that it is cheaper in the long run, and more effective, to subsidize a mother's care of her own young children than to force her to work and compromise her role as a parent. If this point of view gains a wider following, it is bound to stimulate further discussion of ways to integrate the roles of workers and family members.

Workfare and Welfare Reform

Issues related to family and child well being always seem to bring back the familiar question of the proper role of women. Should the private family (when its income is sufficient) or the state (when the family's income is insufficient) subsidize mothers' work at home so that they can forego paid work in order to care for their children? Or should both mothers and fathers be expected to work and share the care of family dependents in some way, either by using outside care, rearranging their schedules, or adopting a division of labor in which one stays at home while the other brings in an income? These questions are intimately related to gender equity in employment, and the American national consensus on how to answer these questions has profoundly changed over the course of the twentieth century.

The presumption underlying mothers' pensions and Aid to Families with Dependent Children (AFDC, formerly ADC, as it was called when instituted in 1935) was based on a family model with a male breadwinner and a female homemaker (Skocpol, 1992). As ever more married women and mothers became active in the labor force, it became increasingly difficult for voters and the general public to justify some women staying at home to care for their children while other women managed both paid work and family work. In this context, AFDC and welfare assistance began to seem more like unemployment insurance, and the implication was that the recipients of such assistance should be required to work if work was available (Orloff, 2001).

Concurrent with the change in gender role expectations was an evolution in thinking about how best to overcome poverty and thereby reduce the welfare rolls. The 1964 Moynihan Report (Rainwater and Yancey, 1967) documented the growth of long-term welfare case loads and the transmission of welfare dependence to the next generation. Charles Murray's (1984) *Losing Ground* went much further to argue that the very existence of welfare programs actually encouraged their use and perpetuated an expectation that a woman and her children would be supported whether or not she had ever worked. The response to Murray's argument was a decade of scholarly efforts by economists, sociologists, and policymakers to invent new, more effective programs and evaluate new methods of providing assistance so that able-bodied people could eventually find work and become self-supporting. Of particular concern in the old welfare program was the disincentive to work that the AFDC benefit provided (which in 1993 was the current equivalent of $469 per month plus food stamps for an average family of three). The cash grant was reduced dollar for dollar by any income brought in. The Family Support Act of 1988 had instituted certain important changes that reflected the new thinking on welfare. Training for basic skills and jobs was provided to eligible families along with transitional assistance in child care and medical care. Recipients, except those with a disability or an infant, were required to engage in job searches and training. Eventually, the delay of work, even for training, began to seem less effective than on-the-job training as a means of improving work habits and getting experience. The result was a shift in priorities to "work first" rather than further investment in training (Turner and Main, 2001).

The result of these two forces—the change in women's roles and the critique of "welfare as we know it"—was the new welfare law, the Personal Responsibility and Work Opportunity Reconciliation Act (PRWORA), passed in 1996 as a result of bipartisan support. This new legislation set up cumulative time limits of no more than five years total for receiving assistance, and required job search or work, or (in a few states) participation in education or training in order to be eligible for financial assistance. The old AFDC program was gone, and in its place stood the program for Temporary Assistance to Needy Families (TANF) (Blau, Ferber, and Winkler, 2002).

Many advocates for women and poor families criticized the new law. Gwendolyn Mink (1998) sees the legislation as being profoundly hostile to women's maternal roles, as well as being class-bound and racist. Frances Fox Piven (2001) interprets the reform as yet another assault on poor people and a tool of capitalists to keep labor costs low in the global economy. Linda Gordon (2001) sees the new law as the result of a reluctance to help lone mothers even while trying to help poor children. Ann Orloff (2001), however, subordinates all these interpretations to an overarching explanation that points to changing gender roles, and particularly the expectation that all women will work: "[E]mployment was defined as central to the strategy of achieving women's equality, and also as the proper mode for supporting families and caregiving. The logic is that if all must work to support households—and this furthers women's prospects—women on welfare, too, should be employed" (153).

Despite criticism, the results of the 1996 welfare reform have been dramatic. In the short term, as a result of the booming economy of the 1990s, the changes were mostly positive. There was, on average, a 50 percent reduction in the welfare rolls. The number of AFDC/TANF families with earnings tripled from 7 percent in 1993 to 21 percent in 1998. The number of recipient families with a teen parent was cut in half from 8 percent to 4 percent, a trend that appears to be directly related to the new requirement that teen parents, to be eligible for assistance, must continue in school and live with a parent. At the same time, however, there is considerable worry among expert observers that negative outcomes (such as use of low-quality child care, or the decreased use of Medicaid and food stamps) are present but hidden, because some administrators discourage applications even though a family is eligible. In addition, the downturn in the economy since 2001 has made finding and maintaining employment much more difficult (Blau, Ferber, and Winkler, 2002).

Finally, an obvious question is how any low-wage mother can support her family and live in safe housing on the minimum wage, even if she does find work as a waitress, hotel maid, or home health aide. This was the question that writer Barbara Ehrenreich (2001) constantly asked herself as she undertook several such short-term low-wage jobs in Florida, Maine, and elsewhere to understand what they were like and how people made ends meet. The logic of welfare reform and the goal of self-sufficiency rested in part on the idea that women's wages were converging on men's and were therefore capable of supporting a family. But according to Waldvogel and Mayer (2000), the ability of low-wage women to be self-sufficient has been declining since 1980, and the convergence has been in the opposite direction. The sex differential is smaller, not because women's incomes have risen, but because low-wage men's incomes have declined.

Summary

Laws and policies affecting gender equity in employment reflect the shift from a rural to an industrial economy and the growing participation of women in the labor force. During the decades following the establishment of the United Nations in 1948, various UN resolutions and ILO conventions endorsed human rights and equal rights for men and women. In the United States, the model of family life changed from that of a breadwinner-homemaker couple with children to one in which families were much more diverse, and both women and men were expected to work. Laws based on a theory that women were different and needed to be protected gave way to equal rights laws. With only a few exceptions, differential treatment of men and women became suspect in employment, education, and the integration of work and family responsibilities.

In the realm of employment, the equal rights tradition gradually superseded protectionism of women in hiring, promotion, and pay. The Equal Pay Act of 1963 and the Civil Rights Acts of 1957 and 1964 prohibited discrimination on the basis of sex.

Throughout the late 1960s and 1970s, the Equal Employment Opportunity Commission investigated complaints of sex discrimination in employment and threatened the withholding of federal contracts if employers did not comply. The judgment rendered against AT&T in 1972 was an important landmark for the women who had charged sex discrimination in hiring, job assignment, and pay. Equal rights legislation gave rise to affirmative action by employers to achieve goals and timetables for a more representative work force. The concept of comparable worth was explored, especially in municipal jobs, but it stalled as a result of a negative judicial decision in the 1980s. Sexual harassment came to be recognized as a significant form of sex discrimination that turned a worker into an object and created a hostile atmosphere.

The issue of equal rights in education was brought to the fore by the passage of Title IX of the Higher Education Amendments of 1972. Perhaps the most visible effect of this legislation was to challenge male domination of athletics and sports in the schools. But the law was also extremely important in changing the sex composition of college faculties and in raising issues of sex discrimination in a host of educational matters including admissions, curriculum, financial aid, and housing. In elementary and high schools, the law called into question the unequal treatment of boys and girls as students, thereby raising awareness of sexual harassment of girls and harsh discipline of boys.

When it comes to the integration of work and family, it is difficult to know how to implement equal rights, given that women still bear disproportionate responsibility for child care and household maintenance at the same time as being employed. Social policies have been developed on three fronts to deal with the tension between parenting and employment. First, with respect to the provision of child care, there has been a gradual movement toward public support of a more universal system of subsidies and services to all families, regardless of income or mother's employment status. Second, work and family programs have evolved to offer a number of options from flextime to telecommuting. Of all such innovations, parental and family leave, paid and unpaid, has emerged as the option that commands the largest consensus and most government support. Third, the welfare reform of 1996 took place against the backdrop of these trends in child care and maternal employment. The rise of women's labor force participation among all income groups made it difficult to justify subsidies to poor mothers to stay at home rather than also join the work force. Rather than assistance from AFDC that would permit mothers to be supported without being employed, the new legislation requires them to search for and find work before time runs out on their temporary assistance. Although the reform has resulted in a dramatic drop in the welfare rolls, there is a question of whether the trend can be sustained in a less favorable economy. In addition, the very low wages that are available to poor women make it unclear whether work alone can ever be sufficient to support a lone mother and her children.

In sum, the past fifty years of growth in women's labor force participation and the expansion of equal rights legislation have together resulted in quite visible progress toward gender equity in employment. Although sex discrimination persists, and working women still have heavier burdens of family care than working men, the positive experience of recent decades shows that the problems are being recognized, especially among the nonpoor, and that progress is likely to continue. Whether the same can be said for workers at the bottom of the income distribution, however, is still to be seen.

References

"Alumnae Show Strong Support for Professorship." 2002. *Radcliffe Quarterly* (Spring/Summer): 3.

American Association of University Women Legal Advocacy Fund. 2000. *A License for Bias: Sex Discrimination, Schools, and Title IX.* Washington, DC: Author.

Bailyn, Lotte. 1993. *Breaking the Mold: Women, Men, and Time in the New Corporate World.* New York: Free Press.

Baker, Douglas D., and Dana L. Stover. 1996. "Sexual Harassment: Legal and Policy Issues." Pp. 264–267 in *Women and Work: A Handbook.* Edited by Paula J. Dubeck and Kathryn Borman. New York: Garland.

Ball, Michael. 1996. "Women in the People's Republic of China (1949–the Present)." Pp. 492–495 in *Women and Work: A Handbook.* Edited by Paula J. Dubeck and Kathryn Borman. New York: Garland.

Barnett, Rosalind. 1999. "A New Work-Life Model for the Twenty-First Century." *Annals of the American Academy of Political and Social Science* 562 (March): 143–158.

Bell, Carolyn Shaw. 1972. "A Full Employment Policy for a Public Service Economy." *Social Policy* 3 (September-October): 12–19.

Belluck, Pam. 2002. "Massachusetts Democrats Pick Nominee for Governor." *New York Times,* September 18, 2002: A20.

Berger, Marshall J. 1992. "The Department of Labor's Glass Ceiling Initiative." *Labor Law Journal* (July): 421–429.

Bergmann, Barbara R. 1996. *Saving Our Children from Poverty: What the United States Can Learn from France.* New York: Russell Sage.

Blau, David M. 2001. *The Child Care Problem: An Economic Analysis.* New York: Russell Sage.

Blau, Francine D., Marianne A. Ferber, and Anne E. Winkler. 1998. *The Economics of Women, Men, and Work.* 3rd ed. Saddle River, NJ: Prentice-Hall.

———. 2002. *The Economics of Women, Men, and Work.* 4th ed. Upper Saddle River, NJ: Prentice-Hall.

Blum, Linda M. 1991. *Between Feminism and Labor: The Significance of the Comparable Worth Movement.* Berkeley: University of California Press.

Bond, James T., Ellen Galinsky, and Jennifer E. Swanberg. 1997. *The 1997 National Study of the Changing Workforce.* New York: Families and Work Institute.

Brownmiller, Susan, and Dolores Alexander. 1992. "How We Got Here: From Carmita Wood to Anita Hill." *Ms.* (January/February): 70–71.

Castro, Ida L. 2001. *Equal Pay: A Thirty-Five Year Perspective.* Washington, DC: U.S. Department of Labor, Women's Bureau.

Christopher, Karen. 2002. "Family-Friendly Europe." *The American Prospect,* April 8: 59–61.

Clark, Charles S. 1991. "How Pervasive Is Sexual Harassment?" *CQ Researcher:* 539, 542–543.

Cohen, Sally Solomon. 2001. *Championing Child Care.* New York: Columbia University Press.

Cornfield, David B. 1996. "Women in the U.S. Labor Movement." Pp. 27–29 in *Women and Work: A Handbook.* Edited by Paula J. Dubeck and Kathryn Borman. New York: Garland.

Crittenden, Ann. 2001. *The Price of Motherhood: Why the Most Important Job in the World Is Still the Least Valued.* New York: Metropolitan.

Cubbins, Lisa A. 1996. "Efforts toward Gender Equity in Sweden." Pp. 468–470 in *Women and Work: A Handbook.* Edited by Paula J. Dubeck and Kathryn Borman. New York: Garland.

Education Amendments of 1972, 20 U.S.C. Section 168.

Ehrenreich, Barbara. 2001. *Nickel and Dimed: On (Not) Getting by in America.* New York: Metropolitan.

England, Paula. 2000. "The Pay Gap between Male and Female Jobs: Organizational and Legal Remedies." *Law and Social Inquiry* 25 (3, summer): 913–931.

England, Paula, and Nancy Folbre. 1999. "Who Should Pay for the Kids?" *Annals of the American Academy of Political and Social Science* 563: 194–207.

Feminist Daily News. 2001. "U.S. Supreme Court Refuses to Hear Affirmative Action Case. *Feminist Daily News,* June 25. http://www.feminist.org/news/newsbyte/uswirestory.asp?id=5612. (accessed October 6, 2002).

Feminist Majority Foundation. 2002. "California Civil Rights Initiative Ballot Language." http://www.feminist.org/other/ccri/catext.html (accessed October 6, 2002).

Firestone, David. 2003. "Bush Presses House's Republicans on Credits for Poor." *New York Times,* June 10, p. A26.

Freeman, Jo. 1975. *The Politics of Women's Liberation: A Case Study of an Emerging Social Movement and Its Relation to the Policy Process.* New York: McKay.

———. 1990. "From Protection to Equal Opportunity: The Revolution in Women's Legal Status." Pp. 497–481 in *Women, Politics, and Change.* Edited by Louise A. Tilly and Patricia Gurin. New York: Russell Sage Foundation.

Friedan, Betty. 1963. *The Feminine Mystique.* New York: Norton.

Giele, Janet Zollinger. 1978. *Women and the Future: Changing Sex Roles in Modern America.* New York: Free Press.

———. 1980. "Crossovers: New Themes in Adult Roles and the Life Cycle." Pp. 3–15 in *Women's Lives: New Theory, Research, and Policy.* Edited by D. G. McGuigan. Ann Arbor: University of Michigan, Center for Continuing Education of Women.

———. 1995. *Two Paths to Equality: Temperance, Suffrage, and the Origins of Modern Feminism.* New York: Twayne.

Giele, Janet Zollinger, and Mary Gilfus. 1990. "Race and College Differences in Life Patterns of Educated Women." Pp. 179–197 in *Women and Educational Change.* Edited by J. Antler and S. Biklen. Albany: State University of New York Press.

Goldin, Claudia Dale. 1990. *Understanding the Gender Gap: An Economic History of American Women*. New York: Oxford University Press.

———. 1997. "Career and Family: College Women Look to the Past." Pp. 20–59 in *Gender and Family Issues in the Workplace*. Edited by Francine D. Blau and Ronald G. Ehrenberg. New York: Russell Sage Foundation.

Gordon, Linda. 2001. "Who Deserves Help? Who Must Provide?" *Annals of the American Academy of Political and Social Science* 577: 12–25.

Greenhouse, Linda. 1996. "Military College Can't Bar Women, High Court Rules." *New York Times*, June 27: A1, B8.

Hakim, Catherine. 2000. *Work-Lifestyle Choices in the 21st Century: Preference Theory*. New York: Oxford University Press.

Halberstam, Malvina, and Elizabeth F. Defeis. 1987. *Women's Legal Rights: International Covenants an Alternative to ERA?* Dobbs Ferry, NY: Transnational.

Hall, Roberta M., and Bernice R. Sandler. 1982. "The Classroom Climate: A Chilly One for Women." Washington, DC: Association of American Colleges, Project on the Status and Education of Women.

———. 1984. "Outside the Classroom: A Chilly Campus Climate for Women?" Washington, DC: Association of American Colleges, Project on the Status and Education of Women.

Han, Shin-Kap, and Phyllis Moen. 1999. "Work and Family over Time: A Life Course Approach." *Annals of the American Academy of Political and Social Science* 562: 98–110.

Hancock, Cynthia Riffe. 1996. "Women in the Military (1890–1990)." Pp. 209–211 in *Women and Work: A Handbook*. Edited by Paula J. Dubeck and Kathryn Borman. New York: Garland.

Hareven, Tamara K., and Randolph Langenbach. 1978. *Amoskeag: Life and Work in an American Factory-City*. New York: Pantheon.

Harrington, Mona. 1999. *Care and Equality: Inventing a New Family Politics*. New York: Knopf.

Hartmann, Susan M. 1982. *The Home Front and Beyond: American Women in the 1940s*. Boston: Twayne.

Hewlett, Sylvia Ann. 2002. *Creating a Life: Professional Women and the Quest for Children*. New York: Talk Miramax.

Hochschild, Arlie Russell. 1975. "Inside the Clockwork of Male Careers." Pp. 47–80 in *Women and the Power to Change.*" Edited by Florence Howe. New York: McGraw Hill.

———. 1983. *The Managed Heart: Commercialization of Human Feeling.* Berkeley: University of California Press.

Hofferth, Sandra L. 1999. "Child Care, Maternal Employment, and Public Policy." *Annals of the American Academy of Political and Social Science* 563: 20–38.

Jones, Jacqueline. 1998. *American Work: Four Centuries of Black and White Labor.* New York: W. W. Norton.

Kahne, Hilda. 1985. *Reconceiving Part-time Work: New Perspectives for Older Workers and Women.* Totowa, NJ: Rowman & Allanheld.

Kanter, Rosabeth Moss. 1977. *Work and Family in the United States: A Critical Review and Agenda for Research and Policy.* New York: Russell Sage Foundation.

Keefe, Bob. 2002. "Paid Family Leave Signed in Calif.; Funds to Come from Workers' Tax." *The Atlanta Journal and Constitution,* September 24: 3A.

Kiernan, Denise. 2001. "The Little Law that Could." *Ms.* (February/March): 18–25.

Lapidus, Gail W. 1992. "The Interaction of Women's Work and Family Roles in the Former USSR." Pp. 140–164 in *Women's Work and Women's Lives: The Continuing Struggle Worldwide.* Edited by Hilda Kahne and Janet Z. Giele. Boulder, CO: Westview Press.

Liljestrom, Rita, Gunilla Furst Mellstrom, and Gillan Liljestrom Svensson. 1978. *Roles in Transition: Report of an Investigation Made for the Advisory Council on Equality between Men and Women.* Stockholm: LiberForlag.

Lindgren, J. Ralph, and Nadine Taub. 1993. *The Law of Sex Discrimination.* 2nd ed. Minneapolis/St. Paul, MN: West.

Loder, Natasha. 2000. "U.S. Science Shocked by Revelations of Sexual Discrimination." *Nature* 405: 713–714.

MacKinnon, Catharine A. 1979. *Sexual Harassment of Working Women: A Case of Sex Discrimination.* New Haven, CT: Yale University Press, 1979.

Meyers, Marcia K., and Janet C. Gornick. 2001. "Gendering Welfare State Variation: Income Transfers, Employment Supports, and Family Poverty." Pp. 215–243 in *Women and Welfare: Theory and Practice in the United States and Europe.* Edited by Nancy J. Hirschmann and Ulrike Liebert. New Brunswick, NJ: Rutgers University Press.

Michel, Sonya. 1999. *Children's Interests/Mothers' Rights: The Shaping of America's Child Care Policy.* New Haven, CT: Yale University Press.

Mink, Gwendolyn. 1998. *Welfare's End.* Ithaca, NY: Cornell University Press.

Moen, Phyllis. 1992. *Women's Two Roles: A Contemporary Dilemma.* New York: Auburn House.

Morse, Susan L. 1992. "Women and Sports." *Congressional Quarterly Researcher* 2: 194–215.

Murray, Charles A. 1984. *Losing Ground: American Social Policy, 1950–1980.* New York: Basic.

Nelson, Robert, and William Bridges. 1999. *Legalizing Gender Inequality.* New York: Cambridge University Press.

Neumark, David, and Wendy A. Stock. 2001. *The Effects of Race and Sex Discrimination Laws.* Cambridge, MA: National Bureau of Economic Research.

Oppenheimer, Valerie Kincade. 1970. *The Female Labor Force in the United States: Demographic and Economic Factors Governing Its Growth and Changing Composition.* Berkeley: Institute of International Studies, University of California.

Orloff, Ann Shola. 2001. "Ending the Entitlements of Poor Single Mothers." Pp. 133–176 in *Women and Welfare: Theory and Practice in the United States and Europe.* Edited by Nancy J. Hirschmann and Ulrike Liebert. New Brunswick, NJ: Rutgers University Press.

O'Toole, Laura L. 1996. "The Advancement of Women in Post-Secondary Educational Administration." Pp. 354–357 in *Women and Work: A Handbook.* Edited by Paula J. Dubeck and Kathryn Borman. New York: Garland.

Padavic, Irene. 1996. "Women in Blue-Collar Occupations." Pp. 147–151 in *Women and Work: A Handbook.* Edited by Paula J. Dubeck and Kathryn Borman. New York: Garland.

Pedersen, Susan. 1993. *Family, Dependence, and the Origins of the Welfare State: Britain and France, 1914–1945.* New York: Cambridge University Press.

Pharr, Susan J. 1981. *Political Women in Japan: The Search for a Place in Political Life.* Berkeley: University of California Press.

Piven, Frances Fox. 2001. "Globalization, American Politics, and Welfare Policy." *Annals of the American Academy of Political and Social Science* 577: 26–37.

Presser, Harriet B. 1998. "Toward a 24-Hour Economy: The U.S. Experience and Implications for the Family." Pp. 39–47 in *Challenges for Work and Family in the Twenty-First Century.* Edited by Dana Vannoy and Paula J. Dubeck. New York: Aldine de Gruyter.

Rainwater, Lee, and William L. Yancey. 1967. *The Moynihan Report and the*

Politics of Controversy. Including the full text of *The Negro Family: The Case for National Action* by Daniel Patrick Moynihan. Cambridge, MA: M.I.T. Press.

Rapoport, Rhona, and Lotte Bailyn. 1996. *Rethinking Life and Work: Toward a Better Future.* New York: Ford Foundation.

Roth, Silke. 2003. *Building Movement Bridges: The Coalition of Labor Union Women.* Westport, CT: Praeger.

Rudolph, Hedwig. 1992. "Women's Labor Market Experience in the Two Germanies." Pp. 169–186 in *Women's Work and Women's Lives: The Continuing Struggle Worldwide.* Edited by Hilda Kahne and Janet Z. Giele. Boulder, CO: Westview Press.

Sadker, Myra, and David Sadker. 1995. *Failing at Fairness: How Our Schools Cheat Girls.* New York: Touchstone.

Schor, Juliet. 2002. "Why Americans Should Rest." *New York Times,* September 2: A17.

Schwartz, Felice N. 1989. "Management Women and the New Facts of Life." *Harvard Business Review* 67 (no. 2, January-February): 65–76.

Sennett, Richard. 1970. *Families against the City: Middle Class Homes of Industrial Chicago, 1872–1890.* Cambridge, MA: Harvard University Press.

Skocpol, Theda. 1992. *Protecting Soldiers and Mothers: The Political Origins of Social Policy in the United States.* Cambridge, MA: Harvard University Press.

Smelser, Neil J. 1959. *Social Change in the Industrial Revolution: An Application of Theory to the Lancashire Cotton Industry, 1770–1840.* London: Routledge & Paul.

Stebbins, Leslie. 2001. *Work and Family in America: A Reference Handbook.* Santa Barbara, CA: ABC-CLIO.

Stith-Willis, Annie M. 1999. "Analysis of the Status of Women Faculty in the United States since the Enactment of Equality Legislation in the 1970s: What Do the Numbers Suggest?" Unpublished Ph. D. dissertation, Virginia Commonwealth University.

Stone, Pamela. 2000. Unpublished research. Department of Sociology, Hunter College, New York.

Sullivan, Gerard, and Karen Herne. 1996. "Australian Women in Paid Employment." Pp. 445–447 in *Women and Work: A Handbook.* Edited by Paula J. Dubeck and Kathryn Borman. New York: Garland.

Tidball, M. Elizabeth. 1980. "Women's Colleges and Women Achievers Revisited." *Signs* 5 (no. 3, spring): 504–517.

Treiman, Donald J., and Heidi I. Hartmann, eds. 1981. *Women, Work, and Wages: Equal Pay for Jobs of Equal Value.* Washington, DC: National Academy Press.

Turner, Jason A., and Thomas Main. 2001. "Work Experience under Welfare Reform." Pp. 291–310 in *The New World of Welfare.* Edited by Rebecca M. Blank and Ron Haskins. Washington, DC: Brookings Institution Press.

Vogel, Lise. 1993. *Mothers on the Job: Maternity Policy in the U.S. Workplace.* New Brunswick, NJ: Rutgers University Press.

Waldvogel, Jane, and Susan E. Mayer. 2000. "Gender Differences in the Low-Wage Labor Market." Pp. 193–232 in *Finding Jobs: Work and Welfare Reform.* Edited by David E. Card and Rebecca M. Blank. New York: Russell Sage Foundation.

Ware, Susan. 1982. *Holding Their Own: American Women in the 1930s.* Boston: Twayne.

Welter, Barbara. 1976. *Dimity Convictions: The American Woman in the Nineteenth Century.* Athens: Ohio University Press.

White, Merry. 1996. "Contemporary Japanese Women: Family, Education, and Workplace." Pp. 464–466 in *Women and Work: A Handbook.* Edited by Paula J. Dubeck and Kathryn Borman. New York: Garland.

Wilson, R. 1999. "An MIT Professor's Suspicion of Bias Leads to a New Movement for Academic Women." *Chronicle of Higher Education* 3 (December).

Zuo, Jiping, and Shengming Tang. 1994. "Policy, Economy, and Changing Status of Women in China." Pp. 123–142 in *Marriage and the Family in Chinese Societies.* Edited by Phylis Lan Lin, Ko-wang Mei, and Huai-chen Peng. Indianapolis, IN: University of Indianapolis Press.

Court Cases Cited

AFSCME v. Washington, 770 F.2d 1401 (1985)

Breedlove v. Suttles, 302 U.S. 277 (1937)

Brown v. Board of Education, 349 U.S. 294 (1954)

Bundy v. Jackson, 641 F.2d 934 (1981)

California Federal Savings and Loan v. Guerra, 55 U.S.L.W. 4077 (1987)

Carnes v. Tennessee Secondary School Athletics Association, 415 F. Supp. 569 (1976)

Clark v. Arizona Interscholastic Association, 695 F2d 1126 (1982)

Commonwealth by Packel v. Pennsylvania Interscholastic Athletic Association, 334 A.2d 839 (1975)

Corning Glass Works v. Brennan, 417 U.S. 188 (1974)

Craig v. Boren, 429 U.S. 190 (1976)

Frontiero v. Richardson, 411 U.S. 677 (1973)

Garrett v. Board of Education of the School District of Detroit, 775 F. Supp. 1004 (1991)

Geduldig v. Aiello, 417 U.S. 484 (1974)

General Electric v. Gilbert, 429 U.S. 125 (1976)

Goesaert v. Cleary, 335 U.S. 464 (1948)

Griggs v. Duke Power Co., 401 U.S. 424 (1971)

Gunther v. Washington, 101 S. Ct. 2242 (1981)

Hoyt v. Florida, 368 U.S. 57 (1961)

Lochner v. New York, 198 U.S. 45 (1905)

Meritor Savings Bank v. Vinson, 477 U.S. 57 (1986)

Mississippi University for Women v. Hogan, 458 U.S. 718 (1982)

Muller v. Oregon, 208 U.S. 412 (1908)

O'Connor v. Board of Education of School District 23, 545 F. Supp. 376, U.S. Dist. (1982)

Reed v. Reed, 404 U.S. 71 (1971)

Roe v. Wade, 410 U.S. 113 (1973)

Rosenfeld v. Southern Pacific Company, 444 F.2d 1219 (1971)

Shultz v. Wheaton Glass, 398 U.S. 905 (1970)

Texas v. Hopwood, 116 S.Ct. 2581 (1996); 999 F. Supp. 872, 877 (1998)

Tomkins v. Public Service Electric Gas Company, 568 F.2d 1044 (1977)

United States v. St. Clair, 240 F. Supp. 338 (1968)

United States v. Virginia, 518 U.S. 515 (1996)

United Steelworkers v. Weber, 443 U.S. 193 (1979)

Vorcheimer v. School District of Philadelphia, 400 F. Supp. 326 (1976)

Weeks v. Southern Bell Telephone and Telegraph Company, 408 F.2d 228 (1969)

West Coast Hotel v. Parrish, 300 U.S. 379 (1937)

Williams v. McNair, 316 F. Supp. 134 (1970)

3

Chronology

This timeline traces the history of gender equity and employment, primarily in the United States, from the beginning of the
twentieth century through the year 2002. Entries on the timeline demonstrate the growing involvement of women in the paid
labor force, the increases in women's educational attainment, the
gradual narrowing of the pay gap between men and women, and
the degree of occupational segregation that is present, though
gradually declining, throughout the century. Key legal and political events in the United States relating to gender equity and
work are covered, as well as a sampling of cultural events (see
chapter 5 for descriptions of some court cases). Selected entries
regarding voting rights and equal employment laws throughout
the world provide a comparative context. (Dates listed for
women's suffrage in other countries are, in most cases, the first instance in which women won even partial voting rights in a particular country. In many countries, women won partial voting
rights and a number of years later won equal voting rights.)

Though the topic of gender equity and employment overlaps
with women's progress on all fronts, an attempt was made not to
select items having to do generally with the women's movement,
unless the issue was large, for example, women's suffrage, or if it
overlapped to a large degree with an employment-related issue.
All entries are about events in, or people from, the United States
unless otherwise indicated.

Perhaps the timeline entries that best tell the history of gender and employment are the ones about female pioneers who
have broken gender barriers to become the first to work in a particular field. Though the entries on female pioneers are selective,

107

attempts were made to provide a representative sample from a variety of fields such as the sciences, the military, law and politics, and nontraditional jobs, such as the first woman circus clown who managed to break through at Ringling Brothers in 1971.

1900   Women comprise roughly 20 percent of the work force; most female workers are young and unmarried and work in manufacturing for as little as $1.56 for a 70-hour week; 200,000 women work in clerical jobs.

Almost 75 percent of all school teachers are women, a reversal from the previous century, when the majority of teachers were men.

During this decade, women in Australia (1902); Finland (1906); Sweden (1909); Denmark and Norway (1913); and the Netherlands, Belarus, Luxemburg, Ukraine, and Belgium (1919) win voting rights.

The International Ladies' Garment Workers' Union is created. The leadership of the organization is male, but the majority of workers represented are women. Nine years later, more than 20,000 workers in the garment industry strike for recognition of the union and for better wages and working conditions. Many women are arrested, but better wages and higher union membership result from the strike.

Ida Wells-Barnett becomes the first president of the Negro Fellowship League.

The National Association of Colored Women sets its goals, which include "equality of pay," job training, and "care for the children of absentee mothers."

The National Women's Business Association opens its first office in New York.

Kate Chopin publishes her last story, "Charlie," about a woman who refuses to marry and rejects receiving a "woman's" education and instead runs the family plantation.

Winnifred Black disguises herself as a boy in order to be the first outside reporter in Galveston, Texas, after the tidal wave kills thousands of people. She is the only female reporter to cover the event.

1901   Mary Murphy, a teacher in Chicago, is automatically fired when she gets married. She sues and wins, though most school boards ignore the decision, and teachers who marry continue to be fired until after World War II.

Maggie Mitchell Walker opens a bank and becomes the first female bank president in the United States. While running the bank, she also raises three children.

Florence Finch Kelley begins reviewing books for the *New York Times*, initially hiding her identity as a woman with the assistance of her editor. Her career as a successful journalist spans twenty-five years.

1902   Mary Dreier is elected president of the Women's Trade Union League. The organization, under her leadership, becomes very active, and she is arrested during the great garment strike of 1909–1910.

With twenty-five founding members, the National Association of Colored Graduate Nurses is formed. African American nurses are not admitted to either the Army or Navy Nurse Corps until the 1950s, however.

Astronomer Williamina Fleming publishes a study of the 222 variable stars she has discovered. The previous year, she was the first American woman elected to the Royal Astronomical Society.

1903   The Women's Trade Union League is created at the American Federation of Labor convention. It is supported and run largely by educated, wealthy women.

At age seventy-six, Belva Lockwood becomes one of the country's most successful female attorneys. She wins a major case before the Supreme Court, obtaining $5 million for the Cherokee nation.

1904   Annie Turbo Malone launches a successful business that specializes in hair care products for African American women. By 1917, the business has assets in excess of $1 million, and 75,000 women work at selling these products. Another entrepreneur, Sarah Breedlove Walker, opens a separate business with the same type of products. A decade later, she becomes the first African American female millionaire.

1905   Edith Wharton publishes the novel *The House of Mirth*, a critique of the restricted place of women in society.

Nettie Maria Stevens secures a $1,000 endowment to continue her work as a biologist. She later makes the discovery that the X or Y chromosome in the sperm of the father determines the embryo's sex. Her breakthrough takes years to be accepted by the scientific community.

In *Lochner v. New York*, the Supreme Court strikes down a New York law limiting the hours when bakery employees can work, saying the law is an unfair burden on employers. Despite this ruling, laws are passed over the next two decades setting maximum work hours for women of between 48 and 60 hours per week.

President Grover Cleveland writes in the *Ladies' Home Journal*, "The relative positions to be assumed by men and women in the working out of our civilization were assigned long ago by a higher intelligence than ours."

1907   From 1907 until 1967, government policy in Australia mandates that women's wages be lower than men's.

1908   *Muller v. Oregon* is argued before the Supreme Court, which upholds the constitutionality of a state law limiting the hours women may work.

Mary Baker Eddy founds the *Christian Science Monitor*.

More than 140,000 women are enrolled in college. Women make up 70 percent of high school graduates and 40 percent of college graduates.

Ethel Barrymore plays the liberated typist Kate in *The Twelve-Pound Look.*

1909   Nannie Burroughs founds the National Training School for Women and Girls. The goal of the school is to prepare young African American women for employment. The curriculum includes grammar and practical skills. African Americans provide the sole financial support for the school.

The International Brotherhood of Electrical Workers finally allows women to be members—at a time when more than 75,000 women are employed as telephone operators.

Louise DeKoven Bowen, a philanthropist and suffragist, convinces the Pullman Company to improve worker safety and persuades International Harvester to grant female employees a minimum wage.

1910   Of all women, 25 percent are in the labor force; 11 percent of married women are in the labor force. In the United States, 90 percent of employed African American women work as domestic servants or as agricultural laborers.

During this decade, women in Iceland (1915); the Soviet Union and Canada (1917); and Ireland (restricted), Austria, Germany, Poland, Estonia, and Latvia (1918) win voting rights.

A. S. Wells, the first female police officer in the United States, is appointed in Los Angeles.

1911   The Triangle Shirtwaist Factory fire in New York City focuses national attention on dangerous working conditions for women. During the first fifteen minutes of the fire, 146 women die. The event generates support for the International Ladies' Garment Workers' Union, which signs its first contract in 1913. The contract provides women with some advantages, but also formalizes the division of labor that exists in the industry by stating that the more lucrative, skilled jobs are for men and that the less skilled, lower-paying job are for women.

1911,
cont.
The Feminist Alliance sends a letter to President Woodrow Wilson asking for passage of a constitutional amendment prohibiting job discrimination on the basis of sex.

1912   More than 10,000 female textile workers in Lawrence, Massachusetts, strike while their children are housed in foster care. Public opinion lies with the strikers, and they win wage and overtime concessions.

Journalist Ida Tarbell publishes *The Business of Being a Woman,* in which she states that marriage and motherhood are more important than employment and leading a public life.

Hortense Ward, a lawyer from Texas, lobbies successfully for state laws providing worker's compensation, a fifty-four-hour work week for women, and improvements in property rights for married women.

1913   Annette Abbott Adams becomes the first female federal prosecutor in the United States. She serves as attorney general for the Northern District of California.

France first adopts a maternity leave policy.

1914   Businesswoman Marjorie Merriweather Post inherits her father's Postum Cereal Company, though she is not allowed to sit on the board of directors until 1936. Until that time, her husband represents her at board meetings.

Labor organizer Dorothy Jacobs Bellanca becomes the first woman on the executive board of the Amalgamated Clothing Workers of America.

Alice Gertrude Bryant and Florence West Duckering become the first two female members of the American College of Surgeons.

Amalgamated Clothing Workers of America becomes one of the few unions, prior to 1930, to accept female members. The union provides members with health care, housing, adult education, scholarships, and day care centers, but it also agrees to lower wages for female workers, though half its members are women.

Lois Weber is the first woman to write, direct, produce, and star in a movie. She is hired by Universal Studios at the high salary of $5,000 per week. Her film, *Hypocrites,* is extremely popular and controversial and is banned in Boston due to its sexual content. She goes on to create more than 400 films and forms her own movie studio.

Obstetrician and surgeon Bertha Van Hoosen founds, and becomes the first president of, the American Women's Medical Association.

Jeanette Rankin is the first female member of the House of Representatives. A pacifist and feminist, she represents the state of Montana.

1917   The Council of Defense sets up a Committee on Women in Industry to advise them on how to protect the welfare of female workers during the war. In July, the first draft of American men to fight in World War I creates a labor shortage. By fall, the United States Employment Service launches a campaign to replace men with women in "every position that a woman is capable of filling." The committee produces recommendations, including a caveat that they "view with alarm the increase of employment of married women with young children, and believe that efforts should be made to stem this movement as far as practicable, especially as regards night work . . . ."

The Navy, in an attempt to fill clerical jobs while its male employees are at war, agrees to pay women the same as men. More than 12,000 women are hired, but most are employed for less than two years.

Mary Frances Lathrop becomes the first woman admitted to the American Bar Association.

During World War I, more than 1.4 million women are working in war-related industries, including iron and

1917,   steel mills, chemical plants, foundries, lumber mills, mu-
cont.   nitions factories, and automobile factories.

1918   Members of the Union of Streetcar Conductors strike in
Cleveland to protest the hiring of women.

Ford Motor Company institutes the "Five Dollar Day," a
"family wage" twice the going rate for unskilled workers
in the Detroit area. Eligible workers have to be "married
men living with and taking good care of their families" or
single men over twenty-two years of age. Women are not
initially included in the plan at all, though later the plan
is amended to include men and women under the age of
twenty-two who are "the sole support of some next of kin
or blood relative." Other large corporations also institute
some form of family welfare program with the goal of ac-
commodating and controlling workers.

Woman in Industry Service (WIS) is set up by the War
Labor Administration to deal with problems associated
with the rapid introduction of women into industry. WIS
quickly formulates standards for employment of women
in war industries, including a forty-eight-hour work
week, equal pay, lunch breaks, and sanitary and safety
rules. The defense departments include these standards
in war contracts, though many contractors do not observe them. WIS evolves into the Women's Bureau in
1920.

France and the Soviet Union mandate equal pay for equal
work.

1919   The First International Congress of Working Women
meets in Washington, D.C. It later becomes the International Federation of Working Women. Its main priority is
to promote trade union organizing among women.

Thirty-three countries sign the Maternity Protection Convention, which consists of three components: a desig-
nated leave period of twelve weeks, a cash benefit to be
determined by individual countries, and job protection.

1920   At this point, 24 percent of all women are in the labor force; 9 percent of married women are in the labor force. Of all employed women, 87 percent are either secretaries or teachers.

During this decade, women in Albania, the Czech Republic, and Slovakia (1920); Armenia, Azerbaijan, and Lithuania (1921); Burma (1922); and the United Kingdom (1928) win voting rights.

Congress establishes the Women's Bureau, a branch of the Department of Labor with a staff of twenty under the directorship of Mary Anderson. The goals of the bureau are to collect information about women in industry and improve working conditions for women. Although the bureau seeks better opportunities for working women, for the first few decades, it favors preserving the role of women as homemakers, and it does not encourage young mothers to work outside the home unless necessary.

The Nineteenth Amendment is passed, granting women in the United States the right to vote.

In the United States, 283,000 women are in college, making up 47 percent of the total enrollment.

During this decade, there are more female directors of motion pictures than at any other time in history.

Women comprise less than one-half of 1 percent of the 3,855 African American physicians in the United States.

Julia Stimson, a nurse superintendent, becomes the first female major in the U.S. Army.

1921   Engineer and industrial psychologist Lillian Gilbreth becomes an honorary member of the all-male Society of Industrial Engineers.

In the United States, 5 percent of medical students are women, although 92 percent of hospitals refuse to accept women as interns.

1921,   Kate Gleason develops a method of pouring concrete and
cont.   begins selling the first concrete box houses in her low-cost housing development in New York. This development serves as a model for later suburban housing projects.

Margaret Washburn is elected president of the American Psychological Association.

1922   Florence Allen becomes the first female state supreme court judge.

Rebecca Latimer Felton becomes the first female member of the Senate. Appointed by the governor of Georgia to replace a senator who has died, she serves only one day.

Lillian and Clara Westropp establish the Women's Savings and Loan Company of Cleveland, Ohio. The bank has no male employees. In 1965, the assets are in excess of $135 million.

A German court justifies unequal pay for male and female teachers, stating that male teachers educate useful workers, but female teachers educate mere housewives.

1923   The Classification Act of 1923 is passed, introducing the concept of "equal pay for equal work." The new law establishes that government salaries should be determined by job duties, not by gender of the employee.

The National Woman's Party first proposes an Equal Rights Amendment for women. Organized labor and some women's groups oppose the amendment because it threatens to generate more protective labor laws for women. It languishes in committee for decades.

Microbiologist Gladys Henry Dick discovers the causative agent of scarlet fever. Together with her husband George, they develop a diagnostic skin test and an antitoxin for treatment.

In *Adkins v. Children's Hospital*, the Supreme Court overturns a Washington, D.C., minimum wage law for women. The Court finds that the minimum wage law is unconstitutional because it interferes with a woman's right to bargain with her employer on the subject of wages. Earlier court decisions had held that a woman's unique need for protection took precedence over her having the freedom to bargain.

1924　Miriam "Ma" Ferguson is elected governor of Texas, the first American woman to be elected as a state governor. Her husband had previously been removed from office for misusing funds. She is reelected in 1932.

Florence Rood becomes the first female president of the American Federation of Teachers.

1925　The Naval Reserve Act makes it once again impossible for women to work in the U.S. armed forces. During World War I, thousands of women had worked for the Navy and Marines in clerical positions.

Rose Knox, president of Knox Company, producers of gelatin for food and industrial purposes, begins to run her successful business "in a woman's way." She institutes one of the first five-day work weeks and keeps her plants clean and comfortable, winning loyalty and dedication from her workers. Years later, Knox becomes one of the few businesses that avoids layoffs during the Great Depression.

1926　Bertha Knight Landes is the first woman to serve as mayor of a large American city, Seattle.

Physician Alice Hamilton writes *Women Workers and Industrial Poisons,* a report warning of the hazards faced in trades in which women are often employed.

1927　Entrepreneur Alice S. Marriott co-founds a Washington, D.C., restaurant that grows into the billion-dollar Marriott Hotel chain.

The Affiliated Schools for Women Workers is founded to coordinate efforts to educate working women.

1928   Zora Neale Hurston, an anthropologist and writer, becomes the first black graduate of Barnard College.

1929   Philanthropist Abby Aldrich Rockefeller sets into motion plans to establish New York's Museum of Modern Art (MoMA).

Businesswoman Marjorie Merriweather Post goes against the wishes of her board of directors and acquires Birdseye's frozen food patents. The move leads to the formation of General Foods Corporation, the country's largest food company.

1930   Twenty-five percent of all women are in the labor force; 12 percent of married women are in the labor force. More than 80 percent of teachers are women, 95 percent of telephone operators are women, and 98 percent of nurses are women. Most working women (72 percent) are single.

During this decade, women in South Africa (1930; only white women); Spain and Sri Lanka (1930); Chile (restricted) (1931); Uruguay, Thailand, and Maldives (1932); Portugal (restricted), Cuba, and Brazil (1934); Philippines (1937); Uzbekistan (1938); and El Salvador (1939) win voting rights.

Heiress Eleanor Patterson becomes the editor and publisher of the *Washington Herald*. Nine years later, she buys both the *Herald* and the *Washington Times* from William Randolph Hearst and combines them. The *Times-Herald* becomes the best-selling paper in Washington.

A National Education Association survey in the United States reveals that 77 percent of schools will not hire married women as teachers and that 63 percent fire women if they marry.

Dorothy Weeks becomes the first woman to receive a doctorate in mathematics from the Massachusetts Institute of Technology.

A Soviet research study reports that female workers are more productive and less frequently absent than men.

1931   The film *Working Girls*, about two Indiana sisters coming to New York City to look for work, is released. Directed by Dorothy Arzner and starring Frances Dee, the film explores gender roles, work, and marriage.

Minor league pitcher Jackie Mitchell, the first professional female baseball player in the United States, strikes out Lou Gehrig and Babe Ruth in an exhibition game.

China's Factory Law gives women limited rights to equal pay.

1932   Section 213 of the Federal Economy Act requires that one spouse resign if both husband and wife are working for the federal government. A Women's Bureau study later shows that more than 75 percent of those resigning were women. It is one of many public and private pressures on women to give up "pin money" (extra money used for incidentals rather than money essential to running the household) so that men can support families during the Depression.

1933   Frances Perkins becomes the first woman to serve in the United States cabinet. As secretary of labor, she serves for twelve years and assists with many key pieces of legislation including the Federal Emergency Relief Act, the National Labor Relations Act, and the Fair Labor Standards Act.

In Germany most women working in law or civil service positions are fired as Hitler and the Nazi Party rise to power. Three years later, all women in Germany are banned from university teaching.

Camp Jane Addams is one of twenty-eight camps organized following Eleanor Roosevelt's White House Conference on Resident Schools for Unemployed Women.

In all but six U. S. states, there are laws limiting the number of hours women can work.

Ruth Bryan Owen becomes the first woman ambassador

1933,   to represent the United States abroad. She serves as
cont.   envoy to Denmark and Ireland.

1934   Lawyer Florence Allen becomes the first female federal
court judge.

In Cuba, a law is passed requiring "equal pay for equal
work."

1935   Educator Mary McLeod Bethune establishes the National
Council of Negro Women. The following year, President
Franklin D. Roosevelt appoints her to be the director of
the Division of Negro Affairs for the National Youth Administration. She has a strong influence on the racial integration policies of the Roosevelt administration.

Gretchen B. Schoenleber becomes the first female member of the New York Stock Exchange.

The Social Security Act sets up a system of guaranteed retirement benefits for working women and men. It includes several benefits and protections for women and
children.

President Franklin D. Roosevelt appoints Anna Rosenberg director of the National Recovery Administration.

1937   Entrepreneur Margaret Rudkin begins baking and selling
bread at her Connecticut home, Pepperidge Farm. Pepperidge Farm later becomes a multimillion-dollar business.

In *West Coast Hotel v. Parrish,* the Supreme Court permits
a minimum wage law for women.

1938   Crystal Bird Fauset of Pennsylvania becomes the first
black woman in the United States to be elected to a state
legislature.

The company manual at Westinghouse states that no
man, regardless of his position in the company, will be
paid less than the highest-paid woman in the company.

The Fair Labor Standards Act sets minimum wages and maximum hours standards to protect workers in the most poorly paid jobs. The act calls for an end to sex- and age-based wage differentials.

1939   A survey reveals that the majority of insurance, banking, and public utility companies in the United States have policies against hiring women.

1940   Twenty-seven percent of all women are in the labor force; 16 percent of married women are in the labor force. About 90 percent of working women are employed in 11 of 451 types of jobs. Women constitute 91 percent of domestic servants, 94 percent of typists and stenographers, and 98 percent of nurses. There are no women employed as railroad conductors, firefighters, sailors, or soldiers.

During this decade, new limited or full voting rights were won for women in the Dominican Republic (1942); Bulgaria and Jamaica (1944); France, Croatia, Indonesia, Italy, Japan, Senegal, and Ireland (1945); Palestine, Liberia, Cameroon, North Korea, Guatemala, Panama, Romania, Venezuela, Yugoslavia, and Vietnam (1946); Bulgaria, Malta, Pakistan, Singapore, Mexico, and Argentina (1947); Israel, Iraq, South Korea, Niger, and Suriname (1948); and Bosnia, Herzegovina, China, Costa Rica, Chile, Syrian Arab Republic, and India (1949).

The Lanham Act is passed to provide funds for building defense-related industries. Federal funds for child care facilities are included under the act to support working mothers who are joining the war effort. Though only a small percentage of the children of working mothers attend these centers, it sets a precedent for federal involvement in child care funding. At the height of the program, 13 percent of children needing care receive federal assistance. The Children's Bureau criticizes the child care centers, calling them "baby parking stations."

The film *His Girl Friday* debuts, starring Rosalind Russell as a hard-boiled reporter choosing between quiet married life and her rewarding, fast-paced career.

1941 The United States enters World War II. A Fair Employment Practices Commission is established to help alleviate discrimination against black people in war production. Black women especially want to escape from
domestic and agricultural jobs into better-paying factory
work.

1942 The National War Labor Board rules that Brown and
Sharp Manufacturing cannot pay women only four-fifths
of what they pay men for the same work. The board supports giving women equal pay for the same quantity and
quality of work in similar jobs.

The draft begins to decimate the ranks of male workers,
and the government issues a nondiscrimination directive,
reversing Depression-era restrictions on employment of
women, especially married women. For the first time,
employers actively seek out female workers for nontraditional jobs, and some offer day care, meals, and transportation to make it easier for women with families to
work.

Women enter several branches of the armed forces following legislation creating the Women's Auxillary Army
Corps, including the Women's Army Corps (WAC) and
the Women Accepted for Voluntary Emergency Service
(WAVES). In WAC, women receive equal status and pay
with male reservists. In addition to WAC and WAVES,
more than 1,000 women are admitted to the elite
Women's Air Force Service Pilots (WASPs).

Rhode Island becomes the first state to offer paid family
leave under its Temporary Disability Insurance program.

The National War Labor Board issues General Order 16,
which urges voluntary equalization of men's and
women's wages.

1943 Oveta Culp Hobby becomes the first director of the
Women's Army Corps (WAC). In her thirties and the
mother of two children, she works fourteen-hour days,
seven days per week.

Myra Logan becomes the first American female surgeon to perform a heart operation.

1944 Between 1940 and 1944, more than 6 million women join the civilian labor force, though fully 75 percent of all women working for wages during the war had worked before the war.

Argentina passes a minimum wage law for piece work done in the home. Women benefit from the new law.

Women in the U.S. Army Nurse Corps win better pay, and ranks that are equivalent to those of men doing similar work. Pay differentials remain significant, however.

The USS *Sanctuary* becomes the first Navy ship to have women on board with men. Two female officers and sixty enlisted women serve on the ship.

1945 No women serve in the U. S. Senate this year, the first time since 1931 that there have been no female members in the Senate.

Business executive Dorothy Shaver becomes president of the Lord & Taylor department store. Her salary of $110,000 is the highest salary on record for any woman in the United States.

During the war, women work as riveters, lumberjacks, welders, crane operators, toolmakers, cattle handlers, police officers, and taxi drivers. Many black women have quit domestic service to enter new jobs. Women working in manufacturing make roughly 65 percent as much as their male counterparts. After the war, many women are forced out of their nontraditional jobs.

Eleanor Roosevelt becomes a delegate to the United Nations and chairs the U.N. Commission on Human Rights. Three years later, she becomes a key player in the passage of the landmark United Nations Declaration of Human Rights.

1946   An equal pay clause is added to the French constitution.

Roughly 80 percent of Americans, including 75 percent of the women surveyed, believe that a woman should not work if her husband is employed.

1947   Italy's new constitution includes the provision of equal pay for equal work, and equal access to promotions for men and women, while continuing to adhere to the principle that a woman's family role is essential.

Senators Claude Pepper and Wayne Morse introduce a bill that would require equal pay for male and female factory workers. The bill fails to pass the Senate.

1948   Alice Dunnigan becomes the first black woman to work as a White House correspondent.

Women comprise 9.4 percent of Olympic athletes.

Architect Eleanor Raymond and chemist and engineer Dr. Maria Telkes invent the first solar-heated house.

Argentina's 15,000 female textile workers win the legal right to equal pay with men.

1949   Simone de Beauvoir publishes *The Second Sex,* a study of women's marginalization in male-dominated society. Her book contributes to a resurgence of the women's movement in the coming decades.

The movie *Adam's Rib* premieres, starring Katharine Hepburn and Spencer Tracy as lawyers who are married to each other and are facing off in a high-profile court case. In addition to showing a woman working as a competent attorney at a time when there were very few female attorneys, the movie raises questions about traditional social roles and the limitations of gender stereotypes.

1950   In the United States, 23 percent of all women participate in the labor force; 28 percent of women with children aged six to seventeen and 12 percent of women with children under age six are employed outside of the home.

During this decade women in Haiti and Barbados (1950); Antigua, Nepal, and Grenada (1951); Greece, Lebanon, and Bolivia (1952); Hungary, Guyana, and Bhutan (1953); Ghana, Colombia, and Belize (1954); Cambodia, Ethiopia, Peru, Honduras, and Nicaragua (1955); Egypt, Somalia, Comoros, Mauritius, Mali, and Benin (1956); Zimbabwe (1957); and Madagascar and Tanzania (1959) win voting rights.

In the early 1950s, hospitals in the United States face a critical shortage of nurses. Surveys find that enough nurses are being trained, but that many women leave nursing when they become mothers. Nursing administrators at many hospitals set up successful on-site day care centers. This sets the stage for employer-sponsored child care in other corporate settings.

Harvard Law School admits women.

The Senate passes the proposed Equal Rights Amendment by a vote of 63–19, and it is passed on to the House of Representatives. Two years later, the Republican Party includes a plank supporting the Equal Rights Amendment.

Anna M. Rosenberg becomes the first female assistant secretary of defense.

Soia Mentschikoff becomes the first woman to teach at Chicago Law School.

1951   The pay gap between women and men working year-round full-time in the United States is 36.1 percent.

In Israel, the Women's Equal Rights Act is passed, banning gender discrimination.

Maggie Higgins is the first woman to win a Pulitzer Prize for international reporting for her coverage of the Korean War, where she is the only female correspondent.

1951,
cont.

Barbara McClintock first publicly presents her discovery that genetic fragments are transposable, which she had recognized as early as the 1930s, long before the structure of DNA had been understood. Her report is so poorly received that for decades she works without publishing and does not receive widespread recognition for her contributions until the 1970s. In 1983, she wins the Nobel Prize in medicine.

1952

Grace Hopper invents the first computer compiler, revolutionizing the development of computer programs by eliminating the need to write basic instructions for each new program. In 1966, a year after she retires, the U.S. Navy recalls her to help standardize their computer operations.

The National Committee for Equal Pay is established from a coalition of women and labor organizations.

Toni Stone becomes the first woman to play as a regular on a men's major league baseball team, as a reserve for the Indianapolis Clowns of the Negro League. In 1954 she plays second base for the Kansas City Monarchs.

President Eisenhower appoints Oveta Culp Hobby to serve as the first secretary of Health, Education, and Welfare.

1953

Clare Boothe Luce is appointed ambassador to Italy, the first woman to represent the United States to a major foreign power.

Fae Margaret Adams becomes the first commissioned female doctor in the regular U.S. Army.

1954

In a dispute with American Airlines, the Airline Stewards and Stewardesses Association appeals for mediation regarding the company's policy that stewardesses must retire at age thirty-two.

Millions of people regularly watch Lucille Ball's comedy television show, *I Love Lucy*. Her character on the show frequently tries to subvert her husband's refusal to allow her to work outside the home. The actress Lucille Ball serves as a role model for working mothers by continuing to work throughout her pregnancy, which is visible on screen and is worked into the plot of the show.

1955   The Department of Labor sponsors the White House Conference on the Effective Use of Womanpower, to explore expanding women's opportunities in the labor market, including greater participation in nontraditional fields.

The formerly all-female U.S. Army Nurse Corps begins to accept the first male nurses.

The AFL and the CIO merge into a single union, to some degree improving the situation of female wage earners. The new AFL-CIO supports the Equal Rights Amendment.

President Eisenhower calls for "equal pay for equal work without discrimination because of sex" in his State of the Union message.

Bette Nesmith Graham, a secretary, invents Liquid Paper in her kitchen. A formula she later patents, it is a quick-drying liquid used to paint over typing errors. In 1979, she sells Liquid Paper to Gillette Corporation for almost $50 million.

1956   *Life* magazine publishes interviews with five male psychiatrists who believe that female ambition is the root of mental illness in wives, emotional upsets in husbands, and homosexuality in boys.

Josephine Bay becomes the first woman to head a New York Stock Exchange member company, as the president and chair of the brokerage house A.M. Kidder and Company.

1957   Austria provides women with sixteen weeks of paid maternity leave, and women are allowed up to one year of unpaid leave from work.

1958   Pakistan gives women twelve weeks paid maternity leave.

1959   Mabel Newcomer reports in *A Century of Higher Education for Women* that although the proportion of women among college students had increased in the United States to 47 percent in 1920, by 1958 it had dropped to 35 percent. Fewer than 10 percent of doctorates were awarded to women in 1958, compared with 17 percent in 1920. Three out of five women attending coeducational colleges are taking secretarial, nursing, home economics, or education courses.

Less than 6 percent of medical school graduates in the United States are women.

Egypt provides married women with fifty days of maternity leave at 70 percent of their regular pay.

1960   Thirty-one percent of all women are in the labor force; 39 percent of women with children aged six to seventeen and 19 percent of women with children under age six are in the labor force. One-third of all wage-earning women hold clerical jobs. Nearly 80 percent of wage-earning women hold jobs stereotyped as "female."

The annual pay of women relative to men working year-round full-time in the United States is 60.7 percent.

During this decade, women in Cyprus, Gambia, and Tonga (1960); Burundi, Paraguay, Rwanda, and Sierra Leone (1961); Algeria, Monaco, Uganda, and Zambia (1962); Morocco, Congo, the Islamic Republic of Iran, and Kenya (1963); Sudan (1964); Afghanistan, Botswana, and Lesotho (1965); and Ecuador (1967) win voting rights.

In the United States, women are 1 percent of engineers, 6 percent of physicians, 12 percent of college teachers, 3 percent of mail carriers, 4 percent of butchers, 10 percent of insurance agents, 11 percent of bartenders, and 12 percent of bus drivers.

The Canadian Bill of Rights is amended to prohibit sexual discrimination. Six years later, the Committee for Equality of Women and the Royal Commission on the Status of Women are created.

Computer programmer Phyllis Fox codevelops the artificial intelligence language LISt processor and writes the manual for the new language.

Tennis player Billie Jean King wins a doubles title at Wimbledon; it is the first of twenty Wimbledon titles for King.

1961   Women hold 2.4 percent of all executive positions in the Kennedy administration, roughly the same percentage they held under the two previous administrations.

Mary Tyler Moore stars on *The Dick Van Dyke Show* as the housewife Laura Petrie. The popular sitcom also includes a middle-aged character named Sally Rogers (portrayed by Rose Marie) who works full time as a writer for a comedy show but longs to get married.

At the urging of Eleanor Roosevelt, President John F. Kennedy establishes the President's Commission on the Status of Women by Executive Order 10980. The commission is charged with investigating the participation of women in key areas of society including employment, and with eliminating discrimination against working women. The following year, based on recommendations from the commission, President Kennedy directs that women and men should be considered on an equal basis for promotions.

1962   Catalyst, an organization to foster women's career development, is founded.

1963   Congress passes the Equal Pay Act, requiring most companies to pay equal wages regardless of sex to all those performing equal tasks. The act cites equal opportunity for women in employment as a national goal.

1963, cont. The President's Commission on the Status of Women issues the report *American Women* recommending equality in employment opportunities, wages, and educational opportunities. The report calls for government-assisted day care centers and government-mandated maternity leave.

Katharine Graham takes over as president and publisher of the *Washington Post* following her husband's death.

Betty Friedan writes *The Feminine Mystique*. The book helps spark the second wave of the women's movement. Based on surveys of her classmates at Smith College, Freidan found that many women were unhappy in their roles as wives and homemakers. Friedan later helps establish the National Organization for Women, which advocates for more child care centers, legalized abortion, and an end to sex segregated employment advertising, in addition to other issues.

1964 Congress passes the Civil Rights Act of 1964. The act includes Title VII, which prohibits firms with fifteen or more employees from discriminating on the basis of sex, among other characteristics. Congress also establishes the Equal Employment Opportunity Commission (EEOC) to coordinate efforts to implement the law and to conciliate disputes. Shortly thereafter, the EEOC is flooded with sex discrimination complaints.

The Society of Engineers gives its Achievement Award to computer programmer Grace Murray Hopper.

Marietta Tree becomes the first woman to serve as a permanent United States ambassador to the United Nations.

Marlene Sanders becomes the first woman to serve as anchor on a television network's evening newscast (ABC News) when she fills in for the regular anchor.

1965 Patsy Mink is the first Japanese American woman elected to Congress.

Patricia Harris becomes the first black ambassador for the United States. She serves as ambassador to Luxembourg. In 1977, she becomes the first black woman in the cabinet when she is appointed secretary of Housing and Urban Development (HUD); in 1979, she becomes secretary of Health, Education, and Welfare (HEW).

Guatemala's constitution guarantees women equal pay for equal work.

Mary Draper Janney and Jane Phillips Fleming create Wider Opportunities for Women (WOW). The organization assists women in gaining job skills, breaking into nontraditional fields, and locating day care.

In the United States, 54 percent of male managers and 50 percent of female managers say they believe women do not want or expect power.

Constance Baker Motley becomes the first black female United States federal judge.

1966   The National Organization for Women (NOW) is founded, and Betty Friedan serves as its first president. The goal of NOW is to bring about full equality between men and women.

1967   Hungary passes a law providing women who stay home with children a monthly pension for three years.

The United Nations adopts the Declaration on the Elimination of Discrimination against Women.

The Boston Marathon refuses to accept a female runner. Katherine Switzer registers for the running race as K. Switzer. When she shows up for the race, officials attempt, but fail, to keep her from running. She finishes the race, and in 1972, becomes the first woman to officially participate in the race.

Stockbroker Muriel Siebert is the first woman to own a seat on the New York Stock Exchange.

1967,   Kathy Kusner is the first American woman granted a
cont.   jockey's license to race thoroughbred horses.

Ghana passes a labor law guaranteeing women twelve
weeks of maternity leave at half salary and job security if
they take their leave. Women who nurse their babies are
given nursing breaks during work.

Executive Order 11246, as amended by Order 11375, prohibits discrimination in employment on the basis of sex,
among other characteristics, by all employers with federal contracts higher than $10,000.

1968   Shirley Chisholm is the first black woman elected to
Congress.

Yale University announces that it will begin admitting
women. Vassar College, previously all-female, announces it will begin admitting men.

Elizabeth Boyer founds the Women's Equity Action
League.

Daisy Fields founds the organization Federally Employed Women. The goal of the organization is to achieve
equality and equal opportunity for women in the federal
government.

1969   *Bowe et al. v. Colgate-Palmolive* overturns weightlifting restrictions that had applied only to women workers. All
employees will now have the opportunity to prove their
suitability for the more physically demanding jobs available at the company.

A survey of engineering consulting firms finds that 99
percent of the 1,000 firms surveyed hire no women
engineers.

1970   Forty-one percent of all women are in the labor force; 49
percent of women with children aged six to seventeen
and 30 percent of women with children under age six are
in the labor force.

The annual pay of women relative to men working year-round full-time in the United States is 59.4 percent.

During this decade, women in Yemen (1970); Switzerland (1971); Bangladesh (1972); Bahrain (1973); Jordan and the Solomon Islands (1974); Angola, Cape Verde, and Mozambique (1975); Portugal (1976); and the Republic of Moldova (1978) win voting rights.

In the United States, women are awarded 3 percent of all M.B.A. degrees and 10 percent of all medical degrees.

Mexico passes a law requiring equal pay for women and men.

Caroline Bird writes *Born Female.* In the book, she documents the unequal status and lower pay of women in the workplace during the 1960s. She also demonstrates that young women need higher grades than men to be accepted by colleges and are relegated to low-paying, sex segregated industries after graduation. She later publishes a number of other books, including *The Two-Paycheck Marriage* in 1979.

Anne Thompson becomes the first black woman prosecutor in the United States. Women in the United States earn 8 percent of all law degrees.

The Women's Strike for Equality march is held. Women demonstrate across the United States, including 20,000–50,000 women in New York City.

Anna Mae Hays and Elizabeth Hoisington become the first female brigadier generals in the United States.

The Mary Tyler Moore Show begins its seven-year run, winning a record twenty-seven Emmy awards during its run. The comedy is about an independent, idealized career woman who is single and not constantly in search of a husband.

Billie Jean King and Gladys Heldman organize the Virginia

1970,   Slims Tennis Circuit. The circuit is organized in reaction to
cont.   the small awards women receive in comparison to men at
national and international tennis tournaments. The following year, King becomes the first female athlete to earn
$100,000 in one year. In 1973, she defeats male player
Bobby Riggs in a widely publicized "Battle of the Sexes."

1971   The Women's Legal Defense Fund (later known as the
National Partnership for Women & Families) is founded
to help women and men meet the dual demands of work
and family. The organization takes a lead role in the passage of the Pregnancy Discrimination Act of 1978, and it
writes the first draft of the Family and Medical Leave Act
in 1984.

The National Press Club votes to admit women. Prior to
their membership, female reporters were not allowed to
use the club's wire machines to transmit stories, and they
were relegated to the balcony of the club when press
briefings and speeches were being conducted.

The Association for Women in Mathematics is founded to
encourage women to study, and have active careers in,
mathematics.

Peggy Lenore Williams joins the Ringling Brothers and
Barnum and Bailey Circus, becoming the first female circus clown in the United States.

The Department of Labor establishes guidelines prohibiting sex discrimination in the workplace.

The Supreme Court overrules the lower courts' finding in
Phillips v. Martin Marietta Corporation. Ida Phillips had
been denied a job at Martin Marietta because she had
young children. The Supreme Court rules that the company cannot have different hiring policies for men and
women. However, the Court leaves open the possibility
that gender might be considered a bona fide occupational
qualification (BFOQ) if parenting could be shown to have
a lesser impact on a man's job performance than on a
woman's job performance.

1972   Congress passes Title IX of the Education Act. The law prohibits sex discrimination in any federally assisted educational program or activity. The law has far-ranging effects on women's education and sports.

The Equal Employment Opportunity Commission rules that employment policies that exclude women violate Title VII of the 1964 Civil Rights Act.

Shirley Chisholm is a candidate for the Democratic presidential nomination. She is the first black person to be a recognized candidate.

The National Women's Law Center is created to protect and advance the progress of women and girls in school, at work, and in other aspects of their lives. The center focuses on family economic security, health, employment, and education.

A Board of Education ruling requiring pregnant teachers to take a six-month leave without pay after their fifth month of pregnancy is overturned by a Chicago district court.

Australia passes an equal pay law for women.

1973   The American Stock Exchange adopts an affirmative action hiring policy.

The Supreme Court upholds the decision in *Pittsburgh Press v. Pittsburgh Commission on Human Relations* that ends the practice of running sex segregated want ads in newspapers.

The U.S. Civil Service Commission revises discriminatory height and weight requirements that have prevented women from working as park police, fire prevention workers, and narcotics control officers.

AT&T pays more than $38 million in back pay in a landmark class-action lawsuit brought by 13,000 women of various races and 2,000 men of color, who sue over discrimination in the workplace.

1973, Pamela Douglas becomes the first black woman producer
cont. at a major motion picture studio, Universal Studios.

Marianne Burge is the first female partner at a Big Eight
accounting firm when she is promoted to partner at Price,
Waterhouse & Company.

Emily Howell begins flying as the first commercial airline
pilot in the United States. She is employed by Frontier
Airlines.

Bonnie Tiburzi becomes the first female jet pilot hired by
a major airline: American Airlines.

Patricia Wiener patents one of the first memory systems
to be contained on a single silicon computer chip.

The organization 9 to 5, the Association of Working
Women, is created as a grassroots organization that supports working women.

1974 The Alliance for Displaced Homemakers (later renamed
the National Displaced Homemakers' Network in 1978)
is established and encourages men and women to view
homemaking and child rearing as occupations. They also
try to help women who are not supported by their husbands to find employment.

Congress amends the Fair Labor Standards Act to include
domestic workers under the minimum wage law.

The Coalition of Labor Union Women is founded to work
toward the goals of affirmative action in the workplace,
increasing women's labor union membership, and encouraging participation of women within their labor
unions.

Katharine Graham, publisher of the *Washington Post*, is
the first woman to be named to the eighteen-member Associated Press Board.

The Women's Educational Equity Act is established to

help schools eliminate sex bias. The act provides funding for programs that support girls in math and science study.

Hanna Gray becomes the first female provost of Yale University. She will later be the first female president, serving on an interim basis at Yale. She later serves as president of the University of Chicago.

An attorney for an employee at Cornell University first uses the term *sexual harassment* when filing a claim with the Equal Employment Opportunity Commission.

Cuban women win the right to sixteen weeks of paid and one year of unpaid maternity leave.

Ireland passes the Equal Pay Act, giving women the right to equal pay for equal work with men. The law protects women who file discrimination suits from retribution.

1975   Congress orders military academies to begin admitting women. Debra Houghton becomes the Army's first female tank driver. Women now make up 4.5 percent of the U.S. Army.

Journalist Helen Thomas, White House bureau chief for United Press International (UPI), becomes the first female president of the White House Correspondents' Association.

The Social Security Administration publishes *The Economic Value of a Housewife* by Wendyce H. Broday. The report describes approaches to determining the economic value of work performed by housewives and estimates that the average value of a housewife in 1972 would be $4,705. The average annual earnings for all workers during this time are $6,697.

Politician Barbara Jordan, a former congresswoman, is the first black person and the first woman to give the keynote speech at the Democratic National Convention.

1976   Barbara Walters co-anchors an evening network news

1976, cont.   broadcast. She later becomes the first female anchor to earn more than $1 million per year.

Kentucky's Commission on Human Rights rules that two coal companies must hire women as miners. The commission also orders the companies to pay $29,000 in back wages to two women who were denied employment.

The Supreme Court rules in *General Electric v. Gilbert* that a health insurance plan providing sickness and accident benefits for any disability but those arising as a result of pregnancy does not constitute sex discrimination under Title VII, although the Court acknowledges that only women can become pregnant.

Anna J. Harrison becomes the first woman in the history of the American Chemical Society to serve as the organization's president.

Sarah Caldwell becomes the first female conductor of the Metropolitan Opera. She is offered the position when Beverly Sills refuses to sing there unless Sarah Caldwell conducts.

In the United States, 90 percent of 9,000 women surveyed claim that they have been sexually harassed.

Eight Denver nurses file the first pay equity lawsuit seeking equal pay for jobs of "comparable worth." The nurses sue the city and county of Denver for paying its tree trimmers, painters, and tire-service men more than its nurses. The nurses lose the case but raise awareness about the issue of comparable worth.

In *Franks v. Bowman Transportation Company,* the Supreme Court holds that Title VII requires an employer to hire a victim of unlawful discrimination with seniority starting from the date the individual was unlawfully denied the position.

1977   Juanita Kreps becomes the first female secretary of commerce.

Lawyer Eleanor Holmes Norton becomes the first woman to head the Equal Employment Opportunity Commission.

Rosalyn Yallow wins the Nobel Prize for medicine for her invention of radioimmunoassay (RIA). RIA revolutionizes the process of medical diagnosis for many diseases.

The National Broadcasting Corporation (NBC), in a settlement with the Equal Employment Opportunity Commission, agrees to provide back pay to female employees and create mobility programs for women.

1978   The Pregnancy Discrimination Act passes, categorizing discrimination based on pregnancy as a type of sex discrimination and requiring employers to treat pregnancy as a temporary disability. Prior to the act, pregnant women were sometimes fired, were demoted, or lost seniority.

Female sports writers in the United States win the right to enter major league baseball locker rooms.

Sally Ride and five other women become NASA's first female astronaut trainees.

New York City admits some women to its firefighting ranks if they are able to pass a strenuous test that male firefighters must also pass. The physical test involves non-job-related challenges that are judged subjectively and seem designed to screen out women. All seventy-nine women taking the original physical test fail and a successful class action suit is filed by Brenda Berkman. The new test focuses on job-related activities such as forcing doors and raising ladders. Berkman and forty-three other women successfully pass the new test and forty-one women including Berkman become firefighters in New York City.

1979   Legal scholar Catharine MacKinnon writes a book about the sexual harassment of working women. The book provides a legal framework for dealing with sexual harass-

1979,
cont.

ment. MacKinnon argues that sexual harassment is a form of sex discrimination and is therefore covered by Title VII of the 1964 Civil Rights Act. One year later the Equal Employment Opportunity Commission changes its guidelines so that sexual harassment is covered by Title VII.

The film *Norma Rae* debuts, with Sally Field winning an Oscar for her role as a poor textile worker who helps unionize a southern mill. Also opening this year are *The China Syndrome,* starring Jane Fonda as a heroic television reporter uncovering the dangers of nuclear power plants, and *Kramer vs. Kramer,* about a man who must cope with balancing fatherhood duties and employment after his wife deserts the family. The film *Kramer vs. Kramer* wins Best Actor, Best Picture, Best Screenplay, and Best Supporting Actress awards.

A U.S. court of appeals rules that employers may not require female employees to wear uniforms if men in comparable jobs are allowed to wear standard business clothes.

The National Committee on Pay Equity is created to work to eliminate sex- and race-based wage discrimination. Their goal is to achieve pay equity.

Women make up 14 percent of the paid work force in Guatemala. Women make up 33 percent of the total work force in El Salvador.

More women than men enter college in the United States this year. Women earn 95 percent of home economics degrees and 94 percent of library science degrees.

Austria and Sweden pass equal pay laws. Canada passes a law providing paid maternity leave to women.

1980

Fifty-two percent of all women are in the labor force; 68 percent of women with children aged six to seventeen and 50 percent of women with children under age six are in the labor force. Labor force participation rates for white women now equal the participation rates of black women.

The annual pay of women relative to men working year-round full-time in the United States is 60.2 percent.

During this decade, women in South Africa (1984; non-white women and men) and the Central African Republic (1986) win voting rights.

Women earn 48 percent of law degrees, but a study by Harvard Law School finds that 25 percent of men and only 1 percent of women are partners in law firms seven years after their graduation from law school.

Michaela Walsh founds Women's World Banking, an organization that provides loans to women around the world. By 1991 the organization will have helped 500,000 female entrepreneurs in many different countries.

In the United States, women earn 21 percent of all M.B.A.s.

Female elementary school teachers make 82 percent as much money as male teachers. Female lawyers make 71 percent as much as male lawyers, and female engineers make 68 percent as much as male engineers. In France, female workers make 69 percent as much as men, in Israel, female workers make 78 percent as much as men, and in Peru, female workers make 50 percent as much as men.

The first female firefighter in Iowa City is awarded damages after a court battle over whether she can breast-feed her baby while at work.

The United Nations first World Conference on Women opens in Copenhagen. The United States and fifty-two other nations sign an agreement to end discrimination against women.

Ford Motor Company pays $23 million in a settlement for a job discrimination case. The money is used to develop

1980, special job training programs for female and minority
cont.   employees. Ford also agrees that women will be hired for
        30 percent of all its job openings for nonskilled workers.

        Dolly Parton, Jane Fonda, and Lily Tomlin star in *9 to 5*, a
        film about women who get even with a boss who has sex-
        ually harassed them.

        Women are 19 percent of the paid work force in
        Afghanistan.

        West Germany, Sweden, and the Netherlands pass laws
        against gender discrimination in the workplace.

1981   An Equal Employment Opportunity Commission report
        finds that women make 60 cents for every dollar earned
        by men.

        Working Mother magazine begins publication in New
        York.

        Women earn 37 percent of all B.S. degrees and less than 5
        percent of all engineering degrees.

        A strike in San Jose, California, ends when the city agrees
        to bring women's pay up to the level of men's for com-
        parable work.

        Sandra Day O'Connor becomes the first female justice of
        the U.S. Supreme Court.

        In the United States, men are 2 percent of all kindergarten
        and preschool teachers, 3 percent of all dental assistants,
        and 8 percent of all telephone operators.

1982   United Airlines is ordered by a federal district court to re-
        hire 1,800 female flight attendants who lost their jobs
        when they married.

        The Supreme Court rules that Trans World Airlines flight
        attendants who were fired prior to 1971 because of preg-
        nancy are entitled to back pay and retroactive seniority.

1983   Christine Craft is awarded damages after a television station in Kansas City, Missouri, fires her from her position as news anchor for being "too old, unattractive, and not deferential enough to men."

Physicist Sally Ride becomes the first U.S. woman in space, serving aboard the *Challenger* space shuttle.

Connie Chung is one of the first female minority news anchors in the United States. In the following decade, she wins several Emmy awards.

1984   France passes a law that provides for fines and imprisonment for those who violate equal pay laws. The new law only applies to full-time workers; 82 percent of female workers in France work part-time.

Democrat Geraldine Ferraro is the first female nominee for vice president from a major political party.

Talk show host Oprah Winfrey becomes host of *AM Chicago*, later called *The Oprah Winfrey Show*.

Business Week magazine estimates that in the United States, women hold only 2 percent of the top 50,000 management jobs.

Title IX protection against bias in education is greatly weakened by the Supreme Court ruling in *Grove City College v. Bell*. The Court states that Title IX only applies to programs receiving funds, not entire institutions.

1985   Penny Harrington becomes the first female chief of a major U.S. police department. She serves as chief in Portland, Oregon.

The Equal Employment Opportunity Commission rejects any cases of job discrimination based on comparable worth.

Basketball player Lynette Woodard becomes the first female member of the Harlem Globetrotters.

1985,   The ABC network pays Cecily Coleman an out-of-court
cont. settlement of $500,000 in a charge brought against former
        ABC network executive James D. Abernathy for sexual
        harassment.

        Women in Iceland go on a twenty-four-hour strike to
        protest unequal wages.

        In the United States, 47 percent of male managers and 82
        percent of female managers say they would be comfort-
        able working for a female boss.

        The World Conference on Women is held in Kenya. Pay
        equity, child care, and flexible working schedules are top
        agenda items.

1986   The term *glass ceiling* is first used in a *Wall Street Journal*
        article describing the invisible barriers that prevent
        women from rising to upper management positions.

        In *Meritor Savings Bank v. Vinson,* the Supreme Court rules
        that sexual harassment of employees violates federal law.

1987   In *California Federal Savings and Loan Association v. Guerra,*
        the United States Supreme Court rules that a woman has
        a right to job security following maternity leave. Writing
        for the 6–3 majority, Justice Thurgood Marshall says that
        the legislation "promotes equal employment opportu-
        nity" because "it allows women, as well as men, to have
        families without losing their jobs."

        Wilma Mankiller becomes the first female leader of the
        Cherokee Nation.

        Twenty-eight states introduce parental/family leave bills.
        Connecticut, Minnesota, Oregon, and Rhode Island pass
        parental/family leave legislation.

        Women own 30 percent of businesses in the United
        States.

        In *Johnson v. Transportation Agency,* the Supreme Court

upholds the constitutionality of voluntary affirmative action programs for women in employment fields from which they had previously been excluded.

1988   Congress passes the Civil Rights Restoration Act. The new law reaffirms that Title IX applies to all educational programs in an institution, not just those that draw federal funds.

1989   The term *mommy track* enters the popular lexicon with the publication of an article in the *Harvard Business Review* by Felice Schwartz. Schwartz proposes that some women should be able to choose a slower track during years when they have children at home, in order to keep valuable women in the labor force from dropping out completely while raising children. The media distorts Schwartz's proposal and suggests that women with children are better suited to part-time and less demanding work labeled the "Mommy Track."

The Supreme Court rules that once a woman presents direct evidence of having been denied promotion because of illegal sex stereotyping, her employer must prove that there were other legitimate reasons for denying the promotion.

1990   Fifty-seven percent of all women are in the labor force; 74 percent of women with children aged six to seventeen and 57 percent of women with children under age six are in the labor force.

The annual pay of women relative to men working year-round full-time in the United States is 71.6 percent.

The U.S. Supreme Court rules that the University of Pennsylvania must make relevant files relating to tenure decisions available to federal investigators. Rosalie Tung had accused the university of discriminating on the basis of sex and national origin.

The State Department settles a lengthy sex discrimination suit by giving some female Foreign Service officers

1990,   priority in obtaining assignments previously denied
cont.   them on the basis of sex.

Sharon Pratt Dixon of Washington, D.C., becomes the first black female mayor of a major city in the United States. Ann Richards wins the governorship of Texas, and Barbara Robert is elected governor in Oregon.

The Guerrilla Girls, an anonymous group of masked women, protest discrimination against women and minorities in the art world. They use posters, personal appearances, and performances as part of their campaign.

President George Bush vetoes the Civil Rights Act of 1990, a bill that would have protected women and minorities from discrimination in the work force.

In Pittsburgh, two male disc jockeys are ordered to pay a female news director almost $700,000 in damages for making sexually explicit remarks about her on the air.

The National Commission on Working Women reports that women make up only 15 percent of producers, 25 percent of writers, and 9 percent of directors in network television.

Dozens of states put together task forces to investigate gender bias in the court system. One report from California documents serious bias against women as litigants, lawyers, and court employees. Other task forces discover similar problems.

The Directors' Guild of America reports that women made 23 of the 406 feature films produced under guild contracts this year.

Marguerite Ross Barnett becomes the first woman president of the University of Houston and the first African American woman to head a major American university.

1991   Sexual harassment becomes prominent news when Anita Hill testifies that Supreme Court nominee Clarence

Thomas sexually harassed her. In the year following her testimony, reports of sexual harassment cases almost double from 6,883 to more than 12,000 by 1993.

Twenty-six female active duty officers of the U.S. Navy are sexually assaulted by at least seventy navy aviators at a Las Vegas convention of the Tailhook Association. Lt. Paula Coughlin reports the incident and later resigns, citing stress as the reason. Her coming forward leads to the early retirement of the secretary of the Navy and several other senior officers. Coughlin is later awarded $6.7 million for sexual assault damages.

Women are 22 percent of lawyers and judges in the United States. Women are 18 percent of doctors in the United States.

Frances Conley, a medical school professor at Stanford University, resigns her post to protest sexual harassment. She later returns to the school to fight sexual harassment from within. At the time, only 15 percent of the medical school's faculty are women; about 25 percent of university faculty nationwide are women.

Japan's child care leave law allows either parent to take a leave of absence from work for one year following the birth of a child.

The courts order Continental Airlines to rehire Terri Fischette, who was fired for not wearing makeup.

In Switzerland, 400,000 women stage a one-day strike for equal pay.

The Supreme Court rules in *Automobile Workers v. Johnson Controls* that employers cannot exclude women from jobs in which exposure to toxic substances could harm a developing fetus.

The United States Department of Labor releases a study of nine Fortune 500 corporations confirming that women and minorities faced significant "glass ceiling" barriers in

1991,   their careers at far earlier stages than previously believed.
cont.   Exclusion from networking, mentoring, and participation in policymaking committees was widespread.

Jockey Julie Krone ranks number three in the jockey standings in New York. She has won purses totaling $37 million, more than any other woman in horse racing.

AT&T Technologies agrees to pay $66 million as a result of an EEOC lawsuit. AT&T is found to have discriminated on the basis of pregnancy by forcing employees to take leave before medically necessary and by failing to guarantee a return to their positions following pregnancy leave on the same basis as for other temporary disabilities.

1992   The Civil Rights Act of 1992 provides victims of job discrimination the right to a trial by jury and makes employers liable for damages of up to $300,000.

Four women are elected to the U.S. Senate, including Carol Moseley-Braun, the first African American female senator.

Advertising executive Charlotte Beers becomes CEO and chair of Ogilvy & Mather, one of the largest advertising agencies in the world.

A study of sexual harassment in the United States Navy confirms widespread problems. Of the sixty-one female officers interviewed, 40 had experienced harassment.

State Farm Insurance Company agrees to pay $157 million to 814 women who were denied jobs as agents. It is the biggest sex discrimination settlement in United States history under the Civil Rights Act of 1964.

1993   President Clinton signs into law the Family and Medical Leave Act. The new law provides for unpaid leave for the birth, adoption, or foster placement of a child, an employee's own serious health condition, or the serious health condition of an employee's immediate family member. Though a major accomplishment, this law covers only 11 percent of United States employers (those with fifty or more employees), leaving 41 percent of all workers ineligible. In addition, the law does not provide leave to employees with less traditional family arrangements, such as gay and lesbian couples or people in common law marriages.

President Bill Clinton appoints Janet Reno attorney general. She is the first woman to serve in this post. Two previous attempts by Clinton to appoint women were stalled, amid protests of discrimination, when questions arose about the legality of their payments to child care providers.

Ruth Bader Ginsburg becomes the second woman on the United States Supreme Court.

Justice O'Connor writes the landmark, unanimous opinion in *Harris v. Forklift Systems* that in a sexual harassment case the plaintiff does not have to prove concrete psychological harm to establish a Title VII violation.

The first Take Our Daughters to Work Day is organized to introduce girls to possible career options.

Ellen Ochoa becomes the first Hispanic woman in space as part of the five-person crew of the *Discovery* space shuttle.

1994   Vassar College is found guilty of discrimination against married women and pays $400,000 to biologist Cynthia Fisher, a married mother of two whose promotions have not paralleled those of men or of unmarried women with lesser credentials. Vassar has not granted tenure to a married woman in the hard sciences in the past thirty years.

Women account for 6.9 percent of all corporate board seats. Only three of Fortune's top 1,000 companies have female chief executives.

1995   Shannon Faulkner becomes the first female cadet at the Citadel military college. She wins admittance through a lawsuit.

1995,
cont.
The fourth World Conference on Women is held in Beijing, China. More than 4,000 delegate and 30,000 participants attend.

The Senate Ethics Committee recommends the expulsion of Oregon Senator Bob Packwood for a "pattern of sex abuse" of his subordinates that involved at least seventeen women. Packwood resigns.

The CIA settles a major class-action suit involving sex discrimination, with $990,000 going to 450 women in its Directorate of Operations (undercover operations).

The Supreme Court rules in *Adarand Constructors v. Pena* that the federal government must follow the same standards as the states in carrying out affirmative action programs.

The bipartisan Glass Ceiling Commission reports that women and minority groups continue to be little represented in senior management positions and that the glass ceiling remains in place.

The first sexual harassment suit against the United Nations is settled for $210,000. Of 185 member nations, 75 are found to have no women in professional positions.

Sexual harassment lawsuits are won against CEOs at two large companies: W. R. Grace and Del Laboratories. The CEO of Grace is forced to resign. Del pays a record $1.2 million to fifteen women who were mistreated by their CEO.

For the first time in Yale's 182-year history, the medical school admits more women then men in the entering class. Seventeen other medical schools around the country have a majority of women, including Harvard.

Rebecca E. Marier becomes the first female valedictorian at West Point.

Linda Chavez-Thompson becomes the highest-ranking

woman in the labor movement, as well as the highest-ranking person of color in U.S. labor history.

1996   Madeleine Albright is nominated U.S. secretary of state and becomes the first woman to hold the post.

The Supreme Court rules in *United States v. Virginia* that the state-funded Virginia Military Institute has violated the Fourteenth Amendment by refusing to admit women as students.

Donna S. Shirley, head of the Mars exploration project at the National Aeronautics and Space Administration's Space Jet Propulsion Laboratory, launches the Mars probe *Pathfinder,* which includes the exploration robot vehicle *Sojourner,* designed by Shirley.

1997   The new Women's National Basketball Association (WNBA) begins its inaugural season before record-breaking crowds.

The Supreme Court upholds *Brown v. Cohen,* thus strengthening Title IX and requiring Brown University to fund women's and men's sports programs equally.

The Mitsubishi Motor Corporation settles a lawsuit and pays out $9.5 million to twenty-seven women at their Illinois plant who had accused the company of condoning sexual harassment in the workplace. The following year, Mitsubishi agrees to pay $34 million to more than 300 female employees to settle a class-action lawsuit brought by the Equal Employment Opportunity Commission. The settlement is the largest out-of-court settlement of a sexual harassment suit involving a corporation in the United States.

1998   The Supreme Court unanimously rules in *Oncale v. Sundowner Offshore Services* that a federal law against sexual harassment in the workplace applies even in situations when the victim and the perpetrator are of the same gender. The case concerns a male Louisiana oil worker who was subjected to harassment by male colleagues.

1998, The Supreme Court, in *Faragher v. City of Boca Raton* and
cont. *Burlington Industries, Inc. v. Ellerth,* spells out the circumstances in which employers will be held liable for acts
of sexual harassment carried out by their supervisory
personnel.

During his State of the Union address, President Clinton
asks for help ending the backlog of more than 60,000 cases
at the Equal Employment Opportunity Commission.

The New Mothers' Breastfeeding Promotion and Protection Bill is introduced into the U.S. Congress. It fails to
pass.

Boeing Company agrees to pay $4.5 million to about
4,400 women and 1,000 employees of ethnic minority origin who were paid less than white male colleagues for
the same work.

1999 In *EEOC v. Tanimura & Antle,* a class-action sexual harassment lawsuit against one of the country's largest let-
tuce growers, the defendant is ordered to pay female
farm workers nearly $3 million as a result of their suffer-
ing sexual harassment and then suffering retaliation for
complaints.

Thirteen states introduce "paid-leave legislation" over
the next two years, but none of the bills succeed.

2000 At this point, 58 percent of all women participate in the
labor force in the United States, and 79 percent of women
with children aged six to seventeen and 66 percent of
women with children under age six are employed outside of the home.

The annual pay of women relative to men working year-
round full-time in the United States is 73 percent. A report released by the General Accounting Office finds that
between 1995 and 2000, the pay gap has widened for
women in seven of ten industries studied nationwide.

Germany revises a family leave law to encourage fathers

to take leave. The statute permits both parents up to three years off with partial wage replacement.

2001   Princeton becomes the first major research university to have women in the two highest posts when president Shirley Tilghman appoints Amy Guttman to the position of provost. Women hold the presidencies at three of the eight Ivy League institutions: Dr. Tilghman at Princeton, Judith Rodin at the University of Pennsylvania, and Ruth J. Simmons at Brown. Nationwide, 19 percent of American college presidents, more than 400 in all, are women, up from 9.5 percent in 1986.

Female labor union members comprise 42 percent of all labor union members.

2002   There are only twenty-five female firefighters in the New York City Fire Department among a total of 11,500. Of the 1,000 firefighters hired in the past year, only one is female.

Presidential adviser Karen Hughes leaves her influential job in Washington, D.C., to spend more time with her family. She joins a long list of professional women who have left high-powered careers to be with their children.

The Bureau of Labor Statistics reports that female part-time employees earn a median of $1.15 for every $1 male part-timers earn, a reverse of the full-time wage gap.

American Express reaches a settlement with plaintiffs in a sex discrimination lawsuit. The company agrees to pay $31 million to as many as 4,000 women who have worked as financial advisers at the firm over the past three years. The company has also agreed to change how it distributes work, how it handles employee complaints, and how it promotes employees.

The American Association for the Advancement of Sciences releases a survey of the salaries and comparative career happiness among researchers in biology, medicine, and related disciplines. Women employed full-time as

2002,   life scientists earn some $72,000 a year, 23 percent less
cont.   than the $94,000 their male counterparts make. Women
         are more likely than men to count themselves as "fairly"
         rather than "highly" happy with their jobs.

         An overwhelming majority of House Democrats elect
         Congresswoman Nancy Pelosi as Democratic Leader,
         making her the highest-ranking woman in the history of
         the U.S. Congress and the first woman to lead a major po-
         litical party.

References

Bird, Caroline. 1970. *Born Female.* New York: Pocket Books.

———. 1979. *The Two-Paycheck Marriage.* New York: Pocket Books.

Broday, Wendyce H. 1975. *The Economic Value of a Housewife.* Social Security Administration. Washington, DC: Office of Research and Statistics.

Chopin, Kate. 1900. "Charlie." In *The Complete Works of Kate Chopin.* Edited by Per Seyersted. Reprint, Baton Rouge: Louisiana State University Press, 1969.

Cleveland, Grover. 1905. *Ladies' Home Journal.* Vol. 22 (April).

de Beauvoir, Simone. 1949. *Le Deuxieme Sexe.* Reprinted as *The Second Sex.* London: Picador, 1988.

Friedan, Betty. 1963. *The Feminine Mystique.* New York: Norton.

Hamilton, Alice. 1926. *Women Workers and Industrial Poisons.* Washington, DC: Government Printing Office.

MacKinnon, Catharine. 1979. *Sexual Harassment of Working Women: A Case of Sex Discrimination.* New Haven, CT: Yale University Press.

Newcomer, Mabel. 1959. *A Century of Higher Education for Women.* New York: Harper.

President's Commission on the Status of Women. 1963. *American Women.* Washington, DC: Government Printing Office.

Schwartz, Felice. 1989. "Management Women and the New Facts of Life." *Harvard Business Review* 67, no. 2 (January–February): 65–76.

Tarbell, Ida. 1912. *The Business of Being a Woman.* New York: Macmillan Company.

Wharton, Edith. 1905. *The House of Mirth.* New York: Berkley.

Court Cases Cited

Adarand Constructors v. Pena, 515 U.S. 200 (1995)

Adkins v. Children's Hospital, 261 U.S. 525 (1923)

Automobile Workers v. Johnson Controls, Inc., 499 U.S. 187 (1991)

Bowe et al. v. Colgate-Palmolive, 416 F.2d 711 (1969)

California Federal Savings and Loan v. Guerra, 55 U.S.L.W. 4077 (1987)

Cohen v. Brown University, 879 F. Supp. 185 (1995)

Burlington Industries, Inc. v. Ellerth, 524 U.S. 742 (1998)

EEOC v. Tanimura & Antle, Northern District of California Civil Action No. C-99-2008JW (1999)

Faragher v. City of Boca Raton, 524 U.S. 775 (1998)

Franks v. Bowman Transportation Company, 424 U.S. 747 (1976)

General Electric v. Gilbert, 429 U.S. 125 (1976)

Grove City College v. Bell, 465 U.S. 555 (1984)

Harris v. Forklift Systems, 510 U.S. 17 (1993)

Johnson v. Transportation Agency, 480 U.S. 616 (1987)

Lochner v. New York, 198 U.S. 45 (1905)

Meritor Savings Bank v. Vinson, 477 U.S. 57 (1986)

Muller v. Oregon, 208 U.S. 412 (1908)

Oncale v. Sundowner Offshore Services, 523 U.S. 75 (1998)

Phillips v. Martin Marietta, 400 U.S. 542 (1971)

Pittsburgh Press vs. Pittsburgh Commission on Human Relations, 413 U.S. 376 (1973)

United States v. Virginia, 518 U.S. 515 (1996)

West Coast Hotel v. Parrish, 300 U.S. 379 (1937)

4

Biographical Sketches

Individuals described in this chapter have contributed to advances in gender equity in the workplace, whether as pioneers in entering new fields, as activists, or as scholars. (For discussions of some court cases cited here, see chapter 5.)

Pioneers

Madeleine Korbel Albright (1937–)

In 1997, when Madeleine Albright became the sixty-fourth secretary of state, she was the first woman to occupy that office, the highest office ever held by any woman in U.S. government history. A naturalized citizen who was born in Czechoslovakia in 1937, she was extraordinarily well qualified for the post as a result of unique circumstances of birth, childhood, education, marriage, and profession.

Born in 1937 into a family that she much later discovered was Jewish (her parents hid the fact from her to protect her from the Holocaust), she learned English as a small child in London where her father, Joseph Korbel, a Czech diplomat, had taken the family to escape the threat of Hitler. She learned French in a Swiss school while her father served as the Czech ambassador to Yugoslavia. Following the war and the change to a Communist regime in Czechoslovakia, the family came to the United States in 1948 and was granted political asylum. They moved to Colorado in 1949, where Korbel became a professor of international relations at the University of Denver. Madeleine received a scholarship to Wellesley College, from which she graduated in 1959. At Wellesley, she majored in political science and was active on the campus newspaper, of which she became the editor.

Shortly after graduation, she married Joseph Albright, scion of the McCormick-Patterson newspaper family, whom she had met while they both were interning during the summer of 1957 at the *Denver Post*. The couple moved briefly to Chicago, then lived in New York during the 1960s, during which time three daughters were born and Madeleine attended graduate school at Columbia University. Using her knowledge of English, French, Czech, Russian, and Polish, she investigated the role of the press in political change in Czechoslovakia in 1968, for which she received her Ph.D. in 1976.

After the Albrights moved to Washington, D.C., in 1968, Madeleine worked on Senator Edmund Muskie's unsuccessful bid for the Democratic presidential nomination in 1972 and later became his chief assistant for legislation. From 1978–1981 during the Carter administration, she was associated with the National Security Council under the direction of Zbigniew Brzezinski, her old professor from Columbia. Despite the personal upheaval of a divorce in 1983, her career continued to progress. As a fellow at the Woodrow Wilson Center for International Affairs at the Smithsonian in 1981–1982, she completed her research for her 1983 book *Poland: The Role of the Press in Political Change.* Later in the 1980s, while working as a research professor of international relations at Georgetown University, she became known for the high-powered "salons" in her home that fostered conversation on foreign policy among Democratic leaders in government and academia. She became valued as an advisor on foreign affairs to all the Democratic presidential aspirants, from Mondale and Dukakis to Clinton.

From 1989, when she became president of the Democratic Interdisciplinary Center for National Policy, until the election of Bill Clinton, she had an important behind-the-scenes role as an advisor to the Senate Foreign Relations Committee. She was interpreter and advisor to President Vaclav Havel of the Czech Republic during his 1990 state visit to the United States. In 1992, she helped to formulate the Democratic platform and developed position papers on foreign policy for Bill Clinton. She was appointed U.S. Permanent Representative to the United Nations by President Clinton in January 1993 as well as a member of his cabinet and of the National Security Council. In January 1997, she became secretary of state.

Fluent in several key languages and extremely knowledgeable about foreign affairs, Madeleine Albright was able to conduct diplomacy in person in both eastern and western Europe and to monitor peacekeeping operations around the globe. She took a major role in negotiations to bring peace to the former Yugoslavia and to achieve an international ban on chemical weapons. Throughout her career, she has also been especially interested in encouraging women to enter the professions of international relations and foreign policy.

Shirley Chisholm (1924–)

Shirley Chisholm accomplished a series of "firsts" in elective office at the state and national level. In 1964 she became the first black woman elected to the New York state legislature. In 1968, she became the first black female member of Congress when she was elected to the House of Representatives from the Bedford-Stuyvesant section of Brooklyn. In 1972, she was the first woman, black or white, to run for the presidency of the United States.

Born in Barbados in 1924, Shirley St. Hill was brought by her parents to New York City, where her father found factory work and her mother worked as a seamstress. At age four, she was returned to Barbados, where she lived with her grandmother and attended the country's excellent British-run schools. Back in New York in 1933 to live with her parents in Brooklyn, she attended public schools and graduated from Girls' High School in 1942. An excellent student, she was offered scholarships to Oberlin and Vassar, but due to financial constraints, she had to stay close to home and attended Brooklyn College, from which she graduated in 1946 with honors in sociology. While at college, she became a political activist and joined the NAACP, Urban League, League of Women Voters, Bedford-Stuyvesant Political League, and Seventeenth Assembly District Democratic Club. She also married Charles Chisholm, a social worker (from whom she was divorced in 1977).

Chisholm's early career was in child care, first as a teacher's aide in Harlem while she also did graduate work at Columbia and received a master's degree in early childhood education. She then became director of two successive child care centers, and in 1959 she became educational consultant for the Day Care Division of the New York City Bureau of Child Welfare. At the same time, she was active in local politics and helped to found the

Unity Democratic Club, which worked to elect blacks and women to political office. She was drafted by her community and ran successfully for the state legislature in 1964. In 1968, when she ran for the House seat, she won support from her many Hispanic and Latino constituents by speaking to them in the Spanish she had learned on her own initiative. She won the district, and, when assigned a seat on the Subcommittee on Rural Development and Forestry, she protested and was reassigned to the Committee on Veteran Affairs. She wryly observed that there were a lot more veterans than trees in Brooklyn.

In Washington, Chisholm practiced politics according to her conscience as an advocate as well as legislator. She explained, "There isn't much I can do inside Congress in a legislative way . . . There is a great deal I can do for people of my district by using my office and the resources it opens up to me in helping individuals and groups." Thus, she tried to cosponsor legislation that was especially meaningful to her constituency and the poor. She supported employment and educational opportunities for women and minorities, early education for disadvantaged children, antipoverty programs, and women's reproductive rights. One of her more memorable achievements was helping to get domestic workers covered by the 1974 minimum wage law. She strongly opposed the Vietnam War and supported the Equal Rights Amendment. These issues, along with antipoverty and minority concerns, were key elements of her platform when she sought the Democratic nomination for president in 1972. With a motto of "Unbought and Unbossed," she entered the convention with only twenty-five committed delegates but received 152 votes on the first ballot.

Pushed to the margins of action during the Nixon presidency, she once again gained visibility and power during the Carter administration when she served on the House Rules Committee and was elected Secretary of the Democratic Caucus of the House of Representatives. She retired from Congress in 1982. One of her best known statements as both a feminist and an activist for civil rights was that she had faced far more discrimination because she was a woman than because she was black. She was a founding member in 1966 of the National Organization for Women and in 1985 of the National Political Caucus of Black Women. As a black woman, she sought common ground between feminism and civil rights.

Ruth Bader Ginsburg (1933–)

The second woman ever appointed a member of the U.S. Supreme Court, Ruth Bader Ginsburg has, more than any other justice, represented the principle of equal protection as it applies to women and men and the issues of gender and sex discrimination.

From the beginning, Ginsburg was always a top student, from elementary and high school in New York City, to Cornell University and Harvard and Columbia Law Schools, where she served on the law reviews. Nevertheless, despite her superlative scholarship and intelligence, she could not find a job at any law firm in New York City after she finished law school. Her life experience undoubtedly affected the direction of her career and the perspective she brought to the law. She followed her husband, Martin, to Harvard Law School and to Fort Still, Oklahoma, where he completed his military service and where she experienced job discrimination, being employed in a lower-status position than she was hired for because she revealed that she was pregnant. After her husband returned to law school, she also entered Harvard as one of only nine women in a class of more than 500, and she and her husband shared the care of their daughter. When Martin, a tax attorney, took a position in New York, she transferred to Columbia Law School and in 1959 graduated first in her class.

After teaching during the 1960s at Rutgers Law School and bearing a son in 1965, she returned to Columbia Law School, where she became one of the first tenured female law professors in the country. During the 1970s, as director of the Women's Rights Project of the American Civil Liberties Union, she argued six cases before the Supreme Court. Several were landmark decisions. *Reed v. Reed* (1971) struck down an Idaho law that favored men over women as executors of an estate. *Frontiero v. Richardson* (1973) upheld the same right of a servicewoman as a serviceman to claim benefits for a dependent spouse. *Craig v. Boren* (1976) struck down an Oklahoma law permitting sale of alcoholic beverages to women at a younger age than men.

In 1980, President Jimmy Carter appointed Ginsburg to the U.S. Court of Appeals for the District of Columbia, and President Clinton appointed her to the Supreme Court in 1993. She is particularly known for her opinions in the realm of gender equity, especially *Harris v. Forklift Systems* which held that a victim of sexual harassment might sue for money damages without having to claim psychological injury (because the hostile atmosphere was in itself a violation of equal protection). In *United States v. Virginia* (1996), Ginsburg wrote the brief that ruled that Virginia Military Institute, as a publicly funded educational institution, was obligated to admit women and thereby provide "equal protection for Virginia's daughters as well as its sons." A central theme of Ginsburg's career has been to replace the kind of protective laws that held women in check, using the constitutional principle of equal protection that opens opportunities once reserved for one sex to the other. "Motherhood," she has said, "has been praised to the skies; but the greatest praise men can give to that role is for them to share in doing it."

Anita Hill (1956–)

Through her nationally televised testimony to a Senate committee in October of 1991, Anita Hill became a household name and raised national awareness about the issue of sexual harassment. The occasion was the confirmation hearings of Judge Clarence Thomas, an African American, who had been nominated by the Bush administration for a seat on the Supreme Court. The appointment appeared to be proceeding toward confirmation, until a leak to the press revealed that Judge Thomas had a dubious record with regard to equal treatment of female subordinates in two earlier positions, first while he was an assistant secretary for civil rights in the U.S. Department of Education, and later, as head of the Equal Employment Opportunity Commission. Anita Hill, an African American lawyer, was brought to Capitol Hill from her teaching job at the University of Oklahoma College of Law to testify before the Senate Judiciary Committee. She was asked to elaborate the details of allegations that, up to that point, had only been available in a confidential memo.

The atmosphere of the hearings became rancorous as Hill recounted offensive incidents from as far back as 1981 when Hill, a twenty-five-year-old assistant to Thomas, was made uncomfortable by Thomas's conversations full of sexual innuendo and his efforts to involve her in a relationship. Hill had discouraged Thomas's advances and avoided his suggestive conversations, and the offensive behavior had stopped. In the following year, concerned that her job in the Department of Education might be eliminated and believing that Thomas had changed, she had accepted Thomas's invitation to work as his assistant in his new position as head of the EEOC. Unfortunately, Thomas had resumed his unpleasant advances, and Hill had begun to realize that situations similar to hers were the subjects of official complaints before the commission. Rather than press charges, the outcome of which was not at all certain, she had left the job in 1983 to take a position as a member of the law faculty at Oral Roberts University and in 1986 had moved to the faculty of the University of Oklahoma Law School.

The power of the hearings was in the empathy that her story aroused among female viewers. They believed her, but it was also clear that many members of the all-male Judiciary Committee did not. Any woman who had faced sexual harassment could identify with her cause. The following election year, an unprecedented number of women were sent to Congress, an event that many observers directly attributed to the impact of the Hill-Thomas hearings. The number of complaints of sexual harassment to the EEOC also rose by 50 percent.

In her biography, *Speaking Truth to Power,* Hill recounts her feelings on entering the hearing room and introducing the many members of her family who had come to give her support. She grew up as the youngest of eleven children on a farm in Oklahoma. She helped with the work on the farm and attended segregated schools in the early grades. She loved to study and wanted to be a lawyer because she had learned of the important contributions of lawyers to the civil rights movement. After attending Oklahoma State University, she was admitted to Yale Law School. In the aftermath of the Hill-Thomas hearings, her life was transformed, her privacy destroyed. Yet she received thousands of letters and phone calls giving her support. She resolved to transform the experience into one that could help others. Now a professor of social policy and women's studies at Brandeis University, she continues to lecture all over the country on matters directly related to discrimination and civil rights.

Billie Jean King (1943–)

Billie Jean King captured the imagination of the American public in 1973 when she defeated tennis champion Bobby Riggs in the tennis match known as the Battle of the Sexes. For many, King's victory symbolized the rebirth of feminism and women's innate potential to perform as well as men, or even better. King remembers that shortly after her win, when she visited the offices of the

Philadelphia Bulletin, one of the women employees came up to her and said, "Billie Jean, because of you we had the courage to ask for a raise."

King grew up in Long Beach, California, and learned to play tennis on the public courts. When she was seventeen, she won her first Wimbledon match with Karen Hantze in the women's doubles. She went on to win a total of twenty Wimbledon titles, more than any other woman in history. From her position as the leading female athlete in the world, she used her fame and position of leadership to expand opportunities for women not only in tennis but other sports as well. A passionate supporter of Title IX of the 1972 Education Amendments, she believes it is the single most important factor in the expansion of equal opportunities for women through its mandate of equal admissions criteria for women and men, equal scholarship aid, and equal educational and athletic programs for males and females. Through her own professional activities, King has fundamentally changed the place of women in professional tennis by working for equal prize money and equal opportunities to play.

In 1971, along with other female tennis players, she established the women's professional tennis tour which has made women's tennis into a leading spectator sport and which in 2001, paid out more than $50 million in prize money. King herself in 1971 was the first woman professional player to win more than $100,000 in prize money. Other notable pioneering achievements were coaching the first coed professional tennis team in 1974, founding the magazine *womanSports,* establishing the Woman's Sport Foundation, and organizing Team Tennis, the first professional sports league in which women compete on a completely equal basis with men. *Life* magazine named her one of only four sports heroes (along with Babe Ruth, Jackie Robinson, and Mohammed Ali) out of 100 leading Americans of the twentieth century.

Sally Ride (1951–)

More than any other American figure of her generation, Sally Ride, the first American woman to fly in space, represents the possibilities that opened up for women in science at the dawn of the space age. In 1978, she was one of only six women and thirty-five men selected by the National Aeronautics and Space Administration (NASA) out of more than 8,000 applicants to train as an astronaut.

As a mission specialist, Ride helped accomplish the scientific work on two space flights in 1983 and 1984 on the space shuttle *Challenger*. The 1983 mission, with a five-person crew, took off from Cape Canaveral and landed six days later on the lakebed runway at Edwards Air Force Base in California. On this mission, Ride deployed communications satellites, carried out roughly forty scientific experiments, and tested the shuttle's fifty-foot-long mechanical arm. The 1984 mission, with a seven-person crew, took off and landed at the Kennedy Space Center in Florida, and lasted eight days. This mission deployed a special Earth radiation satellite, conducted scientific observations of the Earth, and demonstrated potential for satellite refueling in flight.

Born in 1951 in Encino, California, into a doctor's family, Sally Ride at first thought her future career would be in tennis. She was an outstanding tennis player from the age of ten and achieved national ranking as a junior. After a short time at Swarthmore College, she left to train professionally as a tennis player but soon decided she wasn't good enough. She went back to college, this time to Stanford University, from which she received a B.A. in English and a B.S. in physics in 1973, and a doctorate in physics in 1978. That same year, she was selected by NASA for the astronaut program. After her space flights, she served as the only astronaut on the presidential commission investigating the tragedy of the 1986 *Challenger* explosion. At NASA in 1987, she advocated future lunar bases and exploration of Mars by astronauts. Following her retirement from NASA, she became a Science Fellow at the Stanford University Center for International Security and Arms Control. Two years later she moved to the University of California, San Diego, where she became a professor of physics and was named director of the California Space Institute.

Since 1999, Dr. Ride has participated in a number of web-based educational ventures concerned with science. In 1999–2000 she served as an executive of SPACE.COM, a web site for the space industry. She then initiated EarthKAM, a NASA project that helps middle school classes take photos of the Earth from space. Her current project is Imaginary Lines, a web site to encourage girls at the upper elementary and middle school levels to pursue their interests in science, mathematics, and technology. Her "Sally Ride Science Club" can be found there, sponsored by such corporate partners as the Aerospace Corporation, BlueCross/ BlueShield of Arizona, Hewlett-Packard, Honeywell, Union Bank of California, and the Weather Channel. The club features membership cards that entitle girls to special discounts, a members-only web site, and newsletters and e-mail alerts. Ride is also the author of several children's books about science and adventure: *To Space and Back; Voyager: An Adventure to the Edge of the Solar System; The Third Planet: Exploring the Earth from Space;* and *The Mystery of Mars.* She is married to Steven A. Hawley.

Activists

Linda Chavez-Thompson (1944–)

The first woman to hold national executive office in the AFL-CIO, Linda Chavez-Thompson was the first person of color ever to serve on its executive board. Sponsored by AFL-CIO President John Sweeney, Chavez-Thompson was elected its executive vice president in 1995 as the result of an insurgent effort to revitalize union membership and bring it into closer touch with women and minorities. She became the highest-ranking woman in organized labor.

Chavez-Thompson was born in Lubbock, Texas, one of eight children of sharecroppers of Mexican descent who grew and picked cotton. At times, the whole family worked in the fields to earn collectively thirty cents per hour, and during a period of particular hardship, Linda dropped out of the ninth grade to work in the fields. She married Robert Thompson, a city employee, at the age of nineteen and began to clean houses to supplement the family income. In 1967 she answered an ad from her father's labor union for a bilingual secretary who could speak both English and Spanish, and she won the job.

From the beginning, she was successful in hearing and representing the Spanish-speaking workers' grievances, and she educated herself by taking courses on organization and studying various handbooks on the workings of labor unions. Soon after, she was recruited by the American Federation of State, County, and Municipal Employees (AFSCME) in Austin, Texas, then briefly took a less demanding position in San Antonio to be able to spend time with her daughter (born in 1965; a son was born eleven years later in 1976). Very soon, however, she began to rise through the ranks, becoming the AFSCME international representative from 1971–1973 addressing membership needs in a seven-state region in the southwest. Also in 1973, she become business manager of the AFSCME local 2399 in San Antonio and in 1977 was named its executive director, a post that she held until her election to national office in 1995.

Concurrent with her rise through the ranks of AFSCME was her growing visibility in labor organizing among minorities. In 1986 she was chosen by the Labor Council for Latin American Advancement, an arm of the AFL-CIO, to be its national vice president. In 1988, she was elected a vice president of AFSCME with responsibility for all union efforts in her area. The assignment was especially challenging given the general hostility in the region to union activity. In Texas, for example, it was against the law for government employees to be organized. Chavez-Thompson has reported, "You had to maneuver and 'persuade' state officials that workers' grievances needed to be satisfied, and we had to be creative to make headway against unfriendly politicians."

Linda Chavez-Thompson is a union leader whose efforts are particularly associated with active efforts to increase union membership. In 1996 she organized "Union Summer," an annual event hosted by students, community activists, and union members to recruit unaffiliated workers, organize actions against abusive employers, and walk picket lines. She also pledged 30 percent of the yearly AFL-CIO budget to recruitment efforts. In 1997 alone, the union brought in 400,000 new members. In addition, she herself has been politically active in marshaling support among government officials and elected representatives to improve the welfare system and create new protection for children, low-income people, and those in need of health care. She urges union members to express their interests, to vote, and to consider running for office themselves.

She serves on the boards of the United Way, the Democratic National Committee, and the Institute for Women's Policy Research. A passionate advocate for economic justice and social justice, she has personally taken particular interest in employment of those with disabilities, equal pay for women, increase in the minimum wage, and protection of American jobs against foreign competition.

Betty Friedan (1921–)

If there is any one single American intellectual leader of the modern women's movement who stands out from the rest, it is Betty

Friedan. In her revolutionary book *The Feminine Mystique* (1963), she provided a manifesto for modern middle-class women. She then used her visibility and analysis of women's situation to reframe the issues of women's equal rights and to create a platform for leadership, by spearheading the founding of the National Organization for Women (NOW) in 1966 and by her subsequent efforts on behalf of the Equal Rights Amendment, abortion rights, and family-friendly policies in the workplace.

Earlier life experiences had prepared her for her role as cultural critic and advocate for those on the margins. Born and raised in Peoria, Illinois, Betty Goldstein experienced discrimination as a Jew by being excluded from high school sororities and social life. Her mother, who had given up a career in journalism for homemaking, imparted to her a sense of frustration with the traditional feminine role, along with an encouragement to her daughter to escape that life.

Friedan attended Smith College and graduated summa cum laude in 1942. She became a labor journalist but was fired after her request for a second maternity leave. In the course of having three children and herself working at freelance writing, Friedan developed her powerful critique of suburban women's roles in the 1950s. Women's lives were arranged to devote their full energies to child rearing and housekeeping, but Friedan christened their frustration and depression as "the problem that has no name" and proceeded to dissect the cultural myths, psychological advice, and social science theories of "functionalism" that contained women in "the comfortable concentration camp." *The Feminine Mystique* eventually sold 3 million copies and helped to legitimate women's rising employment and ascent into professional and executive positions.

Both during and after spearheading the founding of NOW in 1966 and serving as its president for five years, Friedan helped to launch many other feminist activities such as the Women's Equity Action League, the National Abortion Rights Action League, the Women's Strike for Peace in 1970, the International Feminist Congress in 1973, and the Economic Task Force for Women in 1974. A consultant to the President's Commission on the Status of Women and a delegate to the 1970 White House Conference on the Family, she also worked for the passage of the ERA. Her book *The Second Stage* (1981) adopted what some critics considered a more moderate stance on sex equality by emphasizing the value of mothers to children and families. In her 1997 book *Beyond Gender:*

The New Politics of Work and Family, she argues that researchers and activists should be concerned with women's earnings and economic equality, a reduced work week, flexible scheduling of work, and benefits for part-time work.

Friedan has been featured in countless stories on the women's movement and in 1994 was awarded an honorary doctorate by Colombia University.

Martha Edna Wright Griffiths (1912–)

Democrat Martha Griffiths served in the U.S. House of Representatives from 1955 to 1974 and during that time distinguished herself as the leading supporter of the sex discrimination clause of the Civil Rights Act of 1964 and of the Equal Rights Amendment that was voted out of Congress in 1972.

Representative Griffiths and her husband, Hick, both graduated from the University of Missouri in 1934 and planned to attend law school. The Harvard Law School, which admitted Hick, did not admit women, so the two attended the University of Michigan, where they obtained their law degrees in 1940. After law school, they worked for the American Automobile Insurance Company and then formed their own law firm with G. Mennen Williams, who was later to become governor of Michigan.

Martha was urged to enter politics and to run for a Democratic seat in the Michigan state legislature. She initially declined, but was encouraged by her husband; she ended up running and won a seat that she held from 1949 to 1953. She then sought a congressional seat as representative from her district. Her first attempt was unsuccessful; in 1953 she was appointed the first woman recorder and judge in the Recorders' Court in Detroit. When she ran again for the House seat in 1954, she won.

Once in Congress, Griffiths's first achievement was getting a pay increase for postal workers. She also supported programs for housing, urban renewal, food stamps, and educational and hospital construction. In 1962, she was named to the powerful Ways and Means Committee where all spending bills must originate. There she benefitted from the support and tutelage of its legendary chairman, Wilbur Mills. Her particular interest was in rationalizing and making more equitable the Social Security laws as they affected single parents, married couples, working wives, and survivors of deceased Social Security beneficiaries.

As early as the 1950s, she had begun introducing equal pay

legislation and was the force behind the passage of the Equal Pay Act in 1963. When the Civil Rights of Act of 1964 was introduced, she believed it would be seriously flawed if it left out discrimination by sex. Opposition to this inclusion came from the AFL-CIO and the Assistant Secretary of Labor, Esther Peterson, who believed that Griffiths's inclusion might threaten passage of the whole bill. Griffiths nevertheless drafted an amendment to add "sex" to the types of discrimination that were prohibited and was pleased when a conservative congressman from Virginia, Howard Smith, agreed to sponsor it. To her dismay, however, the proposal was treated as a farce until she entered the debate and said, "A vote against this amendment today by a white man is a vote against his wife, or his widow, or his daughter, or his sister." The amendment passed 168 to 133 in the House and later passed in the Senate.

Her next challenge was to be sure that the Equal Employment Opportunity Commission (EEOC) enforced the act. She discovered that the EEOC did not take seriously the provision against sex discrimination and had allowed complaints to accumulate. Again she called for action: "What is this sickness that causes an official to ridicule the law he swore to uphold and enforce? . . . What kind of mentality is it that can ignore the fact that women's wages are much less than men's, and that Negro women's wages are least of all?"

Her most memorable achievement was to get the Equal Rights Amendment out of the Judiciary Committee, where it had been languishing for years under the chairmanship of Emmanuel Celler. Griffiths obtained the required signatures to get the amendment to the House floor and bring it to a vote. In August 1970 the amendment passed in the House, only to fail in the Senate. Griffiths introduced the amendment again in 1971, and after fashioning compromises related to timing of implementation and a time limit for ratification, it passed Congress in 1972 and was sent to the states for ratification. Griffiths retired from Congress in 1974, then returned to politics in 1983 when she served as lieutenant governor of Michigan from 1983 to 1991.

Bernice Resnick Sandler (1928–)

The work and career of Bernice ("Bunny") Sandler is almost synonymous with the purpose of Title IX of the Higher Education Act, which prohibits sex discrimination in virtually every aspect of the educational system. Before the passage of Title IX in 1972 Sandler was, more than any other person, responsible for discovering a way of punishing sex discrimination in education by using two little-known Executive Orders (11246 and 11375) that were enforced through the Office of Contract Compliance. After Title IX was passed, a similar method of withholding federal funds was used to enforce that law. Beyond her activist work on sex discrimination, Sandler, with her colleague Roberta Hall, studied the slow attrition of bright girls and women from the ranks of the best students and coined the term *the chilly classroom,* which summed up the subtle and usually unconscious discrimination that teachers practiced in their treatment of boys and girls and of male and female college students.

Sandler graduated from Brooklyn College in 1948, received a master's degree from the City College of New York in 1950, and received a doctorate in education from the University of Maryland in 1969. Just as she was coming to the job market seeking a position in counseling at the University of Maryland, she was passed over in such a manner that she (and her husband) concluded that the problem was sex discrimination. Cleverly and persistently, she uncovered an obscure path to enforcement of the prohibition of sex discrimination in education, a field that was not covered by Title VII of the Civil Rights Act of 1964. A call to a government official resulted in a tip that pointed her in the direction of President Johnson's Executive Order 11246 and its sequel, EO 11375, that prohibited race and sex discrimination by any federal contractor. She had found a means to challenge discrimination against women in academia, and to challenge unfairness in their hiring, promotion, and pay.

Successful use of this device and a new knowledge of the extent of sex discrimination in academia helped lay the foundation for Title IX. Together with activists from the Women's Equity Action League (WEAL) and with Representative Edith Green of Oregon, who introduced the legislation, Sandler used her earlier experience to inform the provisions of the new legislation. Although Sandler wanted to lobby for its passage, Representative Green dissuaded her on the grounds that the law would slip through more easily the less attention that was brought to its full implications. Once it was law, Title IX did have enormous repercussions, most visibly in male and female sports programs, but more fundamentally in the growing representation of women in the higher ranks of academia and in growing awareness of the frequency of sexual harassment of female students and the harsher discipline of male students throughout the schools.

Once Title IX was launched, Sandler turned her attention to the informal behaviors of teachers and peers in classroom settings that tended to silence girls and women and give greater encouragement and latitude to boys and men. Her papers with Roberta Hall about "the Chilly Classroom" and "the Chilly Campus Climate," published in the early 1980s, were based on a review and synthesis of research by others. These articles, distributed widely through Sandler's newsletter, *On Campus with Women*, soon became classics in educational, legal, and feminist literature on sex discrimination in education.

Between 1971 and 1991, Sandler pursued the cause of sex equity in education from her base as director of the Project on the Status and Education of Women at the Association of American Colleges in Washington. Since that time, she has served in a variety of consulting roles, including senior associate at the Center for Women's Policy Studies from 1991–1994 and scholar in residence at the National Association of Women in Education since 1994. She has received numerous awards and honorary degrees and was named one of the "100 Most Powerful Women" in *Washingtonian Magazine* in 1982 and one of the nation's "100 Most Important Women" in *Ladies' Home Journal* in 1988.

Eleanor Smeal (1939–)

More than any other individual woman, Eleanor Smeal perhaps best personifies the active feminist of the modern women's movement. As president of the National Organization for Women (NOW), she led the drive to ratify the Equal Rights Amendment and was instrumental in the passage of other key legislation such as the Pregnancy Discrimination Act, the Equal Credit Act, and the Violence Against Women Act.

A product of public schools in Erie, Pennsylvania, she grew up in a first-generation Catholic Italian American family and was one of the pioneers of her generation in combining higher education and employment with marriage and motherhood. Married in 1963, she and her husband both joined NOW in 1970. After a brief stint as a full-time mother, she returned to school for her Ph.D. and at the same time co-founded and directed the day care center that her daughter attended. From her college days at Duke University (where she was active in civil rights protests against race segregation) to her life in Pittsburgh (where she was active in the League of Women Voters as a young mother), she was constantly expanding her repertoire as organizer and advocate. She quickly rose through the ranks of NOW, from president of her local Pittsburgh chapter to state president in 1972, chairman of the NOW national board in 1975, and first paid national president of NOW from 1977 to 1982, and again from 1985 to 1987. In her first term as president of NOW, she strategized to get Congress to extend the deadline for ratifying the ERA to 1982. Also during this period, she originated and popularized the concept of the "gender gap" as representing the somewhat different priorities and values of women and men, which are reflected in their different voting patterns.

When she retired as NOW president, she co-founded the Feminist Majority Foundation, which has taken progressive stands on a number of issues related to reproductive rights, women in policing, affirmative action (to defeat Proposition 209 in California in 1996), and women in sports. In 1993, the *World Almanac* recognized her as one of the most influential women in the United States. *Time* magazine identified her as one of the fifty "faces for America's future." *U.S. News and World Report* listed her as one of Washington's most influential lobbyists. She continues her activism by lecturing on college campuses and working to educate and mobilize women so that they will seek positions of leadership and thereby transform the larger society.

Gloria Steinem (1934–)

Not married until age sixty-six, not a mother, yet beautiful, smart, and famous, Gloria Steinem embodies the very idea of feminism to many contemporary Americans. Best known as the co-founder of *Ms.* magazine, she has stood in the very center of feminist organizing and activism since the 1960s. Unlike another leading feminist, Betty Friedan, who is ten years older, Steinem never had to live the feminine mystique, but from the onset of her adulthood she set out to act autonomously and to unmask the hidden patriarchy of turning women into sex objects. She has tried to understand why she was drawn to the feminist cause as well as to the movements of all other kinds of oppressed groups. While attending abortion hearings in 1969, the answer at last became clear to her: "I finally understood why I identify with 'out' groups. I belong to one too."

Born in Toledo, Ohio, in 1934, Steinem had a travel-filled early childhood, as her father took the family with him on his travels as an antiques salesman. Later, after her father had left the family, she had to care for her mentally ill mother and experienced horrible living conditions in the run-down home her mother had inherited in Toledo. Fortunately, near the end of high school, she had a respite when her older sister, who was away at college, intervened and her father agreed to care for her mother for a year.

She won a scholarship to Smith College, graduated in 1956 with honors and a membership in Phi Beta Kappa, and spent the next two years in India on a traveling fellowship. This transition period was critical in several respects to her later self-identification as a feminist. She began to understand her mother's depression as the result of having had to give up a career as a journalist for marriage. She herself made a different choice on the eve of her departure for India, when she discovered that she was pregnant and chose to have an abortion. In addition, while in India she was exposed to the work and methods of Gandhi and returned to the United States with a new consciousness of the needs of the poor and of collective ways to seek social justice and social change.

Back in New York in 1960 and in search of a job in journalism, she faced unending discrimination as an attractive woman who wasn't taken seriously. An early assignment in 1963 was to work undercover as a bunny at a Playboy club. The resulting article, which she intended to expose the sexism of the role, was instead read as an amusing piece that further limited her assignments. Finally in 1968, she was able to cover George McGovern's election campaign. This—as well as her column in *New York* magazine, which she co-founded—provided further access to political leaders and interesting stories. While reporting, she was drawn to the cause of farm workers and the table grape boycott in California as well as to civil rights and the women's movement. Together with Shirley Chisholm and Bella Abzug, she founded the National Women's Political Caucus (NWPC) in 1971. She spoke out on the topic of abortion and gave currency to the term *reproductive freedom*. Along with Dorothy Pitman Hughes, an African American who founded one of the first community day care centers for working mothers in New York, Steinem began lecturing all over the country, and together they developed the idea of *Ms.*, a magazine for women, which they launched in 1972.

Steinem has been a member of a wide range of feminist and

human rights organizations. Along with co-founding *New York* magazine, NWPC, *Ms.*, and the *Ms.* Foundation for Women, she was also a co-founder of the Coalition of Labor Union Women. In 1975, she received an honorary doctorate from Simmons College, and she was an International Woodrow Wilson Fellow in 1977. Her writings have been wide-ranging, from an analysis of black power in 1970 that won a prize to a biography of Marilyn Monroe and a best-selling self-help book on self-esteem.

Noted author Carolyn Heilbrun, in her biography of Steinem, tries to uncover how Steinem became a leading icon and proponent of feminism in the United States. The answer, the unique combination of experiences in her life, seems to be contained in the title: *The Education of a Woman: The Life of Gloria Steinem*. Steinem's own definition of feminism is instructive: the simple belief that women are human beings.

Scholars

Barbara Bergmann (1927–)

Born in 1927 in New York, Barbara Berman Bergmann has been a pioneer in the economics of race and segregation in employment. She is best known for her "overcrowding hypothesis," which explains the lower earnings of women as the result of their being crowded into a relatively few female-labeled occupations. The oversupply of women's labor concentrated in a narrow range of jobs results in lower labor demand and lower pay, she contends. She first developed this analysis during the early 1970s, when she was a professor at the University of Maryland, to explain race differentials in pay; the hypothesis was later applied to sex discrimination.

After receiving her B.A. from Cornell University in 1948, Bergmann worked in the New York office of the Bureau of Labor Statistics (1949–1953) until she went to graduate school at Harvard. After receiving her Ph.D. in economics in 1959, she held staff positions at the Council of Economic Advisors (1962–1963), the Brookings Institution (1963–1965), and the Agency for International Development (1966–1967). In 1965, she married Fred Bergmann and joined the faculty at the University of Maryland. She continued there until 1988, when she became a distinguished professor of economics at American University, and in 1997, a professor emerita.

Her book *The Economic Emergence of Women* is an authoritative analysis of the rise in women's labor force participation and the realities of their position in a segregated labor market. She has also been a leading advocate of universal child care and has publicized the excellent example of French child care programs in her books *Saving Our Children from Poverty: What the United States Can Learn from France* (1996), and *America's Child Care Problem: The Way Out* (2002). She has served as president of the Eastern Economic Association, the International Association for Feminist Economics, and the Society for Advancement of Socio-Economics. She is also the mother of two children.

Francine Blau (1946–)

Francine Blau, along with her colleagues Marianne Ferber and Anne Winkler, is the author of a leading textbook, *The Economics of Women, Men, and Work,* now in its fourth edition. This book presents a balanced, comprehensive approach to the various economic theories that have been used to explain women's disadvantaged position in the labor force. Blau's work is distinctive in using an eclectic theoretical framework to understand differentials between men's and women's pay. The textbook compares both individual differences between women and men, such as education and length of experience, and differences between the way they are treated and the jobs and industries in which they are employed. To the extent that a textbook represents a codification of existing knowledge as it is passed on to the next generation, this formulation represents a maturing consensus in economics for explaining gender inequality in employment.

Blau's publications show a strong interest in the changing trends and the underlying demographics of the population that help to explain the rise in women's employment and the concurrent decline in pay differences between the sexes. Together with her husband Lawrence Kahn, she has also investigated international variations in pay differentials, a topic that reveals a strong interest in the impact of national institutions and culture. She is further distinguished among economists by her interest in families and the changing social policies that can affect integration of work and family, as shown in her book (cowritten with Ronald Ehrenberg), *Gender and Family Issues in the Workplace* (1997). Work and family programs, child care, and changes in the welfare law are all of interest to her and are given the same dispassionate economic analysis that she devotes to explaining occupational segregation and gender differences in pay.

Blau was born in 1946 in New York City and graduated from Cornell University in 1966. Her first marriage in 1969 ended in divorce in 1972. She received her Ph.D. in economics from Harvard University in 1975. After four years as an instructor at Trinity College while she was still a graduate student, she worked for a year at the Ohio State Center for Human Resource Research and then at the University of Illinois at Champaign-Urbana, where she taught for almost twenty years from 1975 to 1994, rising through the ranks to full professor. In 1979, she married fellow economist Lawrence M. Kahn, with whom she has had two children. She moved to Cornell University in 1994 to become the Frances Perkins Professor of Industrial and Labor Relations.

Over the course of her career, she has testified before congressional committees on matters related to civil rights, children, youth, and families. She has served as a consultant to the U.S. Commission on Civil Rights, the Equal Employment Opportunity Commission, and the Agency for International Development. In 1991–1992, she was president of the Midwest Economic Association, and in 1996–1997, she was president of the Population Association of America.

Jo Freeman (1945–)

More like an athlete than a scholar, Jo Freeman was something of a public figure before the age of thirty. Perhaps more than any other woman of her generation, she personified the informal younger branch of the new feminist movement that took shape in the 1960s. She was a founder of one of the first consciousness-raising groups that, unlike the formal women's organizations such as NOW or WEAL, was built on informal ties and social networks and focused on women's liberation in their personal lives. It was such groups of women who believed that "the personal is political." Not only did Jo Freeman help to invent, and herself participate in, this new kind of women's group; she was also the movement's intellectual in its early days. She labeled the two branches of the movement informal consciousness-raising groups and formal associations (i.e., NOW). Under her pen name, "Joreen," she wrote an article reprinted countless times entitled "The Theory of Structurelessness," which noted the limitations and the strengths of these leaderless groups.

Jo Freeman came to her pioneering role in the women's movement through a series of formative experiences in the student uprising at Berkeley and the civil rights movement. Born in 1945 in Alabama and taken by her mother to California at a young age, she attended the University of California and graduated in 1965. There she became a student activist and was arrested for her role in a student occupation of the administrative offices. After graduation and civil rights work with the Southern Christian Leadership Conference, she moved to Chicago to continue that work. When it ended, she became a journalist and eventually entered graduate school at the University of Chicago to study political science in 1968. At the same time, she co-founded the Westside women's group; edited its newsletter, *Voice of the women's liberation movement;* and did research for her prize-winning 1973 dissertation, later published as *The Politics of Women's Liberation: A Case Study of an Emerging Social Movement and Its Relation to the Policy Process.* The work is a detailed and authoritative historical and political analysis of the informal policy networks operating among the women's organizations in Washington, D.C., and their contribution to the implementation of the Executive Orders prohibiting sex discrimination. She also documented the political actors and constituencies that shaped the 1972 Higher Education Amendments, which became an important tool of the women's movement for equal educational opportunity and employment.

During the 1976 election, she attended both the Democratic and Republican conventions as a reporter for *Ms.* In 1982 she obtained a law degree and taught for four years at the State University of New York. Since that time she has been a freelance lecturer and writer and has served as legal counsel to pro-choice advocates and to women running for political office. Her books include a widely used reader in women's studies, *Women: A Feminist Perspective,* which was published in five editions between 1975 and 1995; *A Room at a Time: How Women Entered Party Politics* (2000); and *Waves of Protest: Social Movements since the 1960s* (1999). She ran unsuccessfully for the New York State Assembly and was a delegate to the Democratic National Convention. Her honors for her scholarship include selection as a Brookings Fellow and a Congressional Fellow. She has also been recognized in numerous ways for her pioneering political activism on behalf of women and her many other civic contributions.

Claudia Goldin (1946–)

A leading specialist in economic history and currently Henry Lee Professor of Economics at Harvard University, Claudia Goldin has always been something of a prodigy. Graduated at sixteen from the Bronx High School of Science, she finished Cornell in 1968 magna cum laude in economics with distinction in all subjects and went on to the renowned Economics Department of the University of Chicago, where she received her Ph.D. in 1972, writing her dissertation on the economics of slavery.

Goldin is known for her detailed quantitative analyses using historical data, office records, old state census data, and masses of similar documents to spell out the economic processes involved in slavery, women's rising labor force participation, and the role of high school education in economic development and social mobility. Her book, *Understanding the Gender Gap: An Economic History of American Women* (1990), is famous for showing the impact of women's college education on their incentive to delay marriage, limit childbearing, and pursue careers. In her view, Rosie the Riveter and World War II were not the real impetus for women's surge into postwar employment, because women workers were sent home after the war. Instead, it was higher education that raised women's wage rates and the Pill that cut back fertility, thereby giving women an incentive for increased economic activity.

Professor Goldin's characteristic approach to economic and historical questions is to search for written records and concrete statistics to understand why change occurs. In examining the question of how women's careers evolved, she used the successive interviews collected by the National Longitudinal Surveys of Women and painstakingly reconstructed the changing work histories of respondents across different age groups. She has been rewarded for her innovative work by a steady rise through the academic ranks from assistant professor at the University of Wisconsin, to a fellowship at the Institute for Advanced Study at Princeton, a professorship at the University of Pennsylvania, and, in 1990, her appointment at Harvard. Along the way, she has been a fellow at the Center for Advanced Study in Behavioral Sciences at Palo Alto, a visiting fellow at the Brookings Institution, and a grantee of the National Science Foundation, the Spencer Foundation, and the Russell Sage Foundation. She is a fellow of the American Academy of Arts and Sciences and has served on various editorial boards and as president of the Economic History Association in 1999–2000. Married once and then divorced, she has no children. The only tenured woman in economics at Harvard, she believes that it is very difficult for high-achieving women to combine family and career.

Alice Kessler-Harris (1941–)

Kessler-Harris is regarded by her fellow historians as the first to effectively merge the fields of women's history and labor history. Over the course of a thirty-year career, she has steadily focused on the issue of women and work. Her 1982 book, *Out to Work: A History of Wage-Earning Women in the United States,* is a classic of the field. Representing an integration and a culmination of her scholarship, her 2001 book *In Pursuit of Equity: Women, Men, and the Quest for Economic Citzenship in 20th-Century America* won the Bancroft Prize in American history. In it she shows how women's opportunities as workers and their economic rights as citizens were always refracted (or distorted) by the lens of gender so that a tendency toward different treatment outweighed equal treatment in hiring, promotion, pay, pensions, and social benefits.

Alice Kessler-Harris was born in Leicester, England, in 1941 and attended schools in Cardiff, Wales, before coming to the United States while she was still in high school. Her father was a shoe designer, and her mother died at the young age of forty. She credits her Hungarian and Czech ancestry, refugee status, and "foreign" parentage with giving her a powerful interest in history and in searching for her own past. She completed high school in Trenton, New Jersey, graduated from Goucher College in 1961, taught school briefly, did graduate work in history at Rutgers University, and received her Ph.D. in 1968. For the next two decades, she taught at Hofstra University, rising from assistant to full professor and directing the Center for the Study of Work and Leisure from 1976 to 1988. She moved to Temple University as professor of history in 1988 and to Rutgers in 1990. From 1990 to 1995 she was director of Women's Studies at Rutgers and also cofounder of the Labor College for District 65 of the United Auto Workers. She is currently the R. Gordon Hoxie Professor of American History at Columbia University.

Kessler-Harris was an expert witness in the sex discrimination case *Equal Employment Opportunity Commission v. Sears Roebuck and Company* before the U.S. District Court. She has been on the editorial boards of *Journal of American History; Labor History,*

Gender and History, and *Signs* and has received fellowships from the Guggenheim, Ford, and Rockefeller Foundations, the National Endowment for the Humanities, and the Radcliffe Institute for Advanced Study at Harvard University. The mother of a daughter from her first marriage, she has two stepdaughters from her second marriage to Bert Silverman in 1982.

Catharine MacKinnon (1946–)

Lawyer Catharine MacKinnon is famous for her landmark contribution to the legal interpretation of sexual harassment. It was her writing and arguments that in 1986 persuaded the court in *Meritor Savings Bank v. Vinson* that the plaintiff, Mechelle Vinson, had suffered sexual harassment because of a hostile environment that was discriminatory, not just by the demand for quid pro quo sexual favors that had preceded her dismissal. MacKinnon, in her 1979 book *Sexual Harassment of Working Women,* had broadened the legal interpretation of the phenomenon by developing a novel feminist legal theory that a practice is an invidious form of sex discrimination if it "participates in the systematic social deprivation of one sex because of sex."

Catharine MacKinnon grew up in a privileged and politically well-connected family. Her father, George E. MacKinnon, advised the presidential campaigns of Dwight Eisenhower and Richard Nixon, served one term as a congressman from Minnesota, then was appointed to a life term on the Washington, D.C. Circuit Court of Appeals. With her efforts for social change, Catharine departed from the politics with which she grew up. After graduating from Smith College, she attended Yale Law School and earned her J.D. in 1977. In New Haven she became a radical, got involved in the women's movement, worked against the Vietnam War, and became involved with the Black Panthers. She co-founded a law collective and created the first course offered by the Yale Women's Studies Program, where she taught as a lecturer from 1977 to 1980. There followed what she dubbed a "ten-year long job interview" in which she moved from one law school to another, never succeeding in finding a permanent place: Harvard, Stanford, Minnesota, UCLA, University of Chicago, Toronto, and Basel (Switzerland). Then in 1990 she became professor of law at the University of Michigan Law School, where she received a tenured appointment and where its then dean, Lee Bollinger, commended her for "the force of her scholarship and the quality of her mind."

While she was at the University of Minnesota Law School, she collaborated with her friend Andrea Dworkin to develop a legal theory about pornography as a form of discrimination that creates a hostile environment for all women. Both the city of Minneapolis and, later, the city of Indianapolis were interested in using this theory to exclude sex businesses from commercial districts. MacKinnon and Dworkin's main point, however, was not that pornography was harmful to property values but that it was harmful to women. This aspect of MacKinnon's work, on pornography and "hate speech," is extremely controversial because it raises the specter of potential abridgement of the First Amendment right of free speech. Moreover, not all feminists agree with MacKinnon's perspective because they say MacKinnon's arguments are in danger of patronizing women as being only passive and vulnerable rather than capable of resisting such harm. Some legal commentators, however, believe that MacKinnon will ultimately prevail in redefining obscenity to include that which degrades, dehumanizes, and subordinates women, just as she prevailed in her legal theory of sexual harassment.

MacKinnon lives in Ann Arbor with her partner Jeffrey Moussaieff Masson, a former psychoanalyst, and she is currently involved in litigation, legislation, and policy development to promote women's human rights in the United States and abroad. On a pro bono basis, she represents Croatian and Muslim women and child victims of Serbian genocidal sexual atrocities to seek remedies under international law.

Barbara Reskin

A preeminent sociologist of her generation who is committed to social justice as well as social science, Barbara Reskin has illuminated the ways that social structure and social organization create and perpetuate discrimination against women and minorities. The lucky recipient of her first academic job without either making an application or being interviewed, she knows the importance of ensuring open formal hiring processes for encouraging applicants who would never otherwise be considered. Reskin is particularly known for her work on occupational segregation. As a result of her policy work in Washington with the National Research Council and the Women's Research and Education Institute, she published two studies of occupational segregation in 1984, *Sex Segregation in the Workplace: Trends, Explanations, Reme-*

dies, and *Gender at Work: Perspectives on Occupational Segregation and Comparable Worth.* A detailed qualitative study of several occupations that opened up to women followed in 1990, *Job Queues, Gender Queues: Explaining Women's Inroads into Male Occupations.* Nearly a decade later, Reskin directed a study of affirmative action that was sponsored by the American Sociological Association, *The Realities of Affirmative Action in Employment* (1998). Despite the contention of some leading sociologists that such a study risked compromising the scientific neutrality of the discipline, Reskin effectively marshaled the relevant data to show that affirmative action indeed worked to open up informal networks and word-of-mouth chains of communication in a way that succeeded in recruiting more minorities and women.

Reskin grew up in a working-class family and was employed at a variety of manual and pink-collar jobs before she finished college and graduate school. Her father, a Russian immigrant and one-time Communist, was a union organizer in the Seattle area. After he died, her mother made ends meet with a combination of clerical jobs and public assistance. Barbara started college at Reed, but dropped out after seeing how ill-prepared she was by the working-class schools she had attended. Married briefly, she followed her husband to Cleveland where he was a graduate student and she worked in a variety of blue-collar and clerical positions. At that time she became involved in the Congress of Racial Equality (CORE) and became an activist, then eventually returned to college at the University of Washington, where she received her B.A. in 1968 and her Ph.D. in 1973 in sociology. There she learned rigorous quantitative methods that she applied in her dissertation, later published as *Sex Differences in the Professional Life Chances of Chemists.*

Following her graduate work, Barbara circulated through a number of the big ten universities (Indiana, Michigan, Illinois, and Ohio) where over the course of a little more than a decade she rose from assistant to full professor; then she arrived at Harvard in 1997, where she was professor of sociology until 2002 when she became the Frank Miyamoto Professor of Sociology at the University of Washington. In 2001–2002 she was elected president of the American Sociological Association. She is a fellow of the American Academy of Arts and Sciences and a former fellow at the Center for Advanced Study in the Behavioral Sciences in Palo Alto. She has also served as an expert witness before Congress on matters related to race and sex discrimination in employment.

Given her radical upbringing and early history, Barbara did not at first feel at home in the elitist academic culture of Harvard. That changed with her participation in the Living Wage Campaign that was spearheaded by students in the spring of 2001 to raise the low pay of dining hall and maintenance workers at the university. During the campaign, Reskin spoke in front of the administration building and supported her students, who were demonstrating inside. In so doing, she too was connecting scholarship with a passion for social justice and social change. Her partner of many years, Lowell Hargens, is also a sociologist.

References

Albright, Madeleine. 1983. *Poland: The Role of the Press in Political Change.* New York: Praeger.

Association of American Colleges and Universities. *On Campus with Women.* http://www.aacu.org/index.cfm.

Bergmann, Barbara. 1986. *The Economic Emergence of Women.* New York: Basic Books.

———. 1996. *Saving Our Children from Poverty: What the United States Can Learn from France.* New York: Russell Sage Foundation.

Bergmann, Barbara, and Suzanne Helburn. 2003. *America's Child Care Problem: The Way Out.* New York: Palgrove Macmullan.

Blau, Francine D., and Ronald Ehrenberg. 1997. *Gender and Family Issues in the Workplace.* New York: Russell Sage Foundation.

Blau, Francine D., Marianne A. Ferber, and Anne E. Winkler. 2002. *The Economics of Women, Men, and Work.* 4th ed. Upper Saddle River, NJ: Prentice-Hall.

Freeman, Jo. 1972. "The Theory of Structurelessness." *Berkeley Journal of Sociology* (vol. 3): 151–164.

———. 1973. *The Politics of Women's Liberation: A Case Study of an Emerging Social Movement and Its Relation to the Policy Process.* Doctoral dissertation, University of Chicago.

———. 1995. *Women: A Feminist Perspective.* 5th ed. Mountain View, CA: Mayfield Publishing.

———. 1999. *Waves of Protest: Social Movements since the 1960s.* Lanham, MD: Rowman & Littlefield.

———. 2000. *A Room at a Time: How Women Entered Party Politics.* Lanham, MD: Rowman & Littlefield.

Friedan, Betty. 1963. *The Feminine Mystique.* New York: Norton.

———. 1981. *The Second Stage.* New York: Summit Books.

———. 1997. *Beyond Gender: The New Politics of Work and Family.* Washington, DC: Woodrow Wilson Center Press.

Goldin, Claudia Dale. 1990. *Understanding the Gender Gap: An Economic History of American Women.* New York: Oxford University Press.

Hall, Roberta M., and Bernice R. Sandler. 1982. "The Classroom Climate: A Chilly One for Women." Washington, DC: Association of American Colleges, Project on the Status and Education of Women.

———. 1984. "Outside the Classroom: A Chilly Campus Climate for Women?" Washington, DC: Association of American Colleges, Project on the Status and Education of Women.

Heilbrun, Carolyn. 1995. *The Education of a Woman: The Life of Gloria Steinem.* New York: Dial Press.

Hill, Anita. 1997. *Speaking Truth to Power.* New York: Doubleday.

Kessler-Harris, Alice. 1982. *Out to Work: A History of Wage-Earning Women in the United States.* New York: Oxford University Press.

———. 2001. *In Pursuit of Equity: Women, Men, and the Quest for Economic Citzenship in 20th-Century America.* New York: Oxford University Press.

MacKinnon, Catharine A. 1979. *Sexual Harassment of Working Women: A Case of Sex Discrimination.* New Haven, CT: Yale University Press.

"100 Most Important Women." *Ladies' Home Journal.* 105 (November 1987): 47–50.

"100 Most Powerful Women." 1982. *Washingtonian Magazine.*

Reskin, Barbara. 1980. *Sex Differences in the Professional Life Chances of Chemists.* Manchester, NH: Ayer.

———. 1998. *The Realities of Affirmative Action in Employment.* Washington, DC: American Sociological Association.

Reskin, Barbara, ed. 1984. *Sex Segregation in the Workplace: Trends, Explanations, Remedies.* Washington, DC: National Academy Press.

Reskin, Barbara F., and Patricia A. Roos, eds. 1990. *Job Queues, Gender Queues: Explaining Women's Inroads into Male Occupations.* Philadelphia: Temple University Press.

Reskin, Barbara F., Ronnie Steinberg, and Lois Haignere. 1984. *Gender at Work: Perspectives on Occupational Segregation and Comparable Worth.* Washington, DC: Women's Research and Education Institute of the Congressional Caucus for Women's Issues.

Ride, Sally. 1991. *To Space and Back.* New York: Beech Tree Books.

————. 1992. *Voyager: An Adventure to the Edge of the Solar System.* New York: Crown Publishers.

————. 1994. *The Third Planet: Exploring the Earth from Space.* New York: Crown Publishers.

————. 1999. *The Mystery of Mars.* New York: Crown Publishers.

Court Cases Cited

Craig v. Boren, 429 U.S. 190 (1976)

Equal Employment Opportunity Commission v. Sears Roebuck and Company (2001), 243 F. 3d 846 (U.S. App. 2001)

Frontiero v. Richardson, 411 U.S. 677 (1973)

Harris v. Forklift Systems, 510 U.S. 17 (1993)

Meritor Savings Bank v. Vinson, 477 U.S. 57 (1986)

Reed v. Reed, 404 U.S. 71 (1971)

United States v. Virginia, 518 U.S. 515 (1996)

5

Legal Facts and Statistical Data

Legal Facts

Gender equity and employment legislation, case law, and executive orders are made up of several related but different strands that focus on various aspects of the topic:

Protective legislation was devised in the early 1900s to shield and look after the "weaker sex," but later was seen as a tool for discrimination.

Pay equity and comparable worth emerged as legal issues in the 1960s and 1970s, but have met with only limited success in the courts and the legislature.

Prohibition of gender discrimination is the most inclusive category of legal change. It covers the subcategory of sexual harassment and has met with considerable success through the legal process.

From the 1960s onward, *affirmative action policies* have been the main positive or preventive means for achieving equality in employment and education. After showing initially encouraging results, these policies are currently being revisited by the courts.

Prior to 1963, protective legislation dominated the legal landscape. Protective legislation was a legal approach founded on the assumption that workers and employers were not equal in bargaining power and that workers therefore needed legal protection. Though protective legislation originally focused on all workers, the focus shifted to women, and in some cases, children, by the beginning of the twentieth century.

Proponents viewed protective legislation as a way to protect women from unsafe and "immoral" work environments, and some protective legislation served to provide female workers with benefits such as mandatory rest periods, and limits on maximum work hours. In *Muller v. Oregon* in 1908, the Supreme Court upheld the constitutionality of an Oregon maximum hour law asserting that due to their physical structure, women needed to be protected from overly strenuous work and long hours. Much of the later protective legislation, however, resulted in discrimination against women in the work force and limited their employment opportunities. For example, in *Radice v. New York* in 1924, the Supreme Court upheld the constitutionality of a New York law that prohibited women from being employed from 10:00 P.M. to 6:00 A.M. in restaurants. The Court felt the loss of sleep at night would be too difficult for women because of their delicate nature.

The fact that women bear children and were viewed as the weaker sex was treated as a legal justification not only for limiting women's work hours and amount of pay, but for firing women who became pregnant or excluding women from working in certain occupations. The Equal Pay Act of 1963, and Title VII of the Civil Rights Act of 1964, prohibited discrimination in employment on the basis of sex and other characteristics. Both laws represented a dramatic shift away from protective legislation for one sex alone and from "special treatment" of women, toward equal treatment for both men and women in the workplace. These laws have led courts and the legislature to move toward gender-neutral laws that hold men and women to the same standard. For example, in dealing with the issue of pregnancy discrimination and family leave, the courts followed this gender-neutral stance. Pregnancy is treated as a disability, and pregnant workers are subjected to the same standards as other disabled workers. Similarly, under the Family and Medical Leave Act of 1993 (FMLA), all eligible employees with family responsibilities are allowed leave.

Though Title VII and the Equal Pay Act were crucial to increasing the enforcement of equal rights in the workplace, Title VII excluded educational institutions, and the Equal Pay Act did not cover professional and administrative employees. Relying on methods used during the civil rights movement, activists used Executive Order 11246 and its amendments to push the passage of Title IX of the Education Amendments of 1972. Title IX reads "No person in the United States shall, on the basis of sex, be excluded from participation in, be denied the benefits of, or be subjected to discrimination under any educational program or activity receiving federal financial assistance." Several successful suits were later brought against Brown University, Harvard University, and other educational institutions that had very few women in professorial positions, to charge them with sex discrimination. Title IX has also had an enormous impact on college athletics, resulting in substantial growth in women's athletic programs and women's participation in sports.

Throughout the 1980s, another important development in sex discrimination law was the recognition of sexual harassment as an illegal form of sex discrimination under the employment discrimination laws. In the circuit court decision of *Tomkins v. Public Service Electric Gas Company* and later at the Supreme Court level in *Meritor Savings Bank v. Vinson,* the courts defined sexual harassment as sexual discrimination that makes concrete employment benefits conditional upon sexual favors. This is known as "quid pro quo" sexual harassment. Later cases broadened the definition of sexual harassment to include a hostile working environment, same-sex harassment (i.e., including harassment of a man by a man), and harassment regardless of whether the plaintiff could demonstrate any tangible or economic harm.

The comparable worth movement has met with great success in other countries and had some initial limited success in *Gunther v. Washington,* but the momentum was later stalled with the ruling in 1985 from the appellate court in *AFSCME v. Washington.* The court held that pay differentials are not necessarily caused by discrimination but are the result of a number of interacting forces, and that to impose a requirement on the state of Washington that it implement a comparable worth plan would interfere with the functioning of a free market. Affirmative action laws and policies, initially bolstered by the passage of several executive orders in the 1960s, have received mixed results in the courts beginning with the *Regents of the University of California v. Bakke* in 1978. Affirmative action is currently under review again by the Supreme Court in several cases brought in 2002 against the University of Michigan Law School.

The following is a chronological summary of key legislation, important case law, and executive orders that relate to gender equity and employment issues.

Legislation

Women's Bureau Act of 1920 (PL 66–259)
This act created the Women's Bureau, a new agency charged with
conducting research about working women.

Federal Economy Act of 1932 (47 STAT 406)
Section 213 of the Federal Economy Act, the "married persons'
clause," required that one spouse resign if both husband and wife
were working for the federal government in order to limit the
number of federal job holders in each family to one. A Women's
Bureau study later found that more than 75 percent of those resigning were women. The act was one of a number of public and
private pressures on women to give up "pin money" so that men
could support their families during the Depression. Though this
legislation was eventually repealed, by 1939, twenty-six states
had proposed "married persons' clauses," and more than 1,500
women had been discharged while additional women resigned to
protect their husbands' jobs. As recently as 1962, more than forty
states had laws that set maximum daily or weekly hours for
women to work outside of the home. It was not until the passage
of Title VII of the Civil Rights Act of 1964 that these limitations on
women's employment were declared illegal.

Fair Labor Standards Act of 1938 (52 STAT 1060–1069;
29 USC 201)
The Fair Labor Standards Act, popularly known as the "Wages
and Hours Law," mandated a minimum wage, initially twenty-
five cents, and a forty-hour work week for women and men, excluding farm and domestic workers. The law also required employers to pay eligible workers "time and a half," or one and
one-half times the customary pay, for hours worked that exceeded the maximum allowance. One of the original goals of the
law was to discourage employers from requiring employees to
work long hours that might interfere with their personal and family lives. The extra compensation for overtime work applies to
hourly workers but not salaried workers.

Lanham Act of 1940 (PL 76–849)
The Lanham Act provided funds for building defense-related industries. Federal funds for child care facilities were included
under the act to support working mothers who were joining the

war effort. Though only a small percentage of the children of working mothers attended these centers, it set a precedent, along with the emergency aid of the Works Progress Administration in the 1930s, for federal involvement in child care funding. At the height of the program, 13 percent of children needing care received federal assistance. At the end of the war, most of these centers were rapidly phased out.

Equal Pay Act of 1963 (PL 88–38)

The Equal Pay Act of 1963, an amendment to the Fair Labor Standards Act, prohibits unequal pay for equal or "substantially equal" work performed by men and women. It was the first federal law aimed at preventing sex discrimination by making it illegal to pay unequal wages to men and women who work in the same place and whose work requires the same set of skills and responsibilities.

Title VII of the Civil Rights Act of 1964 (PL 88–352; 42 USC 2000e)

Title VII was a major legislative achievement that mandated equal employment opportunity for women. Passed by Congress in 1964 as part of the Civil Rights Act, Title VII prohibits firms with fifteen or more employees from wage discrimination on the basis of gender as well as other characteristics. The provision on banning discrimination based on gender was added as an afterthought by Representative Howard Smith, who opposed the bill and thought that the addition of sex discrimination was so preposterous that the legislation would never be passed. Title VII established the Equal Employment Opportunity Commission to coordinate efforts to implement the law and to resolve disputes. Soon after being established, the EEOC was inundated with sex discrimination complaints.

Economic Opportunity Amendments of 1966 (PL 89–794)

The Economic Opportunity Amendments of 1966 authorized Head Start, a preschool day care program for children from low-income families. This law also required that 23 percent of Job Corps positions go to female workers.

Title IX of the Education Amendments of 1972 (20 USC Section 1681)

The Higher Education Act of 1972, of which Title IX is a part, is one of the amendments to the Civil Rights Act of 1964. Title IX forbids discrimination on the basis of sex in federally aided education programs. Initially, legislators attempted to exempt intercollegiate athletics from the provisions of the act but were unsuccessful. Title IX applies to a wide range of programs of different types, but its effect on college athletics has been the most dramatic. In the ten years following its passage, women's participation in college sports increased more than 570 percent; the number of male participants during this same period increased by just over 13 percent.

Until 1984, enforcement standards for Title IX were strict, and funds were withheld from schools that were found to have discriminated in any department or program within the school. But in *Grove City College v. Bell* (465 U.S. 555), the court interpreted the law more broadly and found that a school that discriminated in one program, such as athletics, could still receive federal funds for another program within the school. In 1988, the Civil Rights Restoration Act (see below) restored the original, stricter reading of the law so that colleges receiving federal funding for one program could not discriminate in any of their programs or departments. In 2003, a Bush administration commission recommended changes that would give schools, colleges, and universities more leeway to favor men's and boys' athletics.

Equal Employment Opportunity Act of 1972 (PL 92–261)

The Equal Employment Opportunity Act of 1972 was passed to provide the Equal Employment Opportunity Commission (EEOC) the power to enforce the provision against job discrimination on the basis of race, color, religion, national origin, or gender under Title VII of the Civil Rights Act of 1964. The National Organization for Women and other groups actively pressed for the passage of this legislation so that the EEOC, which had been reluctant to enforce Title VII, would have the ability to sue employers for compliance. Previously, the EEOC had been limited to requesting only voluntary compliance. In addition, this law expanded the coverage of the Civil Rights Act to include small businesses, government employees, and educational institutions.

Tax Reform Act of 1976, Dependent Care Tax Credit (IRC 21)

The Dependent Care Tax Credit, in essence, provided for a 20 percent tax credit that replaced the child care deduction on federal taxes. With the passage of this law, the view of child care shifted from that of a personal expense to that of an employment-related expense. All taxpayers with children benefit from the law, with a larger credit provided for lower-income earners. The size of the Child Care Tax Credit was expanded in 1988 by a factor of more than 7.5, and the Internal Revenue Code was modified to allow taxpayers to shelter pretax dollars for child care and other dependent care services in a "flexible spending plan." Families choose between flexible spending and the tax credit. These policies are intended to facilitate parent choice for child care and minimize direct involvement by government in specific types of child care.

Pregnancy Discrimination Act of 1978 (PL 95–555; 42 USC 2000e(k))

The Pregnancy Discrimination Act of 1978, an amendment to Title VII of the Civil Rights Act of 1964, prohibits workplace discrimination for pregnancy, childbirth, or related medical conditions. The act states that pregnancy should be treated the same as other disabilities. Congress passed the act to correct a perceived gap in the way the courts were interpreting Title VII.

Civil Rights Restoration Act of 1988 (PL 100–259)

This law established that if federal funds went to any program in an educational institution, the entire institution had to comply with Title IX. Its effect was to prohibit sex discrimination at educational institutions where any subunit was receiving federal funds.

Family Support Act of 1988 (102 STAT 2343)

The Family Support Act (FSA) was one of the most significant changes in the welfare system in the United States in the past fifty years. At a time when more than half of all married women with children under six were in the work force, public support declined for allowing mothers on welfare to remain at home. The notion of welfare-to-work programs was incorporated into the passage of the FSA. The goal of the FSA was to help families on public assistance become self-sufficient, unlike the traditional welfare goal embodied in the AFDC program established by the Social Security Act of 1935, which provided financial support for single-parent families. The FSA emphasizes that the relationship between the welfare system and families is one of "mutual obligations." Recipients are expected to work toward economic independence either through employment or participation in educational or training activities. Under the FSA, states were required to implement a Job Opportunities and Basic Skills (JOBS) Training Program. These programs were designed to assist recipients in supporting their children while working, and recipients were guaranteed child care.

Omnibus Budget Reconciliation Act, Title V: Child Care, 1990 (PL 101–508)

The child care provision of the Budget Reconciliation Act provided grants to states for funding for child care assistance and tax benefits to families.

Family and Medical Leave Act of 1993 (107 STAT 6)

The Family and Medical Leave Act (FMLA) of 1993 requires employers of more than fifty workers to provide unpaid leave for up to twelve weeks in any twelve-month period for the birth or adoption of a child; to care for a child, spouse, or parent with a serious health condition; or for the worker's own serious health condition. The act covers employees who have been working for a particular employer for more than one year, it requires employers to continue to provide health insurance during a worker's leave, and it guarantees workers the same or an equivalent job upon their return. Some have criticized the FMLA as being largely symbolic because it covers only 11 percent of United States employers (those with fifty or more employees), leaving 41 percent of all workers ineligible. The act does not provide leave to members of less traditional households, such as gay and lesbian couples or people in common law marriages, and because the leave is unpaid, many workers cannot afford to take the time off.

Personal Responsibility and Work Opportunity Reconciliation Act of 1996 (PRWORA) (PL 104–193)

PRWORA replaced the federal welfare program with block grants to states that provided financial incentives for moving welfare recipients into the work force. Designed to "end welfare as we know it," the law was the first substantial welfare reform since the enactment of Aid to Families with Dependent Children in 1935. PRWORA specifies that welfare is no longer a right, that some recipients are required to work, and that there is a lifetime limit on welfare eligibility of five years or less. PRWORA also provides assistance for families moving from welfare to work by assisting with child care expenses and ensuring medical coverage for the year following the termination of welfare benefits. Though

PRWORA dramatically decreased the number of families receiving welfare benefits, the success of the law remains controversial. As minimum wage jobs pay below poverty-level wages and do not provide medical coverage, some former recipients remain impoverished and in need of assistance.

Court Cases

Lochner v. New York, 198 U.S. 45 (1905)
Key Issue: Maximum Hour Laws/Protective Legislation
In *Lochner v. New York,* the Supreme Court declared unconstitutional a New York state law limiting bakery workers to no more than ten hours per day or sixty hours per week. In the original case, the state of New York had hoped to limit the degree to which employers could force their employees to work long hours. In this 5–4 decision, Justice Rufus Peckham cited the state's violation of due process and held that the "right of contract between employers and employees" was protected by the Fourteenth Amendment and took priority over the role of the Court to regulate hours, wages, or working conditions.

Muller v. Oregon, 208 U.S. 412 (1908)
Key Issue: Maximum Hour Laws/Protective Legislation
In *Muller v. Oregon,* the Supreme Court upheld the constitutionality of an Oregon law that prohibited the employment of women in any factory or laundry for more than ten hours per day. In previous decisions, such as *Lochner v. New York,* the Court had ruled that the liberty to enter into a contract was more important than protective legislation limiting work hours. However in *Muller,* attorney Louis Brandeis argued, and was able to convince the Court, in his famous "Brandeis Brief" that women were in need of protection by the Court from overwork. The Court upheld the ten-hour work day for women, stating that because women were more fragile and had the special role of motherhood, it was in the public interest to protect women in order to "preserve the strength and vigor of the race," because healthy mothers were essential to "vigorous off-spring." *Muller v. Oregon* was used as a precedent to uphold protective legislation barring women from employment and other opportunities for more than six decades.

Radice v. New York, 264 U.S. 292 (1924)
Key Issue: Protective Legislation

In *Radice v. New York,* the Supreme Court followed the precedent of *Muller v. Oregon* and upheld the constitutionality of a New York statute that prohibited women from being employed between 10 P.M. to 6 A.M. in restaurants in New York City and Buffalo, New York. The Court ruled that women, who were more delicate, would not get enough sleep if they worked between these hours and that this would be injurious to them. Though the Court opted for protective legislation in decisions about employment opportunities, the Court had ruled a year earlier, in *Adkins v. Children's Hospital* (261 U.S. 525), that the minimum wage law for women violated liberty of contract in the due process clause of the Fifth Amendment. The Court could see no linkage between wages and women's health or morals, and therefore felt that protective legislation was not needed.

Breedlove v. Suttles, 302 U.S. 277 (1937)
Key Issue: Protective Legislation
The Supreme Court decision in *Breedlove v. Suttles* reinforced earlier protective legislation that held that women are entitled to special consideration. The Court ruled against a Georgia man who Breedlove claimed objected to paying the Georgia poll tax, because women were exempt from paying it unless they chose to vote whereas men were required to pay it regardless of whether they voted. The man claimed that the Georgia poll tax denied his right to equal protection of the laws under the Fourteenth Amendment and his Nineteenth Amendment right not to be discriminated against in voting on account of sex. The Court held that exempting the elderly, the blind, and women who were not registered voters from the annual poll tax of one dollar was reasonable because the equal protection clause of the Fourteenth Amendment did not require absolute equality. Justice Pierce Butler, writing the unanimous decision, asserted that women were naturally entitled to special considerations that permitted the state to discriminate in their favor "in view of burdens necessarily borne by them for the preservation of the race. . . ."

West Coast Hotel v. Parrish, 300 U.S. 379 (1937)
Key Issue: Freedom of Contract/Protective Legislation
In *West Coast Hotel v. Parrish,* the Supreme Court overturned the 1923 *Adkins v. Children's Hospital* decision and agreed to permit a minimum wage law for women. The state of Washington had a board that set minimum wages for women and children. In this

case, Elsie Parrish, an employee of the West Coast Hotel, asked the Court to enforce the minimum-wage law. The Court agreed that states should be allowed to regulate wages and that women and children were in need of special protection. This case was followed one year later by the passage of the Fair Labor Standards Act of 1938, which called for a minimum wage to be instituted for women and men.

Goesaert v. Cleary, 335 U.S. 464 (1948)
Key Issue: Protective Legislation
In *Goesaert v. Cleary*, the Supreme Court upheld a Michigan law that allowed women to serve as waitresses in taverns but barred them from the better-paying positions as bartenders, except for the wives and daughters of male bar owners. Although the Court voiced some concern that male bartenders were attempting to create a monopoly on these better-paying jobs, the Court found that there were moral and social problems with having women serve as bartenders. Presumably, they said, male bar owners would protect their own wives and daughters from overwork and immorality, hence the exemption for their wives and daughters.

Weeks v. Southern Bell Telephone and Telegraph Company,
408 F.2d 228 (1969)
Key Issue: Protective Legislation
Weeks was the first sex discrimination case to reach the appellate court level. Lorena Weeks challenged Southern Bell's assertion that sex was a bona fide occupational qualification (BFOQ) for the job of switchman. The company argued that the job of switchman was strenuous, that it required late night hours, and that the state of Georgia's protective legislation prevented women from holding jobs that required them to lift more than thirty pounds. The court ruled in favor of Weeks, finding that the requirements of the job did not meet the burden of proof that the job fell within the BFOQ exception. Therefore, Southern Bell was found to be in violation of Title VII. The court stated, "Title VII rejects just this type of romantic paternalism as unduly Victorian and instead invests individual women with the power to decide whether or not to take on unromantic tasks."

Shultz v. Wheaton Glass, 398 U.S. 905 (1970)
Key Issue: Sex Discrimination/Equal Pay
When the Equal Pay Act came into being, there was ambiguity in

what was meant by "equal work." In a series of court decisions beginning with *Shultz v. Wheaton Glass,* the courts made clear that mere difference in name did not make jobs different enough to avoid a charge of sex discrimination if the work performed was substantially similar.

Griggs v. Duke Power Co., 401 U.S. 424 (1971)

Key Issue: Employment Discrimination
After Title VII of the Civil Rights Act of 1964 was enacted, Duke Power developed a new policy requiring all employees to have graduated from high school and to meet minimum grade standards on aptitude tests. The effect was to continue to restrict jobs—to some degree—to white employees only. The requirement was viewed as having a disparate impact on that minority group because a smaller percentage of African Americans had completed high school as compared to whites in North Carolina (where Duke Power was located) at that time. The Supreme Court ruled against Duke Power, stating that the burden rests with the employer to demonstrate that the requirements for the job have a clear connection to job duties. Duke Power was found to be in violation of Title VII of the 1964 Civil Rights Act. (In 1989, *Wards Cove Packing Co. v. Atonio* [490 U.S. 642] shifted the burden of proof to the plaintiff, but the Civil Rights Restoration Act of 1988 put the burden back on employers to prove that requirements were reasonable and related to job performance.)

Phillips v. Martin Marietta, 400 U.S. 542 (1971)

Key Issue: Sex Discrimination
The Supreme Court overruled the lower courts' finding in *Phillips v. Martin Marietta.* Ida Phillips was denied a job at Martin Marietta because she had young children. The Supreme Court ruled that the company could not have different hiring policies for men and women; for example, they could not refuse to hire mothers of small children unless they also refused to hire fathers of small children. But the Court left open the possibility that gender might be considered a bona fide occupational qualification if parenting could be shown to have a lesser impact on a man's job performance than on a woman's job performance.

Reed v. Reed, 404 U.S. 71 (1971)

Key Issue: Sex Discrimination
The U.S. Supreme Court ruled unanimously in *Reed v. Reed* that

an Idaho law giving preference to men as executors of estates could not be allowed to "stand in the face of the Fourteenth Amendment" and was unconstitutional. This was the first time the Court invoked the Fourteenth Amendment to overturn a distinction based on sex, but the Court stopped short of making all laws incorporating sex bias "inherently suspect" as it had on racial issues.

Rosenfeld v. Southern Pacific Company, 444 F.2d 1219 (1971)
Key Issue: Equal Employment Opportunity
In *Rosenfeld v. Southern Pacific,* the federal district court ruled that Title VII superseded California protective labor laws that restricted women from working overtime and from lifting weights in excess of the prescribed limit. The case was considered a landmark advance for women's rights, as it moved away from a protectionist stance.

Frontiero v. Richardson, 411 U.S. 677 (1973)
Key Issue: Sex Discrimination
In *Frontiero v. Richardson,* the Supreme Court ruled that denial of benefits to military husbands was unconstitutional. Sharon Frontiero, an Air Force officer, had sought medical and dental benefits to cover her husband. These benefits were automatically given to male officers for their spouses.

Pittsburgh Press v. Pittsburgh Commission on Human Relations, 413 U.S. 376 (1973)
Key Issue: Sex Discrimination
The Supreme Court upheld a lower court's decision in *Pittsburgh Press v. Pittsburgh Commission on Human Relations,* thereby ending the practice of running sex segregated want ads in newspapers. The Court assumed that segregated ads could only lead to discriminatory hiring practices and upheld the lower court's ruling that it is not unconstitutional to prevent the newspaper in advance from contributing to an illegal situation.

Corning Glass Works v. Brennan, 417 U.S. 188 (1974)
Key Issue: Sex Discrimination/Equal Pay
Corning Glass Works v. Brennan was the first equal pay case to reach the U.S. Supreme Court. The Court found that Corning Glass Works was in violation of the Equal Pay Act because it was paying a higher wage to male night shift workers than it paid to

female workers performing the same tasks during the day shift. Some of the pay differentials dated back to policies originating in the 1930s, when protective legislation prevented women from working night jobs.

Geduldig v. Aiello, 417 U.S. 484 (1974)
Key Issue: Sex Discrimination
The Supreme Court upheld a California law denying disability benefits to pregnant women. The Court stated that the California plan was constitutional and did not discriminate against women because the benefit distinguished between women who were pregnant and women who were not pregnant. Four years later, Congress passed the 1978 Pregnancy Discrimination Act, which set aside this ruling.

Craig v. Boren, 429 U.S. 190 (1976)
Key Issue: Sex Discrimination
In *Craig v. Boren*, the Supreme Court found gender-based discrimination in an Oklahoma law unconstitutional under the Fourteenth Amendment. Under the Oklahoma law, men had to be at least twenty-one years of age to purchase 3.2 percent beer legally, but women could do so at age eighteen. The state cited traffic safety backed up by statistics as the reason for the differential treatment. The Court ruled against the state, explaining, "classifications by gender must serve important governmental objectives and be substantially related to the objectives."

General Electric v. Gilbert, 429 U.S. 125 (1976)
Key Issue: Sex Discrimination
General Electric was providing a disability plan to its employees, but it excluded pregnancy from the covered disabilities. The Supreme Court ruled in favor of the company and found that excluding pregnancy from a disability plan does not violate Title VII of the Civil Rights Act of 1964. The Court reasoned, "Pregnancy-related disabilities constitute an additional risk, unique to women, and the failure to compensate them for this risk does not destroy the presumed parity of the benefits, accruing to men and women alike." Two years later, Congress passed the Pregnancy Discrimination Act of 1978, requiring employers to treat pregnancy the same as other temporary disabilities.

Tomkins v. Public Service Electric Gas Company,
568 F.2d 1044 (1977)
Key Issue: Sexual Harassment
In *Tomkins v. Public Service Electric Gas Company,* the Third Circuit
Court of Appeals prohibited the tangible benefit form of sexual
harassment, stating that it was in violation of Title VII. Adrienne
Tomkins was invited to lunch by her supervisor to discuss her
work and was asked to go out with him several times. When she
declined, she was demoted.

In *Tomkins* as well as the 1977 appellate court decision in the
Barnes v. Costle (561 F2d 983) case, sexual harassment was recognized for the first time as a cause of action. These lower court
cases defined sexual harassment as sexual discrimination that
makes concrete employment benefits conditional upon sexual favors. This is known as "quid pro quo" sexual harassment. It was
not until 1986 that the United States Supreme Court recognized,
in *Meritor Savings Bank v. Vinson,* that sexual harassment is indeed
a form of sexual discrimination that is actionable under Title VII.

Regents of the University of California v. Bakke,
438 U.S. 265 (1978)
Key Issue: Affirmative Action
The Supreme Court held that educational institutions are not to
use quota systems in their admissions policies but may take race
into account in order to increase minority enrollment. Alan
Bakke, a white man, had been denied admission to medical
school at the University of California due to a set-aside program
that admitted a set percentage of minority students even though
their grades and test scores were lower than those of white applicants. A divided Court made two rulings. They struck down the
university's dual system of admissions that accepted black applicants who had lower test scores and grade point averages than
white applicants, which meant that Bakke was accepted into the
medical school, but the Court also declared that schools could
take race into account as one among several factors in order to
promote diversity.

In 1995, the Court also limited the use of race as a factor in
awarding government contracts in *Adarand Constructors v. Pena*
(515 U.S. 200). Two Supreme Court cases in 2003 at the University
of Michigan revisited the use of affirmative action in college admissions. Those cases are *Grutter v. Bollinger University of Michigan
Board of Regents* (No. 02-241, 2003) and *Gratz v. Bollinger University*

of Michigan (No. 02-516, 2003). In *Grutter v. Bollinger* the Supreme Court upheld the University of Michigan Law School's affirmative action policy stressing that race can be used in "a flexible and non-mechanical way" and as just one element of a student's application. On the same day the Court handed down a ruling on *Gratz v. Bollinger* striking down the university's undergraduate admissions policy because it automatically awards 20 points on a 150-point scale for any African American, Native American, or Hispanic student.

United Steelworkers v. Weber, 443 U.S. 193 (1979)
Key Issue: Affirmative Action
The Supreme Court held in this case that private employers could voluntarily establish programs using racial preferences in order to eliminate racial imbalances. Because Title VII of the Civil Rights Act of 1964 made it illegal to discriminate by race, color, religion, sex, or national origin, some federal agencies and companies began using racial imbalance as evidence of possible discrimination that was in need of rectifying. Weber, a white employee of Kaiser Aluminum, sued when he was passed over for a position in a training program that went to a less senior African American employee. The Court found that the company did not violate Title VII because the purpose of the statute was to advance employment opportunities for racial minorities, and setting up an affirmative action program was in keeping with this goal.

Bundy v. Jackson, 641 F.2d 934 (1981)
Key Issue: Sexual Harassment/Hostile Climate
The District of Columbia Court of Appeals held that the District of Columbia Department of Corrections violated Title VII by creating a hostile climate of sexual teasing and propositions by supervisors that made it difficult for Sandra Bundy to perform her job as a vocational rehabilitation specialist for criminal offenders. Over the next few years, other courts followed this holding.

Gunther v. Washington, 101 S. Ct. 2242 (1981)
Key Issue: Comparable Worth
In this case, the Supreme Court confronted the issue of comparable worth for the first time. Although the decision did not explicitly favor comparable worth comparisons, it leaned in that direction. The case involved female prison guards who claimed sexual

discrimination under Title VII for being paid 70 percent of the amount that male guards were making. The Supreme Court ruled that intentional discrimination was occurring, even though the women's job duties were not identical to the men's job duties, thus opening the door for Title VII to provide a remedy for pay disparities related to sexual discrimination.

Mississippi University for Women v. Hogan, 458 U.S. 718 (1982)
Key Issue: Sex Discrimination
Joe Hogan, a male nurse, claimed he was discriminated against by not being admitted to a women's nursing school in Mississippi. The Supreme Court found in his favor and agreed that the state-supported school's women-only policy violated his right to equal protection under the law.

AFSCME v. Washington, 770 F.2d 1401 (1985)
Key Issue: Comparable Worth
AFSCME v. Washington greatly limited the scope of the principle of comparable worth and stalled the comparable worth movement. The appellate court held that pay differentials were not necessarily caused by discrimination but were the result of a number of interacting forces, and that to impose a requirement on the state of Washington to implement a comparable worth plan would interfere with the functioning of a free market.

Meritor Savings Bank v. Vinson, 477 U.S. 57 (1986)
Key Issue: Sexual Harassment/Sex Discrimination
The Supreme Court ruled in *Meritor Savings Bank v. Vinson* that sexual harassment was a form of gender discrimination. This ruling paved the way for employees to sue employers for sexual harassment under Title VII of the Civil Rights Act of 1964. Mechelle Vinson, a former employee of Meritor, claimed that her supervisor had subjected her to constant sexual harassment and that this violated Title VII. While working at the bank, Vinson's supervisor repeatedly asked her on dates and invited her to hotel rooms. Vinson testified that she eventually acquiesced to the demands of her supervisor, sometimes under threat of physical force. The Court agreed with the EEOC guidelines, which recognized claims involving quid pro quo propositions and a broader hostile working environment. The plaintiff was not required to demonstrate any tangible or economic harm, and the Court found that sexual harassment may occur even when sexual activity is voluntary.

California Federal Savings and Loan v. Guerra,
55 U.S.L.W. 4077 (1987)
Key Issue: Sex Discrimination
In this judgment, the Supreme Court upheld a California law requiring leave for new mothers. Justice Thurgood Marshall, writing for the six-to-three majority, said that such legislation "promotes equal employment opportunity" because "it allows women, as well as men, to have families without losing their jobs." The case involved a receptionist that California Federal refused to rehire after she returned from pregnancy leave. The case represents the struggle between proponents of "special treatment" for women, who supported the decision, and those who argued that "equal treatment" for women, in the end, would better serve the goal of equal employment opportunities for men and women. This case was unusual in that it supported the idea of special treatment. Most court cases following the Pregnancy Discrimination act of 1978, and the Act itself, support the notion of gender-neutral treatment of employees.

Automobile Workers v. Johnson Controls, Inc., 499 U.S. 187 (1991)
Key Issue: Sex Discrimination
In this landmark case, the Supreme Court found that Title VII as amended by the Pregnancy Discrimination Act forbids sex-specific fetal protection policies. Johnson Controls, a Milwaukee-based battery maker, was sued by United Automobile workers for excluding women from higher-paying jobs that involve exposure to lead unless the women proved they were sterile. The purported purpose of the regulation was to prevent potential damage to fetuses. Men were allowed to work in these jobs despite some scientific evidence that sperm exposed to lead may also cause birth defects.

   The Court found that decisions about the health and welfare of future children should be left to the parents who conceive and raise them, rather than to employers who hire these parents.

United States v. Virginia, 518 U.S. 515 (1996)
Key Issue: Women and Education/Fourteenth Amendment
In *United States v. Virginia,* the Commonwealth of Virginia defended the single-sex policy at Virginia Military Institute (VMI), an all-male college, because the purpose of the school was to educate men who would serve their country as "citizen soldiers." Following the precedent set in *Mississippi University for Women v.*

Hogan, the Supreme Court held that there must be an "exceedingly persuasive justification" for having a separate male school and that Virginia had not met this standard. The Court found that VMI had violated the equal protection clause of the Fourteenth Amendment, and that its establishment of a parallel women's program at a nearby college was inherently unequal, not "separate but equal." As a result of this decision, the Citadel in South Carolina was also opened to women, overturning *Williams v. McNair* (316 F. Supp. 134, 1970), which had justified sex segregation between the Citadel and Winthrop College for Women on the grounds that the two schools were separate but equal.

Texas v. Hopwood, 116 S.Ct. 2581 (1996); 999 F. Supp.
872, 877 (1998)
Key Issue: Affirmative Action
In this judgment, the Fifth Circuit Court of Appeals invalidated an affirmative action program at the University of Texas Law School. The appeals court held that preferences for minority groups would have to be justified by proof that the minority groups were still being affected by past discrimination; the court held that the goal of diversity was not "compelling" justification for affirmative action. The Supreme Court denied a review of the lower court's decision. Following the ruling, the law school experienced a huge drop in minority admissions, and the state of Texas later adopted a policy of guaranteed undergraduate admission to any public university for those who graduate in the top 10 percent of their high school class. It has been argued that this course of action improves minority admissions, as many minority applicants come from racially homogeneous schools.

Executive Orders

Executive Order 10980 (1961)
Executive Order 10980, signed by President John F. Kennedy, established the President's Commission on the Status of Women. The commission made recommendations for overcoming employment discrimination on the basis of sex and for services to help women in their roles as wives and mothers.

Executive Order 11126 (1963)
Executive Order 11126, issued by John F. Kennedy, established the Interdepartmental Committee on the Status of Women, whose

purpose was to oversee women employed by the federal government. The order also established the Citizens' Advisory Council on the Status of Women to explore women's employment issues in the private sector.

Executive Order 11246 (1965)
Executive Order 11246, signed into law in 1965 by President Lyndon Johnson, barred discrimination on the basis of race, color, religion, or national origin in federal employment and in employment by federal contractors and subcontractors. The order requires executive departments and agencies to "maintain a positive program of equal opportunities." In addition, this Executive Order requires federal contractors and subcontractors to take affirmative action to ensure that employees are treated equally without regard to race, creed, color, or national origin.

Executive Order 11375 (1967)
Executive Order 11375 expanded Executive Order 11246 to include women by banning sex discrimination by federal contractors and subcontractors and by federal employers. It was issued by President Lyndon B. Johnson and is actually an amendment to Executive Order 11246, which prohibited race discrimination. The order contains two sections. The first section applies to federal contractors and subcontractors and is enforced by the Department of Labor's Office of Federal Contract Compliance. (The Department of Labor issued sex discrimination guidelines in 1970.) The second part of the order, dealing with federal employees, was enforced first by the Civil Service Commission and then after 1979 by the Merit Systems Protection Board and the Office of Personnel Management. Executive Order 11375 was used successfully to enforce Title IX by bringing suit against employers who were discriminating on the basis of sex.

Executive Order 11478 (1969)
Executive Order 11478 issued by Richard M. Nixon enjoined affirmative action in federal agencies, to be administered by the U.S. Civil Service Commission. President Clinton later amended this order by expanding it to include banning discrimination on the basis of sexual orientation (E.O. 13087), as well as on the basis of "status as a parent" (E.O. 13152).

Revised Order Number 4 (1971)
Revised Order Number 4, issued by the Labor Department, established regulations pertaining to Executive Order 11375. The Revised Order actually prescribes specific antidiscrimination measures and puts forward new regulations that require federal contractors with fifty or more employees and more than $50,0000 in contracts to plan and enforce affirmative action plans, including goals for hiring women and timetables for achieving these goals.

Statistical Data

Labor Force Participation Rate

All around the world, men are more numerous in the paid labor force than women, and women are more likely to be doing unpaid work. At the same time, women's economic activity rates have increased in many regions while men's have decreased. In 1997, more than 50 percent of women in western Europe and other developed regions were economically active, compared with approximately 45 percent in 1980, while in sub-Saharan Africa and in east and southeast Asia the rates stayed roughly the same, around 60 percent, and in South America they rose from 29 to 45 percent. Over the same period, however, men's activity rates generally fell a few percentage points, from roughly 76 to 72 percent in developed regions, from rates of as high as 88 to 86 percent in sub-Saharan Africa, and from 84 to 82 percent on average in east and southeast Asia (United Nations, 2000: 123, 110).

In the United States, the rising labor force participation rate of women has been a century-long phenomenon. Until the coming of industrialization and urbanization, the primary economic activity for both men and women had been unpaid labor in the home or on farms. Modernization brought women into manufacturing and into women's professions such as teaching and nursing. By 1900, 20 percent of working-age women were in the labor force, mostly young and unmarried women who took jobs in manufacturing and in emerging women's fields such as teaching and nursing. The growth of service industries and the need for teachers, clerical workers, and salespeople in the postwar period increased the demand for women's labor. Smaller families and women's increasing education also increased their labor supply. In addition, the rules of employment began to change to allow married women and women with children to hold jobs. By 1970, more than 50 percent of women ages forty to forty-four (born in 1926–1930) were employed. By 1985, the proportion of women ages forty to forty-four (born in 1946–1950) who were employed had risen to more than 75 percent, as shown in figure 5.1.

The employment rate varies for both men and women by marital status and the age and presence of children. These variables have relatively little effect on fathers' participation rates, which in 2001 tended to vary between 90 and 95 percent whether or not they were married with a spouse present or had younger children present in the home. In contrast, women's rates are strongly affected by their marital status and the ages of their children. Not quite 71 percent of mothers who were married with children under eighteen were in the labor force in 2001, compared with almost 74 percent of women who had no spouse present. Among married mothers with children six to seventeen, the rate rose to 77.7 percent and among single mothers to 80.6 percent. For mothers with children under six, however, the overall rate was lower. In 2001, their economic activity rate was 62.5 percent among married mothers and 69.7 percent among single mothers, as shown in table 5.1.

Closely related to sex, marital, and parental status are differences in rates of full-time and part-time employment. As a rule, many fewer men than women work part-time, and the reasons are largely related to the heavier family obligations of women. The connection is most clearly seen in the much higher part-time rates among women with small children. Among women with infants, only one-third (34 percent) worked full-time in 2000, compared with 43 percent of mothers of preschoolers and 59 percent of mothers with school-aged children (New Strategist, 2002: 242–243).

The overall picture of full-time and part-time work also varies with ages of the individual and within different national economies. Although most U.S. women work full-time, one in four works part-time. Of women aged twenty-five to fifty-four, 81 percent worked full-time in 2000, as compared with only 29 percent of sixteen- to nineteen-year-olds (New Strategist, 2002: 239). The part-time rate among women in Europe tends to be much higher than in the United States. In the Netherlands, for example, more than half of employed women work part-time; and more than one-third work part-time in the United Kingdom and Norway, whereas only 3 to 11 percent of men work part-time in those countries (United Nations, 2000: 132).

Figure 5.1
Trends in Labor Force Participation Rates for Women, 1950–2000, by Birth Cohort

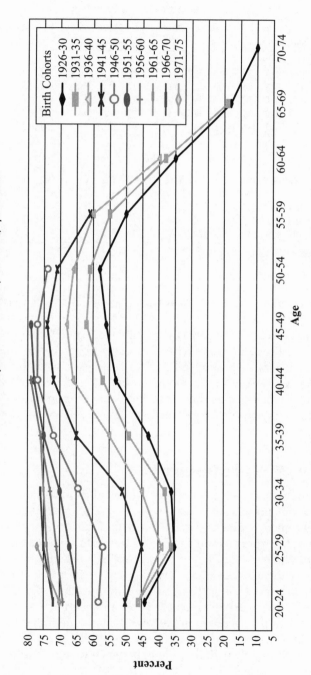

Source: Social Security Administration, 1993; U.S. Department of Labor, Bureau of Labor Statistics, 1996; U.S. Department of Labor, Bureau of Labor Statistics, 2001b.
Compiled by the Institute for Women's Policy Research

Table 5.1

Employment Status of Women by Marital Status and Presence and Age of Children: 1970–2001

Item	Total single/married/other			Total with children single/married/other			With children 6-17 only single/married/other			With children under 6 single/married/other		
In labor force (mil)												
1970	7.0	18.4	5.9	(NA)	10.2	1.9	(NA)	6.3	1.3	(NA)	3.9	0.6
1980	11.2	24.9	8.8	0.6	13.7	3.6	0.3	5.2	1.0	0.3	5.2	1.0
1990	14.0	31.0	11.2	1.5	16.5	4.2	0.6	9.3	3.0	0.9	7.2	1.2
2000	17.8	35.0	13.2	3.1	18.2	4.5	1.2	10.8	3.4	1.8	7.3	1.1
2001	17.9	5.2	13.5	3.0	18.3	4.4	1.2	11.0	3.3	1.8	7.3	1.1
Participation rate (percentages)												
1970	53.0	40.8	39.1	(NA)	39.7	60.7	(NA)	49.2	66.9	(NA)	30.3	52.2
1980	61.5	50.1	44.0	52.0	54.1	69.4	67.6	61.7	74.6	44.1	45.1	60.3
1990	66.4	58.2	46.8	55.2	66.3	74.2	69.7	73.6	79.7	48.7	58.9	63.6
2000	68.6	62.0	50.2	73.9	70.6	82.7	79.7	77.2	85.0	70.5	62.8	76.6
2001	68.4	62.1	50.3	73.8	70.8	83.7	80.6	77.7	86.5	69.7	62.5	76.2

Source: *Statistical Abstract of the United States 2002.*

Race and ethnicity are additional powerful factors that affect labor force activity. In the United States, black women are more likely to be in the labor force than white women (69 versus 60 percent), and Hispanic women are less likely (57 percent). This pattern is especially pronounced during the middle years from ages twenty-five to forty-four. Among women aged sixteen to twenty-four and women over age forty-five, white women are more likely than the other two groups to be employed (New Strategist, 2002: 236–237).

Differentials in Earnings

For a number of reasons that are both understandable and puzzling, women all around the world on average continue to earn less than men. Women's wages in manufacturing as a percent of men's range from as high as 85 to 95 percent in the Scandinavian countries to between 70 and 80 percent in most European countries and the United States, and as low as 50 to 60 percent in Brazil, Bangladesh, and Korea. In addition to the wage differential for similar work, women are likely to spend at least twice as many hours per week on unpaid work as men (United Nations, 2000: 125, 132).

Over time, the pay differential between women and men has

Table 5.2

Median Income by Sex, 1990–2000

(Median income for people aged 15 and older who work full-time, year-round.)

	Median income		Index of women's income
	Women	Men	to men's
2000	$28,820	$39,020	74
1999	28,289	38,836	73
1998	28,338	38,253	74
1997	27,850	37,714	74
1996	27,258	36,662	74
1995	26,698	36,154	74
1994	26,778	36,386	74
1993	26,429	36,554	72
1992	26,657	37,202	72
1991	26,314	37,568	70
1990	26,438	37,208	71
Percent change:			
1990–2000	9.0%	4.9%	—

Source: Bureau of the Census, 2003. "Current Population Survey." *Annual Demographic Supplements.* http://www.census.gov/hhes/income/histinc/p36.html. Accessed June 2003.

generally decreased. In the United States, for example, between 1990 and 2000, as shown in table 5.2, the median income for full-time year-round female workers relative to men's income has risen from 71 to 74 percent. The reasons for the change appear to be women's rising levels of education, the lower fertility rate, and women's greater attachment to the labor market as well as declining opportunities for men in the well-paid manufacturing jobs.

At the same time, women's greater vulnerability to family demands appears to exert a downward pull on their wages as they proceed through life, so that the earnings gap widens substantially by the time women and men are in their early thirties and reaches a maximum when they are in their fifties, a shown in figure 5.2.

The pay gap is further influenced by race and ethnic group. Between 1970 and 1990, white women's wages in the United States rose from 58.70 percent of white men's to 71.58 percent. Although black men did better, rising during the same period from 69.00 to 80.61 percent, Hispanic men did worse, reaching only 61.60 percent of white men's wages in 1999. Hispanic women did even worse, earning only a little more than half (52.11 percent) of white men's annual earnings by 1999, as shown in table 5.3 (Stebbins, 2001: 124).

Despite the pervasive differences in earnings by sex, age,

Figure 5.2
The Female-Male Wage Gap over the Life Cycle (1999 Median Annual Earnings by Age)*

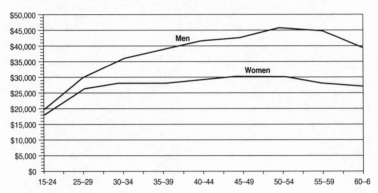

* for full-time, year-round workers.
Source: IWPR, 2001.
Calculated by the Institute for Women's Policy Research.

race, and ethnic group, type of occupation can exert either an accentuating or a dampening effect on the wage gap. Among persons with higher annual incomes in 1998 (in the $500,000 to $1 million category), women had slightly higher average incomes ($670,000 to $668,000) although they were outnumbered by the men 10 to 1 (Johnston, 2002). And among persons with incomes of more than $1 million, women's incomes were 95 percent of men's. Within any given field, the pay gap between women and men may be fairly small, as among engineers, scientists, editors, reporters, high school teachers, and social workers, fields in which female workers earn at least 85 percent of what men earn (New Strategist, 2002: 206–213). What accounts for the much bigger gap between women's and men's incomes is not the differences within occupations in male and female pay but between occupations. The male-labeled occupations (in which at least 60–75 percent of the workers are men) are more highly paid than the occupations in which 60–75 percent of the workers are women.

Related to the gender gap in income is the gender gap in poverty rates. Nationwide in 1998, 12 percent of women aged sixteen and over were living in poverty compared with 8.3 percent of men. For single-mother families, however, the poverty rate was 35.7 percent in 1999 (Institute for Women's Policy Research, 2002: 40–43).

Table 5.3
Changes in the Wage Gap

Year	White Men	Black Men	Hispanic Men	White Women	Black Women	Hispanic Women
1970	100%	69.00%	N/A*	58.70%	48.20%	N/A*
1975	100	74.30	72.10	57.50	55.40	49.30
1980	100	70.70	70.80	58.90	55.70	50.50
1985	100	69.70	68.00	63.00	57.10	52.10
1990	100	73.10	66.30	69.40	62.50	54.30
1992	100	72.60	63.35	70.00	64.00	55.40
1994	100	75.10	64.30	71.60	63.00	55.60
1995	100	75.90	63.30	71.20	64.20	53.40
1996	100	80.00	63.90	73.30	65.10	56.60
1997	100	75.10	61.40	71.90	62.60	53.90
1998	100	74.90	61.60	72.60	62.60	53.10
1999	100	80.61	61.63	71.58	65.05	52.11

*Data not available.
Source: Census Bureau Current Population Reports. 2000. Series P-60, U.S. Commerce Department. http://www.census.gov/prod2001pubs/p60-213.pdf. Accessed June 2003.

Occupational Segregation

Occupational segregation refers to the tendency for many occupations to be sex-typed with a predominance of either men or women. As women's education improves relative to men's and as the service industries (in which women are numerous) have grown, the rate of occupational segregation has decreased.

In other developed countries as well as in the United Sates, most women and men are employed in the service sector as distinguished from agriculture or industry. The service sector has grown with modernization, and with it have grown the opportunities in office work, service work, and government employment, in which almost four-fifths of all women are employed, compared with roughly three-fifths of all men. In the less developed countries of Asia and Africa, however, as many as half of all employed women and men are employed in agriculture (United Nations, 2000: 114).

Historically, there has been a broadening of the range of women's choices as more of them enter formerly male-dominated fields. In the thirty years from 1970 to 1999, certain professions even tipped over from being primarily male to being primarily female. For example, the proportion of personnel and labor relations managers who were women rose from one-fifth to three-fifths, and the proportion of female accountants and auditors grew from one-quarter to more than one-half (Blau, Ferber, and

Table 5.4
Female Workers by Occupation, 2000
(Employed workers aged 16 and older, number and percent distribution of employed women,
and women as percent of total workers, by occupation)

	Total	WOMEN		
		Number (in thousands)	Percent distribution	Share of total
Total employed	135,208	62,915	100%	46.5%
Managerial and professional specialty	40,887	20,345	32.3	49.8
Executive, administrative, and managerial	19,774	8,960	14.2	45.3
Professional specialty	21,113	11,385	18.1	53.9
Technical, sales, and administrative support	39,442	25,154	40.0	63.8
Technicians and related support	4,385	2,267	3.6	51.7
Sales occupations	16,340	8,110	12.9	49.6
Administrative and clerical support	18,717	14,778	23.5	79.0
Service occupations	18,278	11,034	17.5	60.4
Private household	792	757	1.2	95.6
Protective service	2,399	455	0.7	19.0
Service, except private or protective	15,087	9,822	15.6	65.1
Precision production, craft, and repair	14,882	1,351	2.1	9.1
Operators, fabricators, and laborers	18,319	4,331	6.9	23.6
Machine operators, assemblers, and inspectors	7,319	2,697	4.3	36.8
Transportation and material moving occupations	5,557	554	0.9	10.0
Handlers, equipment cleaners, helpers, laborers	5,443	1,080	1.7	19.8
Farming, forestry, and fishing	3,399	701	1.1	20.6

Source: Bureau of Labor Statistics, Employment and Earnings, January 2001. http//www.bls.gov/news.release/ ocwage.toc.htm. Accessed June 2003.

Winkler, 2002: 142). In addition, more women have been able to move up in management and claim more positions as line officers, where they supervise other workers.

In 1972, the index of occupational segregation (the percentage of women and the percentage of men who would have to change jobs in order for the occupational distribution of the two groups to be the same) stood at 41.8. By 1999, it had declined to 32.3 (Blau, Ferber, and Winkler, 2002: 135).

Despite these signs of desegregation, just three occupational groupings continued to claim 90 percent of all women employees in 2000, as shown in table 5.4. Fully 40 percent of all female workers were in technical, sales, and administrative support; another 32.3 percent in management and professions; and 17.5 percent in service occupations.

Similarly, female workers are found in a narrower range of industries than male workers. In 1999, one-third of all women

Figure 5.3
Distribution of Women and Men across Occupations in the United States, 1999

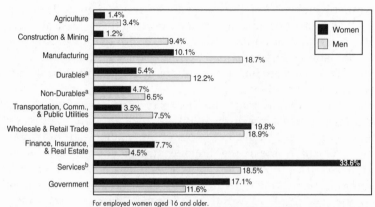

For employed women aged 16 and older.
Percents do not add up to 100% because 'self-employed' and 'unpaid family workers' are excluded.
a Durables and non-durables are included in manufacturing.
b Private household workers are included in services.
Source: U.S. Department of Labor, Bureau of Labor Statistics, 2001a, Table 17. Compiled by the Institute for Women's Policy Research.

were employed in the service occupations, another 19.8 percent in wholesale and retail trade, and 17.1 percent in government. Just these three industries accounted for 70.5 percent of all female employees. The top three industries for males (trade, manufacturing, and services) accounted for only 56 percent of their total, as shown in figure 5.3.

Occupational segregation can also be vertical, in the sense of limiting the upper echelons of an organization to men or only a few women. Women have begun to make progress in opening up the higher echelons of positions as corporate officers. Female corporate officers and top earners have more than doubled since 1995, from 29 women to 77 women in 1999, although the total number of female officers remains small. The women almost doubled their representation among corporate officers, from 8.7 percent in 1995 to 15.7 percent in 2002. In 1997, women of color were corporate officers in 105 companies out of 340 reporting, constituting 1.3 percent of the total officers' pool and 11.2 percent of all female corporate officers in the reporting companies (Catalyst, 1999, 2002).

Educational Attainment

Both internationally and within the United States, the story of women's and men's educational attainment is one of continuing improvement. Literacy has risen, and the gender gap in educational access and attainment has narrowed. More women are able to pursue higher education and to enter professions and specialties that were once almost entirely closed to them. Despite these enormous and continuing gains, there is still room for progress. Women still generally have less education than men, and even when their educational qualifications are equal to men's, they continue to be paid less.

On the international front, the story of improving education begins with basic literacy, the ability to read and write—although here again, women tend to lag behind men. One sign of overall improvement is the rising literacy among younger adults. In northern Africa in 2000, for example, 76 percent of women over age twenty-five were illiterate, compared with only 42 percent of women aged fifteen to twenty-one. For men, the comparable rates were 51 percent illiterate among the men over twenty-five and only 20 percent of those under twenty-five. Comparison of literacy rates in the same region between 1980 and 2000 show a similar pattern: illiteracy among women has fallen 26 percent (from 74 to 48 percent) and 18 among men (from 43 to 25 percent) (United Nations, 2000: 69).

School enrollment of both boys and girls is also on the rise in the developing countries. The gender gap was cut in half in northern Africa between 1980 and 1995, when enrollment had risen to 76 percent of girls and 86 percent of boys who were in school. Enrollments are virtually equal in the developed world and in southern Africa, east Asia, and south America, where rates for both boys and girls range between 90 and 100 percent (United Nations, 2000: 86). An important consequence of mass education appears to be the impact on the fertility rate. A comparative study of seventeen African countries found that the nations with higher levels of education were better able to control population size, and this was especially true if educational improvements were extended to girls (United Nations, 2000: 91).

As more boys and girls have been able to attend school, more of them have also been able to enter higher education and professional training. (In a few rare cases, the gender gap has actually reversed.) In Latin America, roughly equal numbers of men and women (14 to 16 per 1,000) are enrolled in higher education. In western Europe also, the figures are also quite similar for women and men (31 to 32 per 1,000). But there is a clear disparity in a few countries, where women's enrollment in tertiary education is clearly lower than that of men's. In Japan, 27 out of 1,000 women are enrolled in higher education, compared with 36 out of 1,000 men. In Korea, the ratio is only 42 per 1,000 women compared with 70 per 1,000 men (United Nations, 2000: 91–93).

Women's increasing educational attainment has made it possible for them to choose fields traditionally dominated by men. Thus, between 1994 and 1996, almost equal numbers of women were enrolled in law and business in Africa, Latin America, southeast Asia, and eastern and western Europe (United Nations, 2000: 93).

Girls and women in the United States have shared in the worldwide trend toward higher levels of education. Between 1950 and 2000, the proportion of women aged twenty-five and over with a high school diploma rose from 36 to 84 percent, and the proportion of women who were college graduates rose from 5.2 to 23.6 percent over the same period, as shown in table 5.5.

High school completion and college attendance vary considerably by race and ethnicity. Thus, although the overall rate of female high school graduates in 2000 was 84 percent, non-Hispanic white women slightly exceeded that figure (88.4 percent), the proportion of black women was slightly lower (78.3), and the proportion of Hispanic women was significantly lower (57.5). Racial differences were also striking among college graduates. Compared with the national average of 23.6 percent among women in 2000, Asian women had a college graduation rate of 40.7, black women 16.7, Hispanic women 10.6, and white women 25.5 (New Strategist, 2002: 77).

College completion rates, however, tell only part of the story. Currently, almost half of all American women have at least attended college. In addition to those with a bachelor's degree, 17.7 percent have some college, and 8.4 percent have an associate's degree, as shown in table 5.6.

Burgeoning rates of higher education have been associated with U.S. women's more frequent entry into what were once considered male-labeled occupations and fields. Women now constitute about half of all graduating college seniors in business management, administrative services, and marketing (50 percent); parks, recreation, leisure, and fitness (52 percent); and mathematics (47 percent). Nearly half of all new lawyers (46 percent) and medical doctors (43 percent) in 1999–2000 were also women (New Strategist, 2002: 105, 108).

These changes in women's education have already had an

Table 5.5

Percentage of Male and Female Graduates Age 25 and Over, 1950–2000

	Completed 4 years of high school or more			Completed 4 years of college or more		
	Both sexes	Male	Female	Both sexes	Male	Female
2000	84.1	84.2	84.0	25.6	27.8	23.6
1995	81.7	81.7	81.6	23.0	26.0	20.2
1990	77.6	77.7	77.5	21.3	24.4	18.4
1985	73.9	74.4	73.5	19.4	23.1	16.0
1980	68.6	69.2	68.1	17.0	20.9	13.6
1975	62.5	63.1	62.1	13.9	17.6	10.6
1970	55.2	55.0	55.4	11.0	14.1	8.2
1965	49.0	48.0	49.9	9.4	12.0	7.1
1959	43.7	42.2	45.2	8.0	10.3	6.0
1950	34.3	32.6	36.0	6.2	7.0	5.2

Source: U.S. Bureau of the Census. *1952 to 2002 March Current Population Survey.* Washington, D.C.: U.S. Government Printing Office. http://www.census.gov/population/socdemo/education/tabA-2.pdf. Accessed June 2003.

Table 5.6

Highest Level of Educational Attainment by Sex, 2000

(Percent of Population)

	Male	Female
Not a high school graduate	15.8	16.0
High school graduate	31.9	34.3
Some college but no degree	17.4	17.7
Associate's degree	7.1	8.4
Bachelor's degree	17.8	16.3
Advanced degree	10.0	7.3

Source: *Statistical Abstract of the United States,* United States Census Bureau, 2001.

impact in raising women's rate of employment and their pay. In 1998, only 1.3 percent of women holding professional degrees were unemployed, compared with 7.1 percent of those women who did not finish high school. Individuals with a professional degree averaged $72,700 in annual earnings, compared with $19,700 for those with less than a high school degree (U.S. Bureau of Labor Statistics, 2001).

Family Demographics and Household Composition

Simultaneous with the massive changes that have taken place around the world in women's labor force participation and education are large-scale changes in family size and situation. Changes in the family have been driven by modernization and increased education, but a fall in the birthrate and an increase in divorce have also given women more time and incentive to enter the labor force.

Internationally, the main changes in families and living arrangements have resulted in more child-free time for women that has made it possible to extend their education and take employment. Marriage is now occurring later in life, especially in the developed regions, where in 1997 the age at marriage averaged twenty-seven for females and thirty for males. Birthrates have also declined dramatically, to the point at which in 2000 all the developed countries had rates between 1.5 and 1.8 births for women, and women in developing countries wanted fewer children than in the 1980s (three or four in 2000, compared with five to eight in the 1980s). More people are living alone, and one-half to two-thirds of these one-person households are made up of women. Among other households, roughly 30 percent in the developed world are headed by women. The proportion of divorced and separated people has increased, but the increase in the divorce rate appears to have slowed since the 1980s. Between 1980 and the late 1990s, the proportion of divorced and separated women aged forty-five to forty-nine increased from an average of 5 percent in 1980 to 9 percent in the 1990s in Europe, and from 9 to 14 percent in the other developed countries during the same period (United Nations, 2000: 23–43).

A rise in labor force participation has taken place among mothers of young children in Europe, just as in the United States. Of mothers with children under three years of age in 1997, more than 50 percent in Belgium, France, the Netherlands, Portugal, and the United Kingdom were employed, compared with 62 percent in Canada and 58 percent in the United States (United Nations, 2000: 37).

Similar changes in family composition have taken place in the United States. As shown in figure 5.4, married couples with a wife not in the paid labor force have shrunk from constituting two-thirds of all families in 1950 to under 30 percent in 1999. Married couples with an employed wife accounted for only 20 percent of all families in 1950 but grew to half of all families over the same 50-year period. A third group of single-headed and female-headed families has also risen from less than 15 percent to nearly a quarter of all families (Stebbins, 2001: 125).

Figure 5.4
Composition of Families by Family Structure

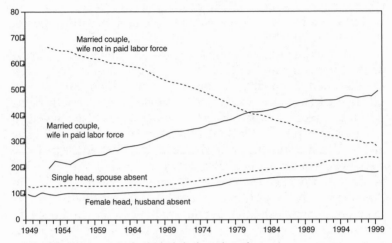

Note: A family is two or more related individuals who reside together.
Source: Economic Report of the President 2000. Washington, DC: U.S. Government Printing Office.
http://w3.access.gpo.gov/usbudget/fy2001/pdf/2000_erp.pdf. Accessed June 2003.

The emergence of these different household forms can be seen in the changing marital histories of American women. Fewer older women have been divorced than younger women. In 1996, 26 percent of women aged sixty to sixty-nine had divorced, compared with 35 percent of women aged fifty to fifty-nine and 37 percent of women aged forty to forty-nine. Nearly one-fifth of all women aged thirty to forty-four in 2000 were living alone or were not independent householders (lived with parents, a relative, or not in a family) (New Strategist, 2002: 283, 288).

The changes in family structure are particularly important for children and their mothers, especially when the mother has to work and also be responsible for home and child care. Prevalence of such living arrangements varies considerably by race and ethnicity among American families. As shown in table 5.7, fully 81 percent of Asian American children live with both parents, compared with 38 percent of black children, 65 percent of Hispanic children, and 78 percent of white children (United States Bureau of the Census, 2001).

Different types of households represent different combinations of earners, caregivers, and dependent children and others needing care. As the proportion of working parents increases,

Table 5.7
Living Arrangements of Children by Race and Ethnicity, 2000
(numbers in thousands)

	Total	Asian	Black	Hispanic	White Total	White Non-Hispanic
Total children	72,012	3,047	11,613	11,613	56,455	45,407
Both parents	49.795	2,454	4,286	7,561	42,497	35,188
One parent	19,220	504	6,080	3,425	12,192	9,046
Mother only	16,162	428	5,596	2,919	9,765	7,095
Father only	3,058	76	484	506	2,427	1,951
Neither parent	2,981	88	1,046	626	1,752	1,161
Percent of children						
Both parents	69	81	38	65	75	78
One parent	27	17	53	29	22	20
Mother only	22	14	49	25	17	16
Father only	4	3	4	4	4	4
Neither parent	4	3	9	5	3	3

Source: "U.S. Bureau of the Census, America's Families and Living Arrangements: March 2000." Current Population Report, P-20-537. http://www.census.gov/population/socdemo/hh-fam/p20-537/2000/tabc2.pdf. Accessed June 2003.

mothers and fathers are likely to feel increasing time pressures, as shown in figure 5.5. In 1998 more families with children had either a single parent who was also employed (25 percent) or two employed parents (49 percent), for a total of 74 percent compared with only 59 percent of all families with children in 1978.

Housework and Child Care

Given the changes in family patterns along with the likelihood that more mothers will be employed, developed countries have constructed a variety of solutions for child care and housework. The basic options involve redistributing labor within the married couple, paying for outside services such as child care, and providing for flexibility in the workplace through maternity leaves and part-time work. All three types of solutions are apparent in other developed countries as well as the United States.

The first solution is redistribution of labor within the household. Internationally, the trend toward more equal sharing of paid work and home-based, unpaid work between men and women in the developed countries is evident in time diaries and surveys from the 1980s and the 1990s. Bielenski and Wagner (2003) report that couples' preferences in fifteen European Union countries

Figure 5.5
Single-Parent and Dual-Earner Families with Children, 1978 and 1998

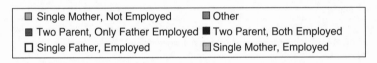

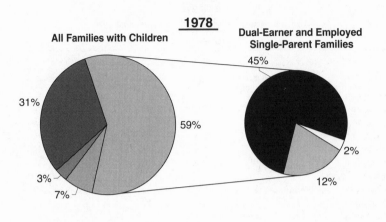

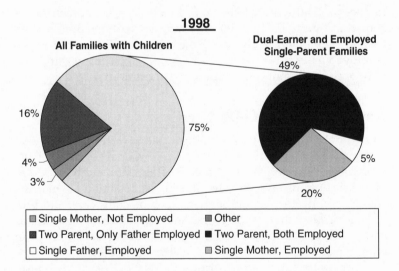

Percentages do not add to 100 percent due to rounding.

Source: Bianchi, Suzanne M. and Marybeth J. Mattingly. 2003. "Time, Work, and Family in the United States," in *Changing Life Patterns in Western Industrial Societies.* Edited by Janet Zollinger Giele and Elke Holst. London: Elsevier Science. Used by permission.

plus Norway are much more egalitarian than actual hours worked. Men, more frequently than women, want to work less (41 percent of men versus 22 percent of women), and more women want to work more (24 percent of women versus 17 percent of men). If couples were to have their preferences, the biggest difference in household division of labor would be to shift from the breadwinner-homemaker model to a dual-earner model in which the men would be employed full-time and the women part-time. Across the sixteen European countries surveyed, the average comes to 29 percent of the respondents who would prefer such an arrangement, as compared with 20 percent who actually have it. Conversely, only 46 percent of couples prefer the traditional breadwinner model, compared with 56 percent who currently live in that form of household; and 48 percent of the respondents would prefer the dual-earner model (in which both partners would be employed either full- or part-time), compared with the 34 percent who currently follow that pattern (Bielenski and Wagner, 2003).

Still another perspective on time use in the family comes from time diaries that compare women's and men's actual time spent on paid work, housework, and child care. Bonke and Koch-Weser (2003), in a study of time use in Sweden, Denmark, France, and Italy, compared the number of hours and minutes spent by childless couples and by couples with two children on paid work, housework, leisure, and "care and needs" (eating, sleeping, grooming, etc.). They discovered that the male-female division of labor in families with and without children was remarkably similar in hours and minutes per day that were devoted to leisure and care and needs. Only in France did women have about an hour less leisure time than men, and there, men spent only 89 percent as much time on care and needs as the women. But in the other three countries, men spent more than 90 percent as much time on care and needs as the women.

Presence of children does, however, affect women's ratio of paid work to unpaid work. A comparison of the effects of children on women's and men's paid and unpaid work in Australia, the Netherlands, and New Zealand between 1995 and 1999 revealed that women's time in unpaid work rose by about 12 percent and men's decreased by 2 percent; conversely, men's paid work rose 10 percent and women's declined by roughly 3 percent (United Nations, 2000: 126). The magnitude and symmetry of these changes suggest an implicit balancing process in the marital division of labor. Bonke and Koch-Weser (2003) found a similar process by which the presence of children is associated with an increase in women's unpaid work and a slight decrease in their paid work, while men make up the difference by a sharper increase in paid work balanced by a decrease in the time doing unpaid work in the home. Only in Sweden was the process somewhat different. There, women in couples with two children spent 20 percent more time in paid work per day than women in couples without children.

Development of child care programs is the second important function that supports the time increase in women's employment and in the number of dual-earner families. By and large, child care in the European Union is widely supported, publicly funded, and available to the large majority of children ages three to six. In 1993, 80 to 99 percent of children this age were enrolled in early childhood education in Belgium, Germany, Denmark, Spain, France, Italy, and Sweden. The United Kingdom enrolled only 53 percent of the children in this age group, and Greece, only 64 percent (Tietze and Cryer, 1999). These figures represented a substantial rise over just five years earlier. Child care provision for children under three is much less widespread, however. Only Belgium, Denmark, France, and Sweden had more than 20 percent of this age group enrolled in early child care in 1993. In the ensuing decade, however, important increases have occurred. In the face of a birthrate below replacement level all over Europe, the EU encourages member states to spend at least 1 percent of gross domestic product on early child care (Tietze and Cryer, 1999). Although this level of investment has not yet been realized, France, for example, has invested heavily in its child care system and now provides paid certified home help, center-based care, and tax credits and subsidies for child care to infants and preschool children. The number of child care places in crèches has increased by about 6,499 places per year between 1980 and 1996, to a total of 201,000 by 1999 (Letablier, 2003).

A third element in the solution of the work-family dilemma is to be found in maternity and parental leave policies and the availability of part-time work. The principle of maternity leave as a basic right of workers was established in 1952 by the International Labor Organization (ILO), which set a standard of at least twelve weeks as the minimum. As of 2000, 119 countries met the standard of twelve weeks or more, and thirty-one countries offered less. In addition to length of leave, another important variable is whether or not the leave is paid. As of 1998, the great majority of countries paid the mother 50 to 100 percent of her normal wages during the period of the leave. Funding for those payments usually came from contributions by the employer, Social Security benefits, or some combination of the two. Parental leave (which is also available to fathers) is available in thirty-six out of 138 member countries in the ILO. In twenty-five of these countries, the leave is paid. The Nordic countries offer the most comprehensive and generous benefits to parents of newborns, with a high level of compensation for wages lost, and 90 percent of couples make use of the benefits, although it is predominately the mothers who do so. But in Australia, New Zealand, and the United States, such leaves are still mostly unpaid (United Nations, 2000: 133–143).

In addition to leave, provisions made by employers for part-time work and flexible hours are important in helping men and women combine work and parenting. In the European Union, Rubery, Smith and Fagan (1999) and Plantenga (2003) have investigated various working-time patterns to discover which are most conducive to women's labor force participation. They suggest that "short" full-time and "long" part-time working hours provide the most favorable circumstances for combining paid work and parenting. "Long" full-time and "unsocial" working hours (nights and weekends), in contrast, are particularly unfavorable to working mothers.

In the United States, the same issues are relevant. Change in the family division of labor has resulted in fathers spending somewhat more time in unpaid housework. Bianchi and Mattingly's (2003) comparison of time diaries from 1965 and 1998 show that women's overall time spent in market work has increased from 7 to 32 percent. Time spent in free time, shopping, and child care has remained virtually the same, and time spent in housework has fallen from 30 to 17 percent. Over the same period, men's amounts of time devoted to free time, shopping, and child care have all increased a few percentage points, but the biggest change is in a decline in market work (from 49 to 40 percent) and a rise in housework (from 5 to 12 percent). One of the chief ways by which couples in 1998 managed to fit in all their activities was by "multitasking," especially by combining child care with other activities such as shopping or housework.

In the United States also, just as in other parts of the developed world, child care outside the home has grown markedly over the last twenty-five years. Although the primary child care arrangement for the majority of preschool children is still with a relative or someone else in the child's own home or another home (75 percent in 1977 and 64 percent in 1994), the most noticeable change is in the number of all preschoolers who are cared for in organized facilities, a proportion that grew from 13 percent in 1977 to 29 percent in 1994 (Stebbins, 2001: 129). A 1999 survey by the Urban Institute of child care arrangements by employed parents found that two-parent families (both high- and low-income) were more likely to rely on parental care, and single parents more often used center-based care for both preschool and school-age children six to twelve. Child care arrangements varied with the age of the child as shown in figure 5.6. Among preschool children up to four, approximately one-quarter each were in the care of parents, family day care or babysitter/nanny, center-based care, or relatives' care. For six- to twelve-year-olds, parent/other care was most common (41 percent), followed by relative care (23 percent), before- and after-school programs (15 percent), and self-care (10 percent) (Sonenstein et al., 2002).

Regarding maternity and parental leave in the United States, the passage of the Family and Medical Leave Act of 1993 represented a major breakthrough. Nevertheless, unlike most countries of the world, the United States' provision for twelve weeks' leave and job protection does not carry with it any guarantee of compensation for lost wages. The leave is available for childbirth, adoption, foster care placement, a serious personal medical condition, or a serious medical condition of an immediate family member. Stebbins (2001: 132) reports the results of a survey by the Families and Work Institute of 1,057 for-profit and nonprofit companies with 100 or more employees. The study found that 88 percent of the companies allowed employees to take time off to attend school and child care functions, and 80 percent allowed employees to return to work on a gradual basis following childbirth and adoption. More than half the companies permitted employees to move between a part-time and full-time schedule, and more than two-thirds permitted four-day flextime schedules. Half the companies had dependent care assistance plans to help employees pay for child care with pretax dollars.

Discrimination and Sexual Harassment

Equal rights legislation as it relates to women's status has grown remarkably in the developed world over the past half century.

Figure 5.6
Primary Child Care Arrangements of Children with an Employed Parent, 1999

Preschool children (0–4)

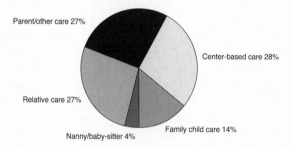

Parent/other care 27%

Center-based care 28%

Relative care 27%

Nanny/baby-sitter 4%

Family child care 14%

Five-year-olds

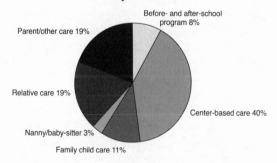

Before- and after-school program 8%

Parent/other care 19%

Relative care 19%

Center-based care 40%

Nanny/baby-sitter 3%

Family child care 11%

School-age children (6–12)

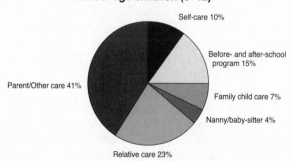

Self-care 10%

Before- and after-school program 15%

Parent/Other care 41%

Family child care 7%

Nanny/baby-sitter 4%

Relative care 23%

Source: Sonenstein, Freya et al. 2002. *Primary Childcare Arrangements of Employed Parents: Findings from the 1999 National Survey of America's Families. Occasional Paper Number 59.* Washington, DC: The Urban Institute. http://www.urban.org/UploadedPDF/310487_OP59.pdf. Accessed June 2003. Used by permission.

The European Union has passed numerous statutes as guidelines for its member nations with respect to equal pay, equal opportunity in the workplace, and sexual harassment. For example, the case of a Belgian airline hostess decided by the European Court of Justice in 1972 set a precedent in striking down a discriminatory policy of laying off female flight attendants when they turned forty but not laying off their male peers (Berghahn, 2003).

In the United States the passage of the Civil Rights Act of 1964 and the institution of the Equal Employment Opportunity Commission (EEOC) created the machinery and set in motion a process for challenging discriminatory practices in the workplace. Statistics on enforcement and litigation of discrimination charges show that charges of sex-based discrimination have averaged between 20,000 to 25,000 cases per year between 1992 and 2002. Merit resolutions, which uphold the charges of the plaintiffs, have resolved roughly 15 to 20 percent of the cases. Over the ten-year period, the monetary benefits have tripled, rising from $31 million to $95 million (U.S. Equal Employment Opportunity Commission, 2003).

Pregnancy discrimination cases have constituted a smaller group of charges that has increased from roughly 3,000 to nearly 5,000 per year over the decade of the 1990s. Merit resolutions have resulted in roughly one-quarter of the cases, and monetary benefits over that period have nearly tripled, from $3.7 million to $10.0 million between 1992 and 2002 (U.S. Equal Employment Opportunity Commission, 2003).

Charges of sexual harassment rose sharply in the four years following the Hill-Thomas hearings (from 10, 572 in 1992 to 15, 541 in 1995) and then leveled off, as shown in figure 5.7. Over the same period, merit resolutions rose slightly, from 27 percent in 1992 to 28 and 29 percent in 2000 and after. Monetary benefits rose from $12.7 million in 1992 to $54.6 million in 2000 and tapered down to $50.3 million in 2002.

There are grounds for believing that charges of sexual harassment have a firm basis in fact. Surveys of federal employees done by the United States Merit Protection Board in 1980, 1987, and 1994 found that approximately one-third of female employees reported being the target of unwelcome sexual remarks and suggestive looks, and one-fourth reported physical touching by a coworker or supervisor. One in six reported pressure for dates, and one in ten, pressure for sexual favors (Fitzgerald, Collinsworth, and Harned, 2001).

Figure 5.7
Sexual Harassment Cases before the EEOC, 1992–2002

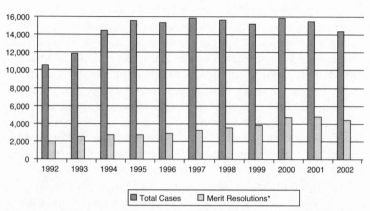

* Merit resolutions include charges with outcomes favorable to the changing parties and/or charges with meritorious allegations. These include negotiated settlements, withdrawals with benefits, successful conciliations, and unsuccessful conciliations.

Source: The U.S. Equal Employment Opportunity Commission, 2003. http://www.eeoc.gov/stats/harass.html. Accessed June 2003.

The Crime Victims' Research and Treatment Center conducted a survey based on a national probability sample of 3,000 women with employment experience. They tried to ascertain prevalence of sexual harassment using a narrower definition of the phenomenon as (1) perpetrated by supervisors; (2) interpreted by the respondent as sexual harassment; and (3) understood by the respondent to lead to negative jobs consequences if reported or rebuffed. By these criteria, the study concluded that the prevalence rate of sexual harassment among employed women was at least 11.5 percent (Fitzgerald, Collinsworth, and Harned, 2001).

In addition to these reports from civilian life, two large-scale surveys by the Department of Defense in 1995 indicated that 78 percent of female military personnel had experienced at least one instance of offensive sex-related behavior in the previous twelve months (Fitzgerald, Collinsworth, and Harned, 2001).

Emerging International Issues of Sex Equality

Beyond the well-documented changes in women's labor force participation and the many signs of progress toward equality between women and men in the workplace, there are a number of emerging but still shadowy topics that have yet to be well documented and understood but should be followed and investigated in the future. Two of these issues were discussed in Chapter 1: first, the exploitation of female workers in Third World countries under sweatshop conditions to meet production quotas and consumer demand that originates in the developed world; and second, the importation of immigrant women from poorer countries to serve as household and child care workers in the homes of the richer countries, thereby depriving these women's own children of their presence and care. A third important issue is trafficking in women that moves them from one country to another for sexual exploitation.

The International Organisation for Migration (IOM) has begun to collect data on the illegal trafficking in women for use as sex workers, sweatshop workers, agricultural slave labor, and domestic servitude. The figures range from estimates of 40,000 to 50,000 women trafficked annually into the United States; 20,000 to 30,000 Burmese women imported to Thailand as prostitutes; 200,000 Bangladeshis taken to Pakistan over the past ten years for a similar purpose; and large numbers of women brought from eastern Europe to western Europe for similar exploitation. The IOM recommends that nations adopt a common framework for getting data and that they then inform law enforcement agencies so that international conventions can be implemented that make such trafficking a crime (United Nations, 2000: 158–159).

References

Berghahn, Sabine. 2003. "The Influence of European Union Legislation on Labor Market Equality for Women." In *Changing Life Patterns in Western Industrial Societies,* vol. 8 of *Advances in Life Course Research.* Edited by Janet Z. Giele and Elke Holst. London: Elsevier Science.

Bianchi, Suzanne, and Marybeth Mattingly. 2003. "Time, Work, and Family in the United States." In *Changing Life Patterns in Western Industrial Societies,* vol. 8 of *Advances in Life Course Research.* Edited by Janet Z. Giele and Elke Holst. London: Elsevier Science.

Bielenski, Harald, and Alexandra Wagner. 2003. "Employment Options of Men and Women in Europe." In *Changing Life Patterns in Western Industrial Societies,* vol. 8 of *Advances in Life Course Research.* Edited by Janet Z. Giele and Elke Holst. London: Elsevier Science.

Blau, Francine D., Marianne A. Ferber, and Anne E. Winkler. 2002. *The Economics of Women, Men, and Work.* Upper Saddle River, NJ: Prentice-Hall.

Bonke, Jens, and Elke Koch-Weser. 2003. "The Welfare State and Time Allocation: Denmark, Italy, France, and Sweden." In *Changing Life Patterns in Western Industrial Societies,* vol. 8 of *Advances in Life Course Research.* Edited by Janet Z. Giele and Elke Holst. London: Elsevier Science.

Catalyst, Inc. 1999 and 2002. *Census of Women Corporate Officers and Top Earners.* New York: Author.

Fitzgerald, Louise F., Linda L. Collinsworth, and Melanie S. Harned. 2001. "Sexual Harassment." Pp. 993–994 in *Encyclopedia of Women and Gender.* Edited by Judith Worell. New York: Academic Press.

Institute for Women's Policy Research. 2002. *The Status of Women in the States.* Washington, DC: Author.

Johnston, David Cay. 2002. "Big Gender Gap for Big Wage Earners; Men Outearn Women in Million-Dollar Salaries." *New York Times,* May 20.

Letablier, Marie-Thérèse. 2003. "Work and Family Balance: Trade-Off in France." In *Changing Life Patterns in Western Industrial Societies,* vol. 8 of *Advances in Life Course Research.* Edited by Janet Z. Giele and Elke Holst. London: Elsevier Science.

New Strategist. 2002. *American Women: Who They Are & How They Live.* Ithaca, NY: New Strategist Publications.

Plantenga, Janneka. 2003. "New Working Time Arrangements in Six European Countries." In *Changing Life Patterns in Western Industrial Societies,* vol. 8 of *Advances in Life Course Research.* Edited by Janet Z. Giele and Elke Holst. London: Elsevier Science.

Rubery, Jill, Mark Smith, and Collette Fagan. 1999. *Women's Employment in Europe: Trends and Prospects.* London: Routledge.

Sonenstein, Freya L., et al. 2002. *Primary Childcare Arrangements of Employed Parents: Findings from the 1999 National Survey of America's Families.* Occasional Paper Number 59. Washington, DC: The Urban Institute.

Stebbins, Leslie F. 2001. *Work and Family in America: A Reference Handbook.* Santa Barbara, CA: ABC-CLIO.

Tietze, Wolfgang, and Debby Cryer. 1999. "Current Trends in European Early Child Care and Education." *Annals of the American Academy of Political and Social Science* 563: 175–193.

United Nations. 2000. *The World's Women 2000: Trends and Statistics.* New York: United Nations. ST/ESA/STAT/Social Statistics and Indicators, Series K, no. 16.

United States Bureau of Labor Statistics. 2001. "Education Pays." In *Working in the 21st Century.* Washington, DC: Author.

United States Bureau of the Census. 2001. *America's Families and Living Arrangements.* Washington, DC: Author.

United States Equal Employment Opportunity Commission. 2003. "Sex-Based Charges; Pregnancy Discrimination Charges; Sexual Harassment Charges, FY 1992–FY 2002." www.eeoc.gov/stats/sex.html; www.eeoc.gov/stats/pregnanc.html; www.eeoc.gov/stats/harass.html (accessed February 23, 2003).

6

Directory of Organizations

Many research, activist, and government organizations are
working on issues related to gender equity and employment. This chapter provides contact information and a con-
cise overview of the activities and research being carried out by
many of the larger organizations and research centers working in
the United States and in other countries on this topic.

This chapter is divided into three sections. The first section
contains an extensive list of organizations in the United States
that are involved in activities related to gender equity and employment. The second section lists academic programs available
in the United States that focus on gender and international development issues and that have gender and employment as one of
their areas of study. The third section provides a selected list of
some of the larger international organizations that focus on multiple countries and are involved in work related to gender equity
and employment.

It is beyond the scope of this book to list the numerous international organizations devoted to gender and human rights or
gender and development. Instead, organizations working on these
broader areas were selected for this chapter if they included substantive work related to employment as part of their objectives.
For more comprehensive lists of international organizations, the
National Council for Research on Women provides a list by country of international centers conducting research on women
(http://www.ncrw.org). The Division for the Advancement of
Women provides a list of nongovernmental organizations involved
in gender equality work (http://www.un.org/womenwatch/

daw). The International Labor Organization provides information organized by country, about groups working on equal employment opportunity and related issues (http://www.ilo. org). And, Michigan State University's Women and International Development Program provides a large list of organizations that focus on women and development work (http://www.isp.msu. edu/WID).

Organizations in the United States

American Association of University Women
1111 Sixteenth Street N.W.
Washington, DC 20036
(800) 326-AAUW
http://www.aauw.org

The American Association of University Women (AAUW) is a national organization that promotes education and equity for women and girls. It is composed of three entities. The Association itself lobbies for equity. It consists of 1,500 local branches across the United States. The Educational Foundation funds research on a variety of topics nationally and internationally. It is the largest source of funding in the world that focuses exclusively on female graduate students. The Legal Advocacy Fund provides support for women seeking judicial redress for sex discrimination in higher education. The AAUW is also affiliated with the International Federation of University Women. The AAUW's web site includes detailed information about their activities and a catalog of publications.

Association for Women in Mathematics
4114 Computer and Space Sciences Building
University of Maryland
College Park, MD 20742–2461
(301) 405–7892
http://www.awm-math.org

The purpose of the Association for Women in Mathematics (AWM) is to encourage women to study and have active careers in mathematics. Founded in 1971, AWM is a nonprofit organization that currently has more than 4,100 members from the United States and around the world. The organization provides a mentor network, awards grants and prizes to students and faculty in mathematics, sponsors an annual lecture, and is involved in policy affecting women in mathematics at the local and national level.

Association for Women in Science
1200 New York Avenue, Suite 650
Washington, DC 20005
(202) 326–8940
http://www.awis.org

Established in 1971, AWIS works to achieve equity and full participation for women in science, mathematics, engineering, and technology. Operating on both a national and local level, this nonprofit organization promotes women's activities in all scientific fields by providing mentoring opportunities, scholarships, job listings, and educational activities in schools and communities. AWIS publishes a magazine and other materials to inform women and girls about science programs and issues. In addition, it is involved in helping shape national policy in the area of women and science.

Business and Professional Women/USA
2012 Massachusetts Avenue N.W.
Washington, DC 20036
(202) 293–1100
http://www.bpwusa.org

The mission statement of Business and Professional Women (BPW) is "To achieve equity for all women in the workplace through advocacy, education, and information." Established in 1956, BPW provides networking opportunities, resources, and educational programs for its members. BPW has a network of more than 2,000 local organizations in the United States. It provides financial assistance to women seeking education to advance their careers or reenter the work force and conducts research on issues affecting women in the workplace. BPW sponsors annual conferences on policy issues and on academic issues relating to women and work.

Catalyst
120 Wall Street
New York, NY 10005
(212) 514–7600
http://www.catalystwomen.org

Catalyst is a nonprofit organization engaged in research and advisory activities that support women's advancement in business. Catalyst works with corporations to develop strategies related to the recruitment, retention, and advancement of women. In addition, Catalyst tracks and quantifies women's leadership development and career advancement. It sponsors an award to businesses engaged in providing opportunities for women to advance, and it provides a speakers' bureau and various publications on issues related to women and work. The organization's web site provides links to related organizations and resources.

Center for Women and Information Technology
1000 Hilltop Circle
University of Maryland-Baltimore County
Baltimore, MD 21250
(410) 455–2822
http://www.umbc.edu/cwit

Established at the University of Maryland-Baltimore County in 1998, the Center for Women and Information Technology (CWIT) seeks to increase the low numbers of women who pursue degrees in computer science and work in the information technology field. The center's mission is to encourage women and girls to study and pursue careers in information technology and to support research concerning the relationship between gender and computers. The center's web site provides curricular resources, a bibliography on women and technology, and information about the organization's speaker series.

Center for Women and Work
Rutgers, The State University
162 Ryders Lane
New Brunswick, NJ 08901–8555
(732) 932–1463 x 647
http://www.rci.rutgers.edu/~cww

The Center for Women and Work (CWW) was founded in 1993 and is part of the School of Management and Labor Relations at Rutgers University. Its mission is to address the needs of working women by conducting and disseminating research on working women and sponsoring educational programs geared toward working women, policymakers, corporate leaders, and activists. The center's work includes the Gender Parity Council, a collaborative effort with the New Jersey State Employment and Training Commission; a "college to career" mentoring program; the Senior Leadership Program for Professional Women; and a data bank with extensive data on women and work in New Jersey.

Center for Women and Work
University of Massachusetts-Lowell
Department of Regional Economic and Social Development
500 O'Leary Library
61 Wilder Street
Lowell, MA 01854
(978) 934–4380
http://www.uml.edu/centers/women-work

The Center for Women and Work (CWW) at the University of Massachusetts-Lowell is working toward improving the conditions of work and enhancing economic opportunities for women through interdisciplinary research, education, and social action. The center is also interested in investigating the relationship between women's work and the well being of communities. CWW is working to enhance women's position in the workplace and in the economy by working to improve the opportunities available to women and the ability of women to pursue these opportunities. Its web site includes extensive links to other organizations doing similar work, a collection of biographical sketches of notable women, a newsletter, and information about its annual forum.

Coalition of Labor Union Women
1925 K Street N.W., Suite 402
Washington, DC 20006
(202) 223–8360
http://www.cluw.org

Founded in 1974, the Coalition of Labor Union Women (CLUW) continues to work toward the goals of affirmative action in the workplace, increasing women's union membership, and encouraging participation of women within their unions. Specific issues that CLUW is involved in include child care, pay equity, national health care, and reproductive freedom. CLUW has more than seventy-five chapters across the country and is involved in public policy work through education, labor negotiations, and political action through the legislative process and the media.

Commission on Women in the Profession
American Bar Association
541 N. Fairbanks Court
Chicago, IL 60611
(312) 988–5522
http://www.abanet.org/women

The Commission on Women in the Profession (CWP) was created in 1987 to review the status of women in the legal profession and identify barriers to advancement. The goal of the commission is to secure the full and equal participation of women in the legal profession and the justice system. CWP develops programs, policies, and publications to assist women in law schools, public and private practice, and the judiciary. It is involved in issues such as gender equity, bias-free evaluation systems, the glass ceiling phenomenon, and other issues affecting women in the legal profession. Its web site includes a list of reports available through the American Bar Association and links to organizations involved in issues related to women and the legal profession.

Employment Policy Foundation
1015 Fifteenth Street N.W.
Washington, DC 20005
(202) 789–8685
http://www.epf.org

The Employment Policy Foundation (EPF) is a small, active think tank funded by corporate and individual donors. Its goal is to provide policymakers with information and analyses that "provide an alternative and more accurate view of the American economy and worker well-being than that portrayed by research studies that promote increased government regulation and other unfunded mandates in the workplace." EPF is actively opposed to the Living Wage Campaign, a local ordinance usually passed by a city to establish a wage floor for a specific group of workers. EPF also opposes paid family leave. Its web site contains numerous press releases and reports on issues relating to employment, including gender equity. In addition, the web site provides analysis questioning the concept of a gender gap in pay.

Equal Rights Advocates
1663 Mission Street, Suite 250
San Francisco, CA 94103

(415) 621–0672
http://www.equalrights.org

Equal Rights Advocates (ERA) was founded in 1974 as a teaching law firm focused on cases relating to sex-based discrimination. The goal of ERA is to protect and secure equal rights and economic opportunities for women and girls using litigation and advocacy. This legal organization uses impact litigation—cases that can affect large groups of women or that have the potential to create new laws. The organization has been involved in landmark cases, such as those involving the San Francisco firefighters and the U.S. Forest Service. Currently, it is involved in the national lawsuit of *Dukes v. Wal-Mart*, a case concerning women who were denied advancement opportunities, paid less than men for comparable work, and subjected to a hostile work environment. ERA also provides a hotline for women and girls to answer questions about sex discrimination and harassment. Its web site provides extensive links to related organizations, detailed information about their legal work, and a newsletter.

Independent Women's Forum
P.O. Box 3058
Arlington, VA 22203–0058
(800) 224–6000
http://www.iwf.org

The Independent Women's Forum (IWF) is a vocal nonprofit advocacy group established in 1992 that believes that individual liberty and the market economy, rather than government interventions, can better rectify inequalities. IWF rejects the view that women are the victims of oppression, challenges what it calls the myths of the glass ceiling and the wage gap, and argues against comparable worth legislation. It also views Title IX, a law established to provide equal educational opportunities to men and women, as being used inappropriately to establish gender quotas in sports. Recent issues of its magazine, *The Women's Quarterly*, and other publications and policy papers are available from the organization's web site.

Institute for Women and Work
16 East 34th Street, 4F
New York, NY 10016
(212) 340–2800
http://www.ilr.cornell.edu/extension/iww/

The Institute for Women and Work (IWW) is a program of the School of Industrial and Labor Relations at Cornell University. This applied research and educational resource center is concerned with issues relating to forces that affect women and work. IWW offers opportunities for women to develop skills, build support systems, and obtain technical assistance. The center's goals include influencing public policy; providing training; hosting seminars; and developing a network among workers, advocates, employers, students, and academics involved with issues concerning women and work. Specifically, it focuses on the restructured workplace and its impact on working families, corporate social responsibility, and labor law reform; and legislative initiatives on child care, contingent work, health care, women in nontraditional employment, and gender equality. Its web site includes research and data from a recent project on women in the construction trade, as well as news and articles issued from the program.

Institute for Women in Trades, Technology, and Science
1150 Ballena Boulevard, Suite 102
Alameda, CA 94501–3682
(510) 749–0200
http://www.iwitts.com

The Institute for Women in Trades, Technology, and Science (IWITTS) is a national nonprofit organization that works to integrate women into the full range of traditionally male careers such as the trades, technology, and science. Founded in 1994 as New Traditions for Women, the group receives funding from foundations, federal and state government contracts, and fee-for-service training. It provides demonstration projects, training for educators and employers, resource publications and videos, and assessments of the workplace environment for employers. Most of its activities are geared toward finding a way to educate, train, recruit, and retain women pursuing traditionally male-dominated careers. Its activities include support for women as well as assistance for workplaces interested in improving their work environment. IWITTS has worked extensively with law enforcement agencies and has also provided assistance in community colleges for technology training for women.

Institute for Women's Policy Research
1707 L Street N.W., Suite 750
Washington, DC 20036
(202) 785–5100
http://www.iwpr.org

The Institute for Women's Policy Research is a nonprofit public policy research organization that focuses on issues that are important to women and their families. Its main areas of interest are poverty and welfare, employment, work and family issues, the economic and social aspects of health care and domestic violence, and women's civic and political participation. The employment issues the institute studies include pay equity, the wage gap, part-time and contingent work, and women in management. The organization works with scholars, public interest groups, and policymakers to conduct and disseminate research on policy issues that affect women and families. The institute is affiliated with the graduate programs in women's studies and public policy at George Washington University.

National Association of Working Women, 9 to 5
231 West Wisconsin Avenue, No. 900
Milwaukee, WI 53203
(800) 522–0925
http://www.9to5.org

Founded in 1973, 9 to 5 is a grassroots organization that supports working women. It provides a hotline to answer questions and provide support on issues such as sexual harassment, family leave, and pregnancy discrimination. The group also advocates for family leave, and it seeks to reduce sexual harassment and other forms of discrimination in the workplace through training programs and changes in public policy. The organization is also involved in welfare policy and treatment of nonstandard (temporary or part-time) workers. Its web site provides facts and statistics about working women, a speaker's bureau, publications for order, and information about women's rights on the job.

National Committee on Pay Equity
1126 Sixteenth Street N.W., Suite 411
Washington, DC 20036
(202) 331–7343
http://www.feminist.com/fairpay

Founded in 1979, the National Committee on Pay Equity is a national membership coalition of more than 180 organizations working to eliminate sex- and race-based wage discrimination. Their goal is to achieve pay equity. The committee is involved in educating the general public about inequities in pay by gender and race. It provides leadership, information, and assistance to pay equity advocates, public officials, employers, the media, and the public. Membership dues and donations fund their activities. Fact sheets and a list of publications that can be ordered are available from the committee's web site.

National Council for Research on Women
11 Hanover Square
New York, NY 10005
(212) 785–7335
www.ncrw.org

The National Council for Research on Women is a working alliance of ninety-two women's research and policy centers, more than 3,000 affiliates, and a network of more than 200 international centers. Founded in 1981, its mission is to strengthen the connections among research, policy analysis, advocacy, and programming on behalf of women and girls. The council embraces a wide variety of research and advocacy topics including women in engineering, healthy development of adolescent girls, and global issues such as the international women's movement. Its web site has an extensive list of international centers for research on women that includes more than 300 organizations in more than eighty countries.

National Council of Women's Organizations
733 15th Street N.W., Suite 1011
Washington, DC 20005
(202) 393–7122
http://www.womensorganizations.org

The National Council of Women's Organizations (NCWO) focuses on promoting public policy issues of interest to the more than 100 organizations and more than 6 million members that it represents. The organization's members include grassroots, research, service, and legal advocacy groups. The council works on a broad spectrum of issues including equal employment opportunity, economic equity and development, education, job training, and health. The board meets bimonthly, and task forces are appointed to work on specific issues. Reports and facts sheets on a wide range of issues are available on the web site.

National Partnership for Women and Families
1875 Connecticut Avenue N.W., Suite 710
Washington, DC 20009
(202) 986–2600
http://www.nationalpartnership.org

Founded in 1971 as the Women's Legal Defense Fund, the National Partnership for Women and Families (NPWF) is a nonprofit organization that uses public education and advocacy to help women and men meet the dual demands of work and family. NPWF works with business, government, unions, and other organizations to develop solutions to work and family issues. It is also involved in promoting fairness in the workplace and working for quality health care. This group assisted in passing the Pregnancy Discrimination Act of 1978, helped win one of the landmark cases that made sexual harassment illegal in 1977, wrote the first draft of the Family and Medical Leave Act in 1984, and worked with other groups to pass that law. Currently, it is working on expanding the coverage of the FMLA to cover more working people.

National Women's Law Center
11 Dupont Circle, Suite 800
Washington, DC 20036
(202) 588–5180
http://www.nwlc.org

The National Women's Law Center (NWLC) was founded in 1972 to protect and advance the progress of women and girls in school, at work, and in other aspects of their lives. The center focuses on family economic security, health, employment, and education. It is active in public policy research, litigation, advocacy, coalition building, and public education. The center's work in the area of gender equity and employment includes strengthening and enforcing the laws and policies against discrimination in the workplace including equal pay, sexual harassment, and pregnancy discrimination. NWLC is also involved in child support enforcement programs, improving Social Security for women who have been the primary unpaid caretakers for their families, working toward ensuring the provision of affordable high-quality child care, and promoting equality in education and health services.

Program on Gender, Work, and Family
American University-Washington College of Law
4801 Massachusetts Avenue N.W.
Washington, DC 20016
(202) 274–4494
http://www.wcl.american.edu/gender/workfamily

The Program on Gender, Work, and Family was founded in 1998 as a research and advocacy center based at American University-Washington College of Law. The program works to decrease the economic vulnerability of parents and children by restructuring workplaces, and it works to change societal norms and practices to assist parents and other family caregivers in pursuing both work and family care goals. The group helps employers to develop family-friendly policies, provides resources for family caregivers, provides technical guidance to policymakers and lawyers, and works with the press to document both common problems facing caregivers and model employer programs that are helping employees meet their dual responsibilities.

U.S. Equal Employment Opportunity Commission
1801 L Street, N.W.
Washington, DC 20507
(800) 669–4000
http://www.eeoc.gov

The Equal Employment Opportunity Commission (EEOC) was established in 1965 to work toward the elimination of illegal discrimination in the workplace by actively enforcing federal legislation prohibiting discrimination in employment. Its web site provides information on federal laws prohibiting job discrimination, how to file a discrimination complaint, federal statistics on job discrimination and related issues, and training and technical assistance programs offered throughout the country.

Wider Opportunities for Women
815 15th Street N.W., Suite 916
Washington, DC 20005
(202) 638–3143
http://www.wowonline.org

Founded more than thirty years ago, Wider Opportunities for Women (WOW) is a women's employment organization that works to achieve economic independence and equality for women and girls. WOW focuses on providing education for women, with an emphasis on literacy, technical training, and nontraditional skills training. WOW oversees three projects: the State Organizing Project for Family Economic Self-Sufficiency, which provides technical assistance; Work4Women, which supports women's access to high-wage nontraditional occupations; and Workplace Solutions, a web-based assistance network that helps employers and unions increase the numbers of women that work in nontraditional jobs.

Women's Bureau
U.S. Department of Labor
200 Constitution Avenue N.W.
Room No. S-3002
Washington, DC 20210
(800) 827–5335
http://www.dol.gov/dol/wb

Established by Congress in 1920, the Women's Bureau is mandated to represent the needs of working women to policymakers. The Women's Bureau identifies issues that are important to working women and investigates ways of addressing these needs. It publishes fact sheets on the status of female workers and provides resources for addressing problems in the workplace. In the past, the bureau has been involved in the issue of pay equity and ending pay discrimination. Under the Bush administration, the bureau is currently focusing its efforts on helping girls and women gain information technology skills in order to provide them with access to better-paying jobs and "to help women balance their work and career goals with the other priorities in their lives." The web site provides access to the full text of recent publications, news, and statistics from the bureau.

Graduate Programs Pertaining to Women and International Development

Clark University, Department of International Development
Carlson Hall, 950 Main Street
Worcester, MA 01610

(508) 793–7201

http://www.clarku.edu/departments/idce/id/grad/index.html

The Department of International Development at Clark involves both an undergraduate and a graduate cross-disciplinary program with an applied research orientation. Using the perspectives of anthropologists, political scientists, economists, historians, sociologists, and geographers, the program focuses on relations between industrialized and developing countries in terms of poverty, equity, justice, and environmental sustainability. The department's web site includes news and information about its program.

Cornell University, Program on Gender and Global Change
310 Triphammer Road
Ithaca, NY 14853–2801
(607) 255–0532
http://www.arts.cornell.edu/womens/G.G.C.htm

The Program on Gender and Global Change is a multidisciplinary and interdisciplinary program focused on comparative historical analyses of changing patterns of gender relations. PGGC is part of the Einaudi Center for International Studies and coordinates its initiatives with the Women's Studies program and the African, Asian, and Latin American Studies programs. PGGC is not a degree-granting program. Its web site includes detailed information about courses, history, and upcoming conferences.

Monterey Institute of International Studies
Gender and Development Certificate Program
Graduate School of International Policy Studies
425 Van Buren Street
Monterey, CA 93920
(831) 647–6519
http://www.miis.edu

The Gender and Development Certificate Program offers certification in this area for graduate students at the Monterey Institute of International Studies, in conjunction with one of their master's degree programs. The web site includes information about the programs.

Ohio State University, Association of Women in Development
Mershon Center for Studies in
International Security and Public Policy
1501 Neil Avenue
Columbus, OH 43201
(614) 292–2161
http://www.womens-studies.ohio-state.edu/osuwid

The Association of Women in Development is a member of the Association for Women's Rights in Development. Housed at Ohio State, it serves as a resource for information on gender issues in development, organizing, jobs, internships, grants, publications, conferences, and other events. Its web site provides links to resources on women in development, activism and organizing, and relevant research and academic programs.

Oregon State University, Women
in International Development Program
Office of International Research and Development
Snell Hall 400
Corvallis, OR 97331–1641
(541) 737–6406
http://www.osu.orst.edu/international/oird/wid.html

The Women in International Development Program at Oregon State University focuses on empowering women through collaborative projects and knowledge exchange. The program runs the WID (Women in International Development) Network, which disseminates information about opportunities, lectures, other events, and publications relating to women and development. The program also assists faculty with curriculum development, organizes and hosts a seminar series, and maintains a library and resource center. Its web site contains additional information about the program.

Rutgers Center for Women's Global Leadership
Douglass College
160 Ryders Lane
New Brunswick, NJ 08901–8555
(732) 932–8782
http://www.cwgl.rutgers.edu

The Center for Women's Global Leadership develops women's

leadership initiatives for women's human rights and social justice worldwide. It is a unit of the Institute for Women's Leadership, a consortium of six women's programs at Rutgers University created to study and promote how and why women lead and to develop programs that prepare women of all ages to lead effectively. Information about the center's two programs (Policy and Advocacy, and Leadership Development and Global Education) are available on its web site. The site also contains the full text of articles, reports and news, and a collection of links related to women's human rights.

University of Arizona, Gender and Development Program
Bureau of Applied Research in Anthropology
Haury Building, Room 316
Tucson, AZ 85721–0030
(520) 621–6282
http://bara.arizona.edu/g_and_d.htm

The Gender and Development Program is part of the Bureau of Applied Research in Anthropology (BARA) at the University of Arizona. Funded in part by the Women in Development Office of USAID (U.S. Agency for International Development) and other development agencies, BARA carries out gender-focused research throughout the developing world. BARA works to promote the valuation of women's and girls' economic contribution in both the formal and informal sectors. The Gender and Development Program collaborates with international researchers to develop programs that enhance women's legal rights and access to education and technology. In addition, the program offers academic coursework that explores the theoretical and practical foundations of gender and development. More information about BARA can be found on its web site.

University of Florida, Center for
Women's Studies and Gender Research
3324 Turlington Hall, P.O. Box 117352
Gainesville, FL 32611
(352) 392–3365
http://web.wst.ufl.edu

The Center for Women's Studies and Gender Research offers a certificate in Gender and Development. The center provides an interdisciplinary forum for the study of gender, its function in cultures and societies, and its intersection with race and class. Information about this program is available from its web site.

University of Illinois at Chicago,
Center for Research on Women and Gender
1640 W. Roosevelt Road, Room 503
Chicago, IL 60608
(312) 413–1924
http://www.uic.edu/depts/crwg/outline.htm

The Center for Research on Women and Gender (CRWG) is a collaborative multidisciplinary program among researchers from the Colleges of Nursing, Liberal Arts and Sciences, Medicine, and Social Work, and the School of Public Health. This program serves in a supportive role to faculty interested in pursuing research in areas related to women and gender. Its web site includes newsletters, center-sponsored events, and detailed information about supported projects.

University of Illinois at Urbana-Champaign,
Women and Gender in Global Perspectives Program
320 International Studies Building
910 S. Fifth Street
Champaign, IL 61820
(217) 333–1977
http://www.ips.uiuc.edu/wggp

Women and Gender in Global Perspectives (WGGP) is an academic unit in the International Programs and Studies division of the University of Illinois at Urbana-Champaign. The program facilitates the development of research, teaching, and service activities focused on the role of women in developing countries and the impact of international development on women, men, and children throughout the world. The program's activities include teaching and mentoring students, supporting and carrying out research projects, and providing opportunities for dialogue through symposia, seminars, and newsletters. Its web site includes a history of the program and an extensive list of sponsored programs and seminars.

University of Minnesota, International
Women's Rights Action Watch
Hubert H. Humphrey Institute of Public Affairs

310 19th Avenue S.
Minneapolis, MN 55455
(612) 625–5093
http://www.igc.org/iwraw

International Women's Rights Action Watch (IWRAW) is an international resource and communications center that serves activists, scholars, and organizations that focus on the advancement of women's human rights. IWRAW is part of the Humphrey Institute of Public Affairs at the University of Minnesota. The program provides technical assistance and research support for women's human rights projects such as law reform, policy advocacy, and monitoring government performance under international human rights treaties. The program sponsors the *Women's Watch* newsletter; provides information, training, and technical assistance to activists, scholars, and other concerned individuals and groups that work at national and local levels on convention implementation; produces reports on women's human rights issues; and sponsors international gatherings for exchange of experience and strategies.

**Women and International Development
Program at Michigan State University**
202 International Center
Michigan State University
East Lansing, MI 48824
(517) 353–5040
http://www.isp.msu.edu/WID

Michigan State's program was established in 1978. It promotes teaching, research, and action on international development as it affects women and gender relations. Its primary focus is the Southern Hemisphere. It is one of the largest and oldest academic centers in the United States focusing on gender and development. In addition to information about the program, its web site includes a working paper series, bulletin, policy briefs, a list of links to women's organizations throughout the world, an audiovisual resource guide, and annotated bibliographies on topics related to women and international development.

**Women in the Informal Economy Globalizing
and Organizing, Harvard University**
Carr Center for Human Rights/Kennedy School of Government

79 John F. Kennedy Street
Cambridge, MA 02138
(617) 495–7639
http://www.wiego.org

Established in 1997, Women in the Informal Economy Globalizing and Organizing (WIEGO) is a worldwide coalition of organizations and individuals working to improve the status of women in the economy's informal sector, which remains largely invisible in official statistics and policies. WIEGO attempts to compile statistics, conduct research, and develop policies relating to this sector. WIEGO is involved in the following areas: urban policies relating to street vendors, the impact of globalization and trade liberalization on female workers, social protection systems for female workers in the informal sector, and organization and representation to strengthen the voice of women in the informal economy. WIEGO also works with the statistical divisions of the United Nations and the International Labor Organization. Its web site includes fact sheets, annual reports, papers, news and events, and links to related web sites.

International Organizations

Coalition for Women's Economic Development and Global Equality

1825 Connecticut Avenue N.W., Suite 800
Washington, DC 20009
(202) 884–8396
http://www.womensedge.org

The Coalition for Women's Economic Development and Global Equality (Women's EDGE) is an activist organization that seeks to mobilize American women and men through educational activities. It provides current information about how women's lives in developing countries are being impacted by U.S. policies relating to trade and development. With both individuals and organizations as members, Women's EDGE promotes equitable international aid and trade policies. Its membership is made up of international aid agencies, domestic women's groups, human rights organizations, and think tanks, and Women's EDGE regularly collaborates with women's organizations from other countries. Its web site includes a list of publications, links to related resources, and current statistics on women and development.

European Women's Lobby
18 Rue Hydraulique
B-1210 Brussels, Belgium
32 2 217 90 20
http://www.womenlobby.org

European Women's Lobby (EWL) is a coordinating body of European nongovernmental women's organizations in the European Union. It consists of more than 3,000 member organizations in the fifteen EU member states. Its goal is to eliminate all forms of discrimination against women and to serve as a link between policymakers and women's organizations at the EU level. Its web site includes detailed information about ongoing policies and campaigns relating to gender equality in employment and many other areas such as health, human rights, violence against women, environmental concerns, education, and the needs of female children. The web site also contains a list of organizations it is affiliated with by country and detailed information about EWL's campaigns.

European Women's Management Development
International Office
Mainzer Straße 52
65185 Wiesbaden, Germany
49 (0) 611 / 900 97 17
http://www.ewmd.org

European Women's Management Development (EWMD) is an international network of individuals and corporations representing all areas of business, education, and politics. Founded in 1984, EWMD works to improve the quality of management with respect to people, age, and cultural diversity, including balancing work and family life. The organization's focus is on local practices. Though it was started in Europe, members now come from more than twenty-five countries around the world. Members share knowledge and experience of management practices that are suitable for all people. EWMD seeks to increase the number of women in management by using benchmarking in all fields, identifying barriers to women's professional development, and promoting and sharing information about best practices for work-life balance.

Global Fund for Women
1375 Sutter Street, Suite 400
San Francisco, CA 94109
(415) 202–7640
http://www.globalfundforwomen.org

The Global Fund for Women is a grant-making foundation that provides assistance to grassroots women's groups around the world. The fund consists of an international network of women and men committed to world equality. It provides grants to seed women's rights groups based outside the United States working to address human rights issues. Its web site includes profiles of supported organizations, grant applications, publications and resources, and links to related sites. The web site is available in seven languages.

Inter-American Commission of Women
Permanent Mission of the United States to the OAS
WHA/USOAS, Suite 5914
Department of State
Washington, DC 20520
(202) 647–9907
http://www.oas.org/cim/default.htm

The Inter-American Commission of Women (CIM) is a specialized organization of the Organization of American States established in 1928. The purpose of CIM is to ensure recognition of the civil and political rights of women. CIM is made up of thirty-four permanent delegates, one for each member nation. The organization plays an important role in making the participation and support of women a legitimate part of governance and international consensus building in the Americas. CIM provides support to national women's movements of all levels. It has provided support for conventions supporting women's equal political participation and against violence directed toward women. The CIM web site includes a history of the organization; key documents, reports, and conventions related to its work; text of assemblies and resolutions; and information about projects that CIM has funded.

International Federation of University Women
8 rue de l'Ancien-Port
CH-1201 Geneva, Switzerland
41 22 731 23 80
http://www.ifuw.org

International Federation of University Women (IFUW) is an international nongovernmental organization of more than 180,000 female university graduates from seventy-two associations throughout the world. Founded in 1919, IFUW works to promote the rights of women and girls to education in order to reach their full potential. The group advocates for the improvement of the status of women and girls and enables graduate women to use their expertise to effect change. IFUW provides a study and action program that allows female graduates a voice in international policymaking settings such as the United Nations, and it assists in creating projects that help women and girls. It provides a network to connect female graduates from around the world to facilitate working toward common goals. Its web page contains newsletters and reports, information about current projects, and links to related organizations and resources.

International Labor Organization
4, route des Morillons
CH-1211 Geneva 22, Switzerland
41.22.799.6111
http://www.ilo.org; http://www.ilo.org/public/english/
bureau/gender/index.htm

International Labor Organization (ILO) is a United Nations specialized agency that "seeks the promotion of social justice and internationally recognized human and labour rights." The ILO is responsible for formulating international labor minimum standards on all kinds of labor rights and work-related issues, including equality of opportunity and treatment. ILO also provides technical assistance in the areas of employment policy, labor law and industrial relations, working conditions, management development, labor statistics, and many other areas. ILO maintains an extensive collection of resources on their web page including e.quality@work, a database containing resources on gender equality laws, policies, and programs. It also sponsors a large bibliographic database, Labordoc, which provides access to 250,000 citations to books, journal articles, and other documents, and Laborsta, a database of labor statistics. In addition, the ILO has a special Bureau on Gender Equality, the goals of which include equal remuneration for work of equal value and a statement against discrimination in employment. The web page for the bureau includes information about the work of the ILO in relation to gender equity issues.

International Labor Rights Fund
733 15th Street N.W., #920
Washington, DC 20005
(202) 347–4100
http://www.laborrights.org

International Labor Rights Fund (ILRF) is an advocacy organization working to achieve humane treatment for workers worldwide. ILRF has numerous campaigns concerning child labor, forced labor, and sweatshops. Its new campaign, "Rights for Working Women," seeks to alleviate labor conditions that disproportionately affect women workers in developing countries; the campaign uses research, education, litigation, and legislative action. One main focus of this campaign is the issue of workplace sexual harassment. The program will focus on Kenya and, later, the Caribbean, Latin America, and southeast Asia. The web site includes news releases, information on current campaigns, publications, and a list of useful links.

Office of Women in Development
Bureau for Global Programs, Field Support, and Research
United States Agency for International Development
Washington, DC 20523–3801
(202) 712–0570
http://www.usaid.gov/wid

Office of Women in Development (WID) was created in 1974 to make sure that women participate and benefit equally from U.S. development programs. WID assists USAID by helping integrate gender concerns into all USAID programs and identifying emerging issues relating to gender. The goals of WID are to enhance the economic status of women in developing countries, expand educational opportunities for women and girls, improve women's legal rights and increase their participation in policymaking, and ensure that gender concerns are attended to throughout USAID programs. Specifically, WID offers technical assistance and training for USAID programs and promotes gender issues through publications and conferences. Its web site contains detailed information about current projects, the full text of newsletters and reports issued by WID, and an extensive list of links to related sites concerning gender issues.

United Nations Development Fund for Women
304 E. 45th Street, 15th Floor
New York, NY 10017
(212) 906–6400
http://www.unifem.org

United Nations Development Fund for Women (UNIFEM) was founded in 1976 to promote gender equality throughout the world. It acts as a catalyst within the United Nations system to ensure the participation of women in all levels of development planning at the country level through the United Nations Resident Coordinator System. UNIFEM has been involved in many projects throughout the developing world that promote improved working conditions and the creation and enforcement of gender-sensitive laws and marketing systems. Using thirteen Regional Program Advisors, UNIFEM works to develop and support female entrepreneurs, increase women's participation in decisionmaking processes, and promote women's human rights. Since the 1995 U.N. Fourth World Conference on Women in Beijing, UNIFEM has also worked to support implementation of the platform developed at that conference. Its web site includes press releases and newsletters reporting on current activities, detailed information about past and upcoming conferences and meetings, and a catalog of publications available for purchase.

United Nations Division for the Advancement of Women
2 UN Plaza, DC2–12th Floor
New York, NY 10017
(212) 963–3463
http://www.un.org/womenwatch/daw

United Nations Division for the Advancement of Women (DAW) advocates for equality for women throughout the world. As a division of the United Nations system, DAW seeks to ensure that women can serve as equal partners with men in all types of activities, including education and employment. DAW conducts research, develops policy options, and provides information to U.N. intergovernmental organizations. It attempts to promote communication between international and national policymaking processes and has been a key player during the World Conferences on Women held every five years. DAW works closely with the Committee on the Elimination of all Forms of Discrimination against Women and with the U.N. Commission on the Status of Women. DAW's web site includes press releases, extensive information from the Beijing + 5 women's conference, text and reports from meetings, an annotated list of publications, and information about various countries and their implementation of U.N. initiatives relating to gender equality.

United Nations Gender in Development Program
UNDP Liaison Office
1775 K Street N.W., Suite 420
Washington, DC 20006
(202) 331–9130
http://www.undp.org/gender

Started in 1987, the United Nations Gender in Development Program (GIDP) advises and facilitates the United Nations Development Programme's gender equality policy and practice and promotes the empowerment of women. GIDP is a unit within the Bureau for Development Policy (BDP). It furthers the BDP mandate to support innovation through pilot country initiatives on gender mainstreaming. GIDP is responsible for ensuring that women and men participate equally in the development process as agents and as beneficiaries. Its duties include the implementation of the Beijing Platform and the Convention on the Elimination of All Forms of Discrimination commitments. The web site includes a detailed description of the role of GIDP, a Gender Briefing Kit, publications and reports produced by GIDP and other United Nations organizations, and a list of links to related resources.

**United Nations International Research
and Training Institute for the Advancement of Women**
Calle César Nicolás Penson 102-A
Santo Domingo, Dominican Republic
(809) 685–2111
http://www.un-instraw.org

United Nations International Research and Training Institute for the Advancement of Women (INSTRAW) was established in 1976 to promote gender equality and women's advancement worldwide through research, training, and communication. It recently developed a methodology called the Gender Awareness Information and Networking System (GAINS), which functions as a "virtual community" using information technology to manage and communicate knowledge and assist researchers in conducting collaborative research and information sharing in the area of gender equality. GAINS consists of four separate networks of organizations from around the world that share and disseminate information. INSTRAW serves at the international level to assist intergovernmental, governmental, and nongovernmental organizations in advancing gender equality. Its web site includes a database of more than 1,000 resources relating to gender research, and a catalog of their publications.

7

Selected Print Resources

This chapter contains descriptions of recently published books related to gender equity and employment and a comprehensive list of journals that frequently publish articles related to this area of study. The book titles were selected with the goal of including recent works that have made significant contributions to the study of gender equity and employment. The list includes titles from a wide variety of disciplines and perspectives within the social sciences.

The selections are categorized by broad subject area.

Books

General Overview and History of Gender and Employment

Amott, Teresa, and Julie Matthaei. 1996. *Race, Gender and Work: A Multi-Cultural Economic History of Women in the United States.* Boston, MA: South End. 454p. ISBN 092168990X, $18.00.

Amott and Mattaei, both economists, provide a broad overview of the social and economic factors that differentiate women's experiences in the labor force. The authors see gender, race and ethnicity, and class as interrelated factors that influence women's experiences in the labor force. The book is organized by different racial and ethnic groups and examines the experiences of the six largest racial/ethnic groups in the United States. Each chapter begins with one group's earliest experiences in the United States and ends in the 1990s. The employment stories of each group are placed in historical context so that the book provides a history of labor, political, and civil rights movements in the United States in addition to telling the story of women and work. The final section of the book is devoted to an analysis of comparative statistics on paid work that highlights the structural inequalities in labor markets and describes the connection between racial and gender discrimination. By demonstrating the diversity of women's experiences in the United States and pulling together the common themes, the authors advocate for a unified front in the battle for equality at work.

Bergmann, Barbara. 1986. *The Economic Emergence of Women.* New York: Basic. 384p. ISBN 0312219415, $17.00.

Bergmann, an economist, uses both economic and sociological theory to explain occupational segregation by sex. Her thesis is that self-interested men (both employees and employers) and some women enforce sex segregated work roles, with the higher-paid jobs going to men. Women are relegated to lower-paying, lower-status positions with less chance for training and advancement. Bergmann draws upon case law and documents, as well as sociological research, to support her work. The book provides extensive policy recommendations for decreasing discrimination and reducing occupational segregation. In particular, Bergmann explores affirmative action and pay equity in detail, explaining the differences between the two policy options. She outlines the key affirmative action measures that have become law, beginning with the passage of Title VII of the Civil Rights Act of 1964, and makes clear what behaviors are considered to be discrimination under Title VII. Bergmann advocates for affirmative action as being more effective than policies for equal pay.

Blau, Francine D., Marianne A. Ferber, and Anne E. Winkler. 2002. *The Economics of Women, Men, and Work.* 4th edition. Upper Saddle River, NJ: Prentice-Hall. 446p. ISBN 0135659795, $68.00.

Blau and Ferber published the first edition of this textbook in 1986. Winkler, also an economist, joins them in this fourth edition of their work. Though the book primarily uses neoclassical economic explanations to describe how the labor market operates, it critiques these theories and brings in other economic and sociological theoretical analyses as well. The book explores the allocation of time between household labor and outside employment, and the complex issues of occupation and earnings differentials between men and women. Chapter 2 provides a comprehensive historical analysis of women's work roles both within the family and in paid employment, using the work of anthropologists and biologists in addition to work by economists and sociologists. Later chapters focus on gender differences in occupations, earnings, and unemployment and the economic theories that attempt to explain these differences. Extensive analyses of supply-side or human capital explanations and demand-side or "discrimination" models are provided. The last chapter gives international comparative data and analysis as well and examines carefully the problems inherent in using comparative analysis. One conclusion the authors draw is that a major obstacle to equality between men and women may lie more with the unequal distribution of labor within the home rather than with problems that occur within the workplace, although they observe that progress is occurring on the home front.

Dubeck, Paula J., and Kathryn Borman, eds. 1996. *Women and Work: A Handbook.* New York: Garland. 592p. ISBN 0824076478, $80.00.

In 150 articles by different authors, this large compilation presents an overview of research on women and work. Included are sections covering labor force participation, different methodologies and approaches to the topic, women in diverse occupations, factors influencing career choice, legal issues relating to women and work, women's work experiences within different organizations, cross-cultural and international comparisons, and work and family issues. The authors have selected articles that reflect the experiences of women from diverse racial, ethnic, and economic backgrounds.

Goldin, Claudia D. 1990. *Understanding the Gender Gap: An Economic History of American Women.* New York: Oxford University Press. 328p. ISBN 0195072707, $34.95.

Goldin, an economist at Harvard, looks at the economic history of American women in the labor market from 1776 to the present, using economic theory, econometrics, and a close examination of the historical literature. In the first part of the book, Goldin uses newly collected data to analyze long-term trends. These trends show a change over time in women's labor force participation that is U-shaped, with a decline until the end of the nineteenth century and an increase (first by single women and later by married women) in the twentieth century. Goldin uses this historical analysis to investigate the pay gap between women and men and concludes that, although the pay gap remained fairly constant between 1950 and 1980, this was a short-term trend. Other than this period, throughout history the pay gap has gradually narrowed over time. The remainder of the book focuses on interpreting the reasons for the pay gap and its gradual decline. Wage discrimination, economic explanations, and the effects of legislation and case law are evaluated against particular historical periods. Goldin is optimistic that the larger trend toward a decrease in the pay gap will continue, though she also points to the need for further legislation and social change.

Kanter, Rosabeth Moss. 1977. *Men and Women of the Corporation.* New York: Basic. 384p. ISBN 0465044549, $22.00.

Kanter, a professor of business administration at Harvard Business School, wrote this seminal book about men and women and their changing roles in corporate America. In it, she argues that productivity, motivation, and career success are determined largely by organizational structure and a person's social circumstances. This means that differences between male and female workers have more to do with how they are treated by the organization than inherent differences in their abilities. Kanter argues that the problem in organizations is that women are not being treated equally for a variety of reasons, including sex-typed beliefs held by managers; the fact that so many women are in lower-status jobs; and the fact that very few women are in the upper levels of management or, when they are, they are such a small minority it is difficult for them to gain legitimacy and acceptance. Kanter recommends that the focus should be on fixing the corporations rather than changing the individuals. Decades have passed since the publication of this important book, and many of Kanter's recommended organizational changes have been implemented to some degree, though there is still a great deal of ground to cover.

Kessler-Harris, Alice. 2003. *Out to Work: A History of Wage-Earning Women in the United States.* 20th anniversary edition.

Oxford, UK: Oxford University Press. 416p. ISBN 0195157095, $19.95.

Historian Kessler-Harris has written a comprehensive history of American wage-earning women. This pioneering work, originally published in 1982, traces women's relationship to paid work from Colonial America to the present, providing an analysis of the research conducted in this area of study. Chapters include such topics as the movement from household manufacturing to outside employment, advances in technology, protective legislation, and the impact of the two world wars and the Great Depression. Kessler-Harris explores the effects of class, ethnic, and racial patterns and the changing perceptions of women in the work force and the relationship between paid employment and family roles. The twentieth anniversary edition has been updated and includes a new afterword by the author.

Reskin, Barbara, and Irene Padavic. 2002. *Women and Men at Work.* 2nd edition. Thousand Oaks, CA: Pine Forge. 227p. ISBN 076198710X, $27.95.

Originally published in 1994, Reskin and Padavic's book concisely summarizes the vast sociological and related literature on gender and work from a broad cross-cultural and historical perspective. They include a history of the sexual division of labor from preindustrial Europe to the present time, though most of the focus is on conditions in the United States. Three types of gender inequality are explored, and the authors give an overview of the explanations and current research on these topics, which include occupational sex segregation, gender differences in promotion and managerial responsibilities, and gender differences in pay. The authors also provide an analysis of the construction of the gendered workplace, and specific examples of sexual harassment incidents serve as illustrations. They conclude with an overview of current research on family and employment and future trends in gendered work roles.

Pay Equity, Occupational Sex Segregation, and Comparable Worth

Acker, Joan. 1989. *Doing Comparable Worth: Gender, Class, and Pay Equity.* Philadelphia: Temple University Press. 272p. ISBN 0877228345, $22.95.

Joan Acker, a professor of sociology at the University of Oregon, links feminist theory to a qualitative analysis of the battle for a comparable worth wage policy for state employees in Oregon. Like many other states working for comparable wage policies for state or municipal employees, Oregon's effort went through several attempts at legislation before a somewhat watered-down version of comparable worth was passed by the legislature in 1987. Acker's analysis looks closely at gender and class conflict in the state wage-setting system. Major stumbling blocks in Oregon included the threat posed by flattening or reducing the hierarchical structure of the organization if most female workers were suddenly paid higher wages, and the issue of most women benefiting and most men not benefiting from this legislation. Acker provides a clear picture of the goals of managers, unionists, and many politicians who link gender subordination to class subordination. This linkage explains why the legislation that finally passed in Oregon, like that in other areas, provided moderate pay increases for some women but did not achieve the broader goal of equal pay for comparable work.

England, Paula. 1992. *Comparable Worth: Theories and Evidence.* New York: Aldine de Gruyter. 346p. ISBN 0202303489, $28.95.

England, a sociologist at Northwestern University, provides a comprehensive interdisciplinary analysis of gender inequity at work and of the use of comparable worth policies to correct this inequity. England is a strong supporter of comparable worth policies, and she garners economic, philosophical, and legal evidence to provide support for these policies. England gives an overview of the major economic and sociological labor market theories explaining pay inequity and questions the ability of market forces to reduce discriminatory practices that have become so culturally ingrained. She then reviews the data used to calculate the pay gap, and concludes that at least 5 to 10 percent of the wage gap is due to gender bias. Occupations that are predominantly female are paid less, not because of the skills involved, but simply because they are female-dominated jobs. In reviewing recent court rulings, England is not optimistic that comparable worth will be accomplished through the legal system. Her final chapter summarizes the stands taken by all the players in this debate by creating a fictionalized dialogue between a corporate executive, a religious conservative, a socialist-feminist, and a sociologist. She concludes that equality requires both women's entry into nontraditional occupations and revaluing and increasing the rewards involved in traditionally female-dominated work.

Jacobs, Jerry A. 1989. *Revolving Doors: Sex Segregation and Women's Careers.* Palo Alto, CA: Stanford University Press. 230p. ISBN 0804718148, $17.95.

Jacobs, a sociologist at the University of Pennsylvania, provides an overview of the extent of occupational segregation by gender that has persisted throughout the past century. He explains and evaluates the two main sociological theories that are used to explain this persistence of occupational segregation: socialization theory and human capital theory. Jacobs then pulls together data from the National Longitudinal Surveys of Young and Mature Women, the Current Population Survey, and additional data to challenge these two theories. He demonstrates that a large number of women move in and out of male-dominated professions during their working lives, which means that socialization is not causing women to choose female-dominated jobs. In addition, Jacobs found that many women aspire to jobs that are male-dominated, even if they do not actually succeed in acquiring these positions. Jacobs also points out that women have historically moved quickly into male-dominated jobs whenever they were given the opportunity. Jacobs's "revolving door" idea refers to the fact that for every eleven women who enter a male-dominated occupation, ten of them end up leaving. The women leave due to discrimination and sexual harassment, and employers perceive it to be in their economic interest to reinforce these conditions. Jacobs extensively documents the effects of the discrimination that occurs when women try to enter male-dominated occupations and elaborates on a social-control perspective to account for the persistence of occupational segregation.

Jacobs, Jerry A., ed. 1995. *Gender Inequality at Work.* Thousand Oaks, CA: Sage. 441p. ISBN 0803956975, $43.95.

This edited volume, written primarily by sociologists, presents quantitative studies demonstrating the continuing pay inequity experienced by women in the workplace. Jacobs has assembled a group of scholars who provide a balanced approach to the issue, with some viewing the glass as half full by highlighting the advances that women have achieved in the workplace, and others seeing the glass as half empty and emphasizing the degree of inequity that remains. This book, which emerged from a special edition of the journal *Work and Occupations*, is organized into four broad areas of research. The first section focuses on the issue of compensation and closely details how pay inequity is measured and analyzed. The second section summarizes the progress women have made in managerial jobs. The third section reviews the gender differences in careers of television writers, considers occupational segregation and the influence of early-career job shifts, and provides an extensive comparative analysis of occupational segregation in fifty-six countries. The last section analyzes occupational resegregation in the fields of academic sociology, computer work, and public school teaching. The final chapter provides a synthesis of the research presented in the entire volume.

Reskin, Barbara F., and Heidi I. Hartmann, eds. 1986. ***Women's Work, Men's Work: Sex Segregation on the Job.*** Washington, DC: National Academy Press. 186p. ISBN 0309034299, $29.95.

Reskin, a sociologist at Harvard, and Hartmann, an economist and currently the president and CEO of the Institute for Women's Policy Research, assembled research from the National Research Council Committee on Women's Employment and Related Social Issues. This groundbreaking book provides a comprehensive analysis of women's labor force participation and the degree and impact of job sex segregation through the early 1980s. The authors differentiate between segregation by job and segregation by occupation. Analyses of occupational segregation tend to underestimate the levels of segregation and thus result in inadequate policies. Job segregation focuses more on discriminatory employment practices and more fully represents the unequal access women experience in the labor market. The authors trace the index of sex segregation over time and for specific jobs and take note of resegregation that may be occurring in certain areas. Reskin and Hartmann provide a comprehensive review of research explanations for sex segregation and present some findings of their own. They also assess past policy attempts to diminish job segregation and suggest future directions.

Reskin, Barbara F., and Patricia A. Roos. 1990. ***Job Queues, Gender Queues: Explaining Women's Inroads into Male Occupations.***

Philadelphia: Temple University Press. 368p. ISBN 0877227438, $24.95.

Analyzing data from the U.S. Census, secondary sources, and original data gleaned from participant observation and interviews, Reskin and Roos investigated occupations or segments of fields that women entered in large numbers in the 1970s. Not surprisingly, they found that these occupations were characterized by declining attractiveness to men in terms of pay or working conditions. Their research shows that little progress has been made in terms of true gender integration of occupations and pay equity. The authors investigated eleven occupations, such as book editing and real estate work, in which women's representation increased more rapidly than average. They then used the "Queue Model" to explain why members of the high-status group (men) hold the most attractive jobs and members of the low-status group (women) have access to the remaining jobs. The majority of the book consists of individual case studies conducted by different researchers, with four chapters devoted to a summary of these studies. The authors assert that the level of sex segregation in an occupation is the result of the combination of employers' labor queues (meaning preferences for particular types of workers) and workers' job queues (meaning preferences for certain occupations). In some cases, antidiscrimination legislation was seen as possibly dampening employers' preferences for men over women. The authors also discovered little change in the female-male wage ratio, as women entered four male-dominated occupations in lower wage and status positions.

Rhode, Deborah L. 1997. *Speaking of Sex: The Denial of Gender Inequality*. Cambridge, MA: Harvard University Press. 352p. ISBN 0674831772, $29.95.

Rhode, a law professor at Stanford, investigates gender inequality from a broad perspective by examining inequality within the family and at work. She demonstrates that problems persist because many people minimize or deny the existence of sex discrimination and gender inequity and rarely address it in their day-to-day lives. Rhode holds that though women have achieved some equality through the courts, many do not perceive the matter as a burning issue and, as a result, less progress has been made recently. Her book explains why a gap exists between public perception and concrete data on gender inequality.

Selective perception is one device that allows those who benefit from discrimination to deny the advantages they gain from its continuation. Women also tend to compare themselves to other women when they take measure of their status or achievements, rather than wondering why men are so far ahead. In addition, many people view discrimination as a set of isolated cases needing individual solutions, like the Anita Hill case, and not as a widespread political phenomenon in need of political solutions. Rhode calls for these political solutions by advocating for changes in workplace structures, family arrangements, and social policies.

International and Comparative Studies

Anker, Richard. 1998. *Gender and Jobs: Sex Segregation in the Occupations in the World.* Geneva: International Labour Office. 444p. ISBN 922109524, $40.00.

Anker, who works for the International Labor Organization, has conducted a detailed and comprehensive analysis of data on occupational segregation by sex for 175 occupations in forty-one countries. Not surprisingly, he finds that occupational segregation by sex is extensive in all of the countries under study. He also finds that there are more male-dominated occupations than female-dominated occupations. Anker's work is exceptional for two reasons. First, he covers so many parts of the world that he is able to draw comparisons between very different types of cultures and economies. Second, he achieves precision in his investigation by breaking down categories within occupations and finding much more widespread segregation than has previously been demonstrated. Comparisons across countries often raise methodological issues, but by using a number of different indicators to investigate the multifaceted nature of occupational segregation, this study was able to minimize the problems of comparability. Generally, Anker finds that about one-half of all workers are in occupations that are dominated either by men or by women. Anker also demonstrates that occupational segregation by sex is greatly influenced by social and cultural factors, more so than by socioeconomic and labor market conditions.

Blossfeld, Hans-Peter, and Sonja Drobnic. 2001 *Careers of Couples in Contemporary Societies: From Male Breadwinner to Dual-*

Earner Families. Oxford: Oxford University Press. 396p. ISBN 019924491, $74.00.

Sociologists Blossfeld and Drobnic have integrated the work of an international team of scholars who made use of longitudinal data on life histories to explore changes resulting from women's increased participation in the labor force. The book includes couples in Germany, the Netherlands, the Flemish part of Belgium, Italy, Spain, Great Britain, the United States, Sweden, Denmark, Poland, Hungary, and China. In particular, the book investigates the transition from male-breadwinner to dual-earner families and the accompanying transformation that has occurred for men and women in their careers. The researchers find that changes in gender roles in couples have been slow but are influenced by the timing, speed, and pattern of the transition in different countries.

The book provides evidence that although women's educational and career opportunities have improved greatly, housework and child care have remained in large part the role of women, resulting in a double burden on women to work both within and outside of the home. Women are often forced to sacrifice their careers for their families or their family needs for their careers. The resistance to change on the home front contributes to gender inequalities in the labor market. The authors examine closely the impact a husband's career has on his wife's pursuit of a career, finding that the impact is significantly different for conservative welfare regimes, market-dominated societies, and social democracies. They also find growing income inequality between households as couples with high-earning partners push up the high end of the income distribution and thereby increase the distance between those at the top and the bottom.

Blossfeld, Hans-Peter, and Catherine Hakim, eds. 1997. *Between Equalization and Marginalization: Women Working Part-Time in Europe and the United States of America.* New York: Oxford University Press. 360p. ISBN 0198280866, $85.00.

This book is the product of a collaborative research effort by a group of European sociologists and economists. It includes case studies and cross-national comparisons of part-time work in the United States, Greece, Italy, France, Germany, the Netherlands, Britain, Denmark, and Sweden and an overview of part-time work in central and eastern European countries. Part-time work is defined broadly as anything from one hour per week to thirty-five hours per week. Part-time work has become increasingly common in industrialized countries, where women make up a large percentage of part-time workers, although the levels of their participation vary considerably from country to country. Variables such as women's education, family stage (whether or not children are living in the home or if there are eldercare needs), child care availability, and systems of taxation are correlated with women's participation in part-time work as revealed through longitudinal studies. The authors challenge the feminist perspective that part-time work hinders equality for women by confining them to marginalized positions.

Kahne, Hilda, and Janet Z. Giele, eds. 1992. *Women's Work and Women's Lives: The Continuing Struggle Worldwide.* Boulder, CO: Westview Press. 324p. ISBN 0813306361, $60.00.

Kahne and Giele have compiled an extensive body of research on women's life and employment experiences around the world. Bringing together researchers from a variety of disciplines including anthropology, economics, political science, history, and psychology, the book investigates how factors such as demographics, cultural and political context, and level of economic development influence women's labor force experiences. Giele, a sociologist, provides the theoretical framework by reviewing current modernization theories and presenting a revised conceptual framework that promotes noneconomic factors such as religion and culture, race and class, and women's access to power. She then demonstrates how the employment situation of women is related to the structure of the state, economic conditions, and family life.

Economists Blau and Ferber provide an overview of the economic status of women throughout the world. Using data on labor force participation, occupational distribution, earnings, education, and time spent on housework duties, they demonstrate that gender inequalities continue to be pervasive. The core of the book contains chapters on women's work and lives in three distinct types of economy—modernizing, socialist transitional, and advanced industrial. Kahne, an economist, summarizes the common themes found in women's roles around the world. She finds that women everywhere experience occupational segregation, pay inequity, and an unfair division of labor within the household. Economic structure, state policy, and social and cultural traditions all have an impact on these experiences.

Ward, Kathryn, ed. 1990. *Women Workers and Global Restructuring*. Ithaca, NY: Cornell University Industrial and Labor Relations Press. 272p. ISBN 087546162, $18.95.

Ward's edited volume is a collection of economic and sociological essays on the effects of global economic restructuring on women's lives. It uses case studies, supported by theory, to analyze gender relations and work and family connections. Most of the studies deal with the effect that laboring for multinational corporations has on women in both developed and developing countries. Coverage includes Colombia, Greece, Java, Taiwan, Mexico, the United States, Japan, and Ireland. Many of the findings echo earlier research demonstrating exploitation of female workers in both the informal and formal sectors of the economy. The contributors to this volume explore the role of paid work in women's lives and the degree to which this work either enhances their economic and household positions or marginalizes them in relationship to men. This volume is able to isolate specific and distinct regional issues such as those found, for example, in a study on female owners of the means of production in Greek garment work who become their own source of exploitation. These studies also show the subtle and diverse ways in which women fight back against exploitation by standing up to managerial control or celebrating rituals in their lives. Ultimately, the book questions whether corporate-led development improves the socioeconomic status of women, who frequently work in unregulated factories or at home-based production. The book shows that for the most part, these women experience low pay, poor working conditions, the double burden of work and household responsibilities, and little control over the wages they earn (which are under the control of male members of the household).

Race, Ethnicity, Gender, and Work

Browne, Irene, ed. 1999. *Latinas and African American Women at Work: Race, Gender, and Economic Inequality*. New York: Russell Sage Foundation. 454p. ISBN 0871541475, $16.95.

This collection of essays breaks important ground by providing both qualitative and quantitative analyses of the frequently overlooked issue of how race, along with gender, affects labor force participation and wages. The majority of contributors are prominent sociologists, with a few representatives from women's studies and economics. In her introduction, Browne, a professor of sociology at Emory University, describes the recent trends in employment and earnings by women of color and reviews the theoretical explanations for gender and racial disparities in labor force participation and pay. In the 1970s, the gaps in labor force participation and wages between white women, African American women, and Latinas were declining, but in the 1980s this trend slowed for Latinas and reversed for African American women. Using extensive statistical documentation to back up theory, section 1 of the book focuses on this decline, with chapters on the wages of women of color over time and the relationship of wages to gender, race, and ethnicity. Barbara Reskin provides the final chapter in section 1, focusing on occupational segregation by race and ethnicity. Section 2 addresses issues specific to the labor force experiences of African American women and Latinas, with attention paid to generational paths into and out of work, racial differences in getting off welfare, and perceptions of workplace discrimination. Section 3 provides critiques of existing research, showing that the interaction that occurs between race and gender in the labor market is frequently left out of the picture. In addition, section 3 provides an overview of the policy implications raised by this book, including educational and wage reforms, and child care and health care subsidies.

Sokoloff, Natalie J. 1992. *Black Women and White Women in the Professions: Occupational Segregation by Race and Gender, 1960–1980.* New York: Routledge. 224p. ISBN 0415906091, $23.95.

Sokoloff, a sociologist, investigates the structural changes that occurred in white-collar work between 1960 and 1980 and challenges the claim that white men have been victimized by "reverse discrimination" as a result of affirmative action policies. The 1978 Supreme Court ruling in the *Bakke* case upheld the decision that medical schools had engaged in "reverse discrimination" in their admissions policy. This decision served to reinforce the perception that "reverse discrimination" was widely practiced in hiring and admissions decisions. Sokoloff challenges this perception and also questions the assumptions that white women have gained employment opportunities at the expense of black men and that black women have benefited the most from affirmative action requirements because they enable employers to meet two hiring requirements in one candidate. Using her Index of Relative Advantage, Sokoloff measures the degree of overrepresentation or underrepresentation of particular race or gender groups by comparisons within a given occupation. She goes beyond human capital and sex segregationist models to provide an analysis of structural changes that have occurred in professional occupations between 1960 and 1980. Using Census Bureau data, she shows that although women and black men did gain greater access to professional occupations as a whole, by the time they had gained access, the quality and level of these jobs had deteriorated in terms of working conditions, earnings, and opportunities for promotion. During these same decades, white men had moved on to jobs that had higher status and pay. Sokoloff demonstrates that the job hierarchies were maintained, with white men occupying the best jobs in terms of pay and working conditions and black women occupying the lower-status and lower-pay positions. She concludes that "reverse discrimination" did not result from affirmative action policies during the decades studied. Sokoloff ends her book with a discussion of the developments in the labor market since 1980.

Tomaskovic-Devey, Donald. 1993. *Gender and Racial Inequality at Work: The Sources and Consequences of Job Segregation.* Ithaca, NY: ILR. 232p. ISBN 0875463053, $18.95.

Tomaskovic-Devey, a sociologist at North Carolina State University, investigates how workplace characteristics and the social organization of the workplace influence earnings, levels of job complexity, and levels of managerial authority. The author analyzes these issues in relationship to both gender and race, documenting the differences and similarities between gender and racial inequality in the workplace. Theoretical explanations include human capital theory and socialization theory. He says that workplace status composition processes are also relevant: that is how most jobs take on a racialized or gendered character that contrasts with the better-paying, higher-status jobs that are held by whites and men. Though the author acknowledges that human capital and social forces affect inequality in the workplace, he asserts that the most important factor is the sex composition of jobs, followed by organizational closure processes that exclude women and minorities from certain positions. He concludes that these organizational closure processes account for most of the race and gender inequality at work. The author then uses these theoretical explanations for job inequities to make concrete policy recommendations for comparable worth, affirmative action, more formalized hiring procedures, government incentives, and leadership from heads of corporations.

Work and Family

Blau, Francine D., and Ronald G. Ehrenberg, eds. 1997. *Gender and Family Issues in the Workplace.* New York: Russell Sage Foundation. 336p. ISBN 0871541173, $42.50.

In this collective work, Blau and Ehrenberg, labor economists from Cornell, have gathered together chapters by a group of economists and sociologists who investigate what factors have impeded professional women's progress in the workplace and what can be done to promote equality. The authors highlight the important role work-family issues play in the maintenance of gender inequality in employment, although workplace discrimination is also a factor. The book also focuses on family leave policies and the emergence of corporate "family-friendly" benefits. A related question is whether these benefits serve to reinforce traditional gender roles and undermine true equality for women in the workplace.

Hakim, Catherine. 2000. *Work-Lifestyle Choices in the 21st Century: Preference Theory.* Oxford: Oxford University Press. 360p. ISBN 0199242100, $24.95.

Hakim, a sociologist and senior research fellow at the London School of Economics, uses preference theory to predict women's choices between market and family work. Hakim identifies five changes that provide women with more freedom of choice: easy access to contraceptives; the growth of white-collar work; the availability of part-time work; the individual freedoms present in a modern society; and the equal opportunities revolution that promised women equal access to occupations and careers. Analyzing sex-role attitude survey data from Europe spanning several decades, Hakim finds that most women do not desire a career-centered lifestyle but prefer some combination of part-time work, household, and child care responsibilities. She does not see women's employment patterns becoming more like men's, but finds three distinct profiles among women: home-centered, work-centered, and adaptive (in giving priority to children over work).

Hakim argues that a single social policy for such a heterogeneous group does not make sense and that preference theory is better for predicting women's employment patterns and policy needs. Her work has caused some controversy among scholars, both for her use of preference theory and for her insistence that the largest group of women is home-centered or adaptive. Women who are work-centered are viewed by Hakim as having the same needs as men and therefore not in need of any particular policy interventions.

Hochschild, Arlie. 1989. *Second Shift: Working Parents and the Revolution at Home.* New York: Viking. 315p. ISBN 0380711575, $13.95.

Hochschild, a sociologist at the University of California-Berkeley, conducted extensive interviews with fifty dual-career couples from working-class to upper-class backgrounds. She found that most men are not sharing the load with their wives in terms of child rearing, cooking, cleaning, grocery shopping, or other household duties. The result is that most wives who are working full-time come home to a "second shift" of household and child care duties. Hochschild cites studies demonstrating that women have fifteen fewer hours of leisure time each week compared to their husbands, so that over the course of a year they work an extra month of twenty-four hour days. Hochschild labels this inequality in home responsibilities the "stalled revolution," and she asserts that men and women are stuck in following traditional "gender strategies" that prevent progress. Though more recent studies provide evidence that at least some men are starting to increase their workload at home, Hochschild found that in the couples she studied, only 20 percent split household and child rearing duties equally. She suggests that the United States adopt more profamily policies such as providing tax breaks to companies that encourage job sharing, part-time work, and flextime for both mothers and fathers.

Kahne, Hilda. 1985. *Reconceiving Part-Time Work: New Perspectives for Older Workers and Women.* Lanham, MD: Rowman & Littlefield. 200p. ISBN 0847675696, $23.00.

Kahne advocates for what she calls "New Concept" part-time work—part-time jobs that are paid on the basis of prorated earnings; include some prorated fringe benefits; are available across a variety of occupations; and have some career potential. Kahne cites a number of factors behind the need for "New Concept" positions, factors that remain valid almost twenty years after her book was written. Relevant trends include the increase in single-parent families, role overload for working mothers, and the shortage of high-quality child care combined with an increase in mothers who have young children and are entering the work force. Kahne demonstrates that it is inevitable that mothers and those nearing retirement will need part-time jobs and concludes that there should be more "New Concept" jobs to meet the needs of these workers. Kahne also sees the stumbling block as more likely to be union-driven rather than employer-driven, because unions view part-time employment as a threat to the positions of full-time workers.

Moen, Phyllis. 1992. *Women's Two Roles: A Contemporary Dilemma.* Westport, CT: Auburn House. 192p. ISBN 0865691991, $23.95.

Moen's research was inspired by Alva Myrdal and Viola Klein's classic study, "Women's Two Roles: Home and Work" (1962), which suggested that women leave the labor force to raise their young children and resume work when their children enter school. Moen sees women today as having more options. She advocates making work more flexible for parents with young children so that they can work reduced hours without losing their seniority. Drawing together a large amount of research on women's home and work roles, Moen argues for restructuring work and rethinking how to sequence education, work, and retirement so that men and women can have more time at home when their children are young. She ultimately views work and family decisions as having no single solution, and she reviews research literature that supports the idea that a mother's attitude about being employed may have more influence on her child's development than whether or not she works outside of the home.

Schor, Juliet B. 1992. *The Overworked American: The Unexpected Decline of Leisure.* New York: Basic. 272p. ISBN 046505434, $16.00.

Schor draws on historical materials, statistical evidence, and other sources to put forward the thesis that Americans are overworked both on the job and at home. Workers are putting in longer hours every week, and in-home technology has not allowed them to spend less time on housework but instead has raised expectations about what should be accomplished. Schor points out that many people now have second jobs, put in more overtime, and take less vacation time. She calls attention to the capitalist underpinnings of these trends—employers save money on benefits and other costs by paying fewer workers to work longer hours, but other people remain underemployed or unemployed. Though some researchers have questioned Schor's analysis, most agree that the issues she raises are important. Schor renews interest in the fight for a shorter work week and also calls attention to what she calls the "consumerist treadmill," a never-ending cycle that results in workers spending more hours working overtime in order to acquire more possessions. Schor also demonstrates how women in particular have suffered from overwork because they have taken on greater roles in the labor market while still being the primary person at home responsible for children and housework.

Spain, Daphne, and Suzanne M. Bianchi. 1996. *Balancing Act: Motherhood, Marriage, and Employment among American Women.* New York: Russell Sage Foundation. 240p. ISBN 0871548151, $16.95.

Balancing Act uses demographic data from the decennial census and other federal statistics, as well as public opinion data, to trace changes in marriage, family structure, and employment for women over the past fifty years. The authors are especially adept at analyzing how work and family changes occur over different groups in succession by breaking apart data on traits of older women in the work force and comparing them with characteristics of women just entering the work force in terms of salaries, types of careers, and other variables. The authors also address race and ethnic differences in earnings and employment histories and provide data for international comparisons. In addition to assembling a comprehensive collection of statistics on women, Spain and Bianchi also cite several alternative theoretical perspectives to interpret some of the more dramatic changes that have occurred in women's lives.

Journals

The following is a list of journals that frequently cover research on gender equity and employment and related issues.

American Journal of Sociology, bimonthly journal publishing articles and review essays on the theory, methods, and practice of sociology. University of Chicago Press, Journal Division, P.O. Box 37005, Chicago, IL 60637; Phone: (877) 705–1878, Fax: (877) 705–1879.

American Psychologist, monthly journal of the American Psychological Association; publishes empirical and theoretical articles. American Psychological Association, 750 1st Street N.E., Washington, DC 20002–4242; Phone: (202) 336–5500, Fax: (202) 336–5568.

American Sociological Review, bimonthly sociology journal covering broad sociological research topics. Pennsylvania State University Department of Sociology, 206 Oswald Tower, University Park, PA 16802; Phone: (814) 863–3733, Fax: (814) 863–3734.

Gender and Society, bimonthly journal covering the theory and research on the study of gender and its relationship to society. Department of Sociology, SS340, University of Albany, SUNY, 1400 Washington Avenue, Albany, NY 12222; Phone: (518) 442–4671, Fax: (518) 442–4936.

Gender, Work, and Organization, quarterly journal covering theory, research, and applications of gender studies at work. Blackwell Publishers, Ltd., 108 Cowley Road, Oxford OX4 1JF, England; Phone: 44–1865–791100, Fax: 44–1865–791347.

Industrial and Labor Relations Review, quarterly interdisciplinary scholarly journal on industrial and labor relations. Cornell University, 201 ILR Research Building, Ithaca, NY 14853–3901; Phone: (607) 255–3295, Fax: (607) 255–8016.

International Journal of Politics, Culture, and Society, quarterly journal of comparative sociology. Human Sciences Press, 233 Spring Street, New York, NY 10013–1578; Phone: (212) 620–8000, Fax: (212) 463–0742.

International Labour Review, quarterly multidisciplinary journal investigating the level, quality, and distribution of employment in different countries. CH–1211, Geneva 22, Switzerland; Phone: 41-22-799-7903, Fax: 41-22-799-6117.

Journal of Labor Economics, quarterly journal containing both theoretical and applied international research examining issues affecting the economy as well as social and private behavior. 1101 E. 58th Street, Chicago, IL 60637; Phone: (773) 702–8607, Fax: (773) 702–2699.

Journal of Occupational and Organizational Psychology, quarterly journal publishing empirical and conceptual papers focused on understanding the relationship between people and organizations. British Psychological Society, Journals Department, St. Andrews House, 48 Princess Road East, Leicester, LE1 7DR; Phone: 0116 254 9568, Fax: 0116 2470787.

Journal of Organizational Behavior, published seven times per year; scholarly journal covering recent research and topics on occupational behavior. John Wiley and Sons, Inc., 605 3rd Avenue, New York, NY 10158; Phone: (212) 850–6000, Fax: (212) 850–6049.

Monthly Labor Review, monthly government serial reporting on labor issues and current labor statistics, P.O. Box 371954, MS4004-MIB, Pittsburgh, PA 15250–7954; Phone: (202) 512–1800, Fax: (202) 691–6325.

Organizational Dynamics, quarterly magazine on organizational behavior aimed at management executives. American Management Association, 1601 Broadway, New York, NY 10019–7420; Phone: (212) 586–8100, Fax: (212) 903–8083.

Personnel Psychology, quarterly journal covering research on industrial psychology employees and the workplace, 745 Haskins Road, Suite D, Bowling Green, OH 43402; Phone: (419) 352–1562, Fax: (419) 352–2645.

Sex Roles, monthly journal containing empirical research on sex roles. Plenum Publishing Corporation, Graduate School, City University of New York, 33 W. 42nd Street, New York, NY 10036; Phone: (212) 642–2514, Fax: (212) 642–1987.

Social Forces, quarterly journal covering sociological research and theory. University of North Carolina Press, IRSS, Manning Hall, University of North Carolina, Chapel Hill, NC 27599; Phone: (800) 848–6224, Fax: (919) 962–4777.

Social Problems, quarterly sociology journal addressing social issues. University of California Press/Journals, 2120 Berkeley Way, Berkeley, CA 94720–0001; Phone: (510) 643–7154, Fax: (510) 642–9917.

Sociological Forum, quarterly journal covering all areas of sociology. Plenum Publishing Corporation, 233 Spring Street, New York, NY 10013–1578; Phone: (212) 620–8000, Fax: (212) 463–0742.

Women's Studies International Forum, bimonthly journal promoting an exchange of feminist research in the multidisciplinary, international area of women's studies. Elsevier Science Regional Office, P.O. Box 945, New York, NY 10159–0945; Phone: (212) 633–3730, Fax: (212) 633–3680.

Women's Studies Quarterly, semiannual journal focusing on feminist research and education. Feminist Press at City University of New York, The Graduate Center, 365 Fifth Avenue, New York, NY 10016, Phone: (212) 817–7920, Fax: (212) 817–1593.

Work and Occupations, quarterly sociology journal covering work, occupations, employment, and labor relations. Sage Publications, 2455 Teller Road, Thousand Oaks, CA 91320; Phone: (805) 499–0721, Fax: (805) 499–0871.

Work and Stress, quarterly journal on employment and stress, health and safety. Taylor and Francis, 325 Chestnut Street, Philadelphia, PA 19106; Phone: (215) 625–8900, Fax: (215) 625–2940.

Work, Employment, and Society, quarterly journal analyzing all forms of work in relation to wider social processes. Cambridge University Press, 40 W. 20th Street, New York, NY 10011–4211; Phone: (212) 924–3900, Fax: (212) 691–3239.

8

Selected Nonprint Resources

The first part of this chapter provides descriptions of videos that focus on issues related to gender equity and employment. Prices reflect the cost of purchasing a video, but many videos listed here are available for rental at significantly lower rates. Selection criteria for the videos included availability, relevance to the topic, and appropriateness for upper-level high school students or for college students. There was also a limit placed on the number of videos listed for any one aspect of gender equity and employment. As a result, the list includes only a few of the many videos available covering sexual harassment issues, but the list includes almost all of the available videos that focus on the international aspects of this topic, due to the dearth of films in this area.

Videos and Web Sites

Activism and Organizing

A Day's Work, A Day's Pay
Type: Videotape
Length: 60 minutes
Date: 2001
Source: New Day Films
          190 Route 17M
          P.O. Box 1084
          Harriman, NY 10926
          Phone: (888) 367–9154

http://www.newday.com
Cost: $240

This is a documentary film about welfare recipients who become leaders in the fight against New York City's workfare program. The film follows three welfare recipients in New York City from 1997 to 2000 as they participate in the Work Experience Program that was instituted after the 1996 welfare reform law.

Economic Equity: Realities, Responsibilities, and Rewards
Type: Videotape
Length: 120 minutes
Date: 1997
Source: Women's Bureau, United States Department of Labor
          200 Constitution Avenue N.W., S3311
          Washington, DC 20210
          Phone: (800) 827–5335
          http://www.dol.gov/dol/wb

This is a video of the National Working Women's Summit hosted by the Women's Bureau in 1997, on equal pay for equal work for women. It includes introductory remarks by Vice President Albert Gore, Labor Secretary Alexis M. Herman, and Women's Bureau Director-Designate Ida L. Castro.

The Secret to Change
Type: Videotape
Length: 38 minutes
Date: 2001
Source: Filmakers Library
          124 East 40th Street
          New York, NY 10016
          Phone: (212) 808–4980
          http://www.filmakers.com
Cost: $195

This film chronicles the life of Mildred McWilliams Jeffrey, who was awarded the Medal of Freedom in 2000. Jeffrey is an activist who has fought for seven decades for equality and opportunity in the workplace. Her work has included organizing textile workers in the 1930s and female factory workers during World War II, and later working with the women's and civil rights movements for social justice.

We Dig Coal
Type: Videotape
Length: 58 minutes
Date: 1982
Source: The Cinema Guild
130 Madison Avenue, 2nd Floor
New York, NY 10016–7038
Phone: (212) 685–6242
ttp://www.cinemaguild.com
Cost: $350

This classic award-winning film examines the lives of female coal miners in the United States and the battles they waged to be hired; the opposition they faced from family, community, and male coworkers; and their day-to-day lives at work.

Women Organize!
Type: Videotape
Length: 32 minutes
Date: 2000
Source: Women Make Movies
462 Broadway, Room 500
New York, NY 10013
Phone: (212) 925–0606
http://www.wmm.com
Cost: $195

This film by the Union Institute Center for Women and the Women and Organizing Documentation Project shows female organizers from across the United States engaged in campaigns relating to decent working conditions, homophobia, and other social justice issues.

Discrimination, the Glass Ceiling, and Gender Issues at Work

Cherry v. Coudert Brothers: The Mommy Track
Type: Videotape
Length: 50 minutes
Date: 1998
Source: Courtroom Television Network (Court TV)
600 Third Avenue
New York, NY 10016

Phone: (800) 888–4580
http://www.courttv.com
Cost: $34.95

This is a documentary film on the *Cherry v. Coudert Brothers* trial, involving a female employee who sued her employer for being fired after returning from maternity leave.

The Glass Ceiling
Type: Videotape
Length: 30 minutes
Date: 1997
Source: Society of Women Engineers
         120 Wall Street
         Eleventh Floor
         New York, NY 10005–3902
         Phone: (212) 509–9577
         http://www.swe.org
Cost: $10 rental (must be SWE member)

This is a video of an inservice program designed to facilitate discussion about gender discrimination against female engineers.

Hill vs. Thomas
Type: Videotape
Length: 45 minutes
Date: 1997
Source: Films for the Humanities and Sciences
         P.O. Box 2053
         Princeton, NJ 08543–2053
         Phone: (800) 257–5126
         http://www.films.com/index.cfm
Cost: $89.95

This video provides archival footage covering the events surrounding the Judiciary Committee and Senate hearings regarding Anita Hill's sexual harassment accusations against U.S. Supreme Court nominee Clarence Thomas. Four CBS commentators provide an analysis of the case.

Invisible Rules: Men, Women, and Teams
Type: Videotape
Length: 34 minutes

Date: 1996
Source: CorVision Media
          3014 Commercial Avenue
          Northbrook, IL 60062
          Phone: (800) 537–3130
          http://www.corvision.com
Cost: $495

This video discusses the differences in cultural perspectives of male and female workers and the ways these different understandings can interfere with successful teamwork.

Out at Work: America Undercover
Type: Videotape
Length: 58 minutes
Date: 1996
Source: Filmakers Library
          124 East 40th Street
          New York, NY 10016; Phone: (212) 808–4980
          http://www.filmakers.com
Cost: $295

This documentary investigates employment policies still being adhered to in forty states that allow employers to fire employees for being homosexual. Using several prominent case studies, this film shows workers who had to deal with serious job discrimination and harassment issues and took action to fight for their rights.

Paving the Way
Type: Videotape
Length: 52 minutes
Date: 1995
Source: Filmakers Library
          124 East 40th Street
          New York, NY 10016
          Phone: (212) 808–4980
          http://www.filmakers.com
Cost: $350

This film presents the stories of four women who were able to break through the glass ceilings imposed on them: Supreme Court Justice Ruth Bader Ginsburg, Major General Jeanne Holm, Reverend Addie Wyatt, and Congresswoman Patsy Mink.

The Power Dead-Even Rule and Other
Gender Differences in the Workplace
Type: Videotape
Length: 36 minutes
Date: 1995
Source: CorVision Media
         3014 Commercial Avenue
         Northbrook, IL 60062
         Phone: (800) 537–3130
         http://www.corvision.com
Cost: $495

Consultant Pat Heim discusses the ways in which male and female cultures are different, why they clash sometimes at work, and how one can learn to speak the language of either culture when trying to communicate and achieve in the workplace.

Risk, Rescue, and Righteousness: How Women Prevent
Themselves from Breaking through the Glass Ceiling
Type: Videotape
Length: 58 minutes
Date: 1995
Source: Kantola Productions (Stanford Executive Briefings)
         55 Sunnyside Avenue
         Mill Valley, CA 94941
         Phone: (800) 989–8273
         http://www.wmm.com
Cost: $95

This film provides a statistical overview of women in management over the past twenty-five years. It reviews recent research on why women have trouble moving into management positions and suggests that personality characteristics and relationship-oriented strategies that women have used as midlevel managers prevent them from being promoted to high-level positions.

Through the Glass Ceiling
Type: Videotape
Length: 17 minutes
Date: 1996
Source: Filmakers Library
         124 East 40th Street
         New York, NY 10016

Phone: (212) 808–4980
http://www.filmakers.com
Cost: $195

This is an animated film that uses humor to discuss women's equality issues in the workplace.

Education and Career Choice

Careers for the Twenty-First Century: Women in Non-Traditional Roles
Type: Videotape
Length: Five programs with varying run times
Date: 1992
Source: Takeoff Multimedia
6611 Clayton Road
St. Louis, MO 63144
Phone: (314) 863–0700
Cost: $495

In this video, women from twenty-two nontraditional professions discuss their careers.

Did I Say Hairdressing? I Meant Astrophysics
Type: Videotape
Length: 15 minutes
Date: 1998
Source: Filmakers Library
124 East 40th Street
New York, NY 10016
Phone: (212) 808–4980
http://www.filmakers.com
Cost: $150

This is an animated video that demonstrates why women are underrepresented in science, engineering, and technology. The film encourages young women to consider training in these fields.

Exercise Your Options
Type: Videotape
Length: 12 minutes
Date: 1999

Source: Films for the Humanities and Sciences
         P.O. Box 2053
         Princeton, NJ 08543–2053
         Phone: (800) 257–5126
         http://www.films.com/index.cfm
Cost: $89.95

This video demonstrates why girls should not avoid taking math classes in school and gives examples of rewarding math-related careers.

Hammering It Out: Women in the Construction Zone
Type: Videotape
Length: 54 minutes
Date: 2000
Source: Women Make Movies
         462 Broadway, Room 500
         New York, NY 10013
         Phone: (212) 925–0606
         http://www.wmm.com
Cost: $195

Hammering It Out is a documentary film about the Century Freeway Women's Employment Program in California. The result of a lawsuit, this program trained women in the traditionally male-dominated building trades. The film explores issues of equality and changing gender roles as women report on their experiences with discrimination, sexual harassment, and other issues such as child care and benefits.

Hard Hats: A 60 Minutes Report
Type: Videotape
Length: 15 minutes
Date: 1998
Source: CBS Video/60 Minutes
         524 W. 57th Street
         New York, NY 10019
         Phone: (800) 848–3256
         http://store.cbs.com/videoarea.php
Cost: $29.95

Hard Hats explores the lives of women who work in the construction industry, including why they became construction workers and the obstacles they face at work. This video originally aired on the television program *60 Minutes* on September 27, 1998.

Intellectual Parity: What Little Girls Are Made Of

Type:	Videotape
Length:	48 minutes
Date:	1998
Source:	Films for the Humanities and Sciences
	P.O. Box 2053
	Princeton, NJ 08543–2053
	Phone: (800) 257–5126
	http://www.films.com
Cost:	$89.95

This film examines the history of intellectual prejudice against women and how that prejudice has impacted opportunities for women in education, particularly in the area of science.

Men in the Workplace: Nontraditional Career Choices

Type:	Videotape
Length:	18 minutes
Date:	1998
Source:	Enter Here Publishing/Thomson Learning
	P.O. Box 6904
	Florence, KY 41022–6904
	Phone: (800) 354–9706
	http://www.enterherepublishing.com
Cost:	$67.95

This video focuses on nontraditional career paths that men can pursue when choosing or changing careers. The video shows young men in careers as nurses, caregivers, and other jobs traditionally considered women's work, and seeks to dismantle stereotypes of what types of occupations are considered most suitable for men.

Women in the Workplace

Type:	Videotape
Length:	21 minutes
Date:	1997
Source:	Enter Here Publishing/Thomson Learning
	P.O. Box 6904
	Florence, KY 41022–6904

Phone: (800) 354–9706
http://www.enterherepublishing.com
Cost: $67.95

This film features the stories of successful women who have created rewarding careers by developing their strengths and following nontraditional career paths.

Women's Work
Type: Videotape
Length: 30 minutes
Date: 1991
Source: Great Plains National
            1800 N. 33rd Street, Box 80669
            Lincoln, NE 68583
            Phone: (402) 472–2007
            http://gpn.unl.edu
Cost: $39.95

This video explores the experiences of women employed in technical careers. In the film, the women discuss the challenges they have had to overcome.

History, Diversity, and International Perspectives

Defying the Odds: Women around the World Create New Roles
Type: Videotape
Length: 29 minutes
Date: 1996
Source: Filmakers Library
            124 East 40th Street
            New York, NY 10016; Phone: (212) 808–4980
            http://www.filmakers.com
Cost: $295

Produced for the Beijing Women's Conference, this video focuses on four women from diverse nations and backgrounds and of different ages who have broken with tradition to pursue and achieve in fields not traditionally open to women from their countries.

The Double Burden: Three Generations of Working Mothers
Type: Videotape

Length: 57 minutes
Date: 1992
Source: New Day Films
190 Route 17M P.O. Box 1084
Harriman, NY 10926
Phone: (888) 367–9154
http://www.newday.com
Cost: $250

This award-winning documentary film interviews three diverse families in which the grandmothers, mothers, and daughters all hold jobs to support the family. The film includes historical footage.

The Double Shift
Type: Videotape
Length: 47 minutes
Date: 1997
Source: Films for the Humanities and Sciences
P.O. Box 2053
Princeton, NJ 08543–2053; Phone: (800) 257–5126
http://www.films.com
Cost: $149

This is a documentary, narrated by Susan Sarandon, on equality for employed women around the world. The video focuses on opportunity, pay, career and family, value placed on traditional activities, exploitation, self-employed women, and househusbands.

Full Circle: The Ideal of a Sexually Egalitarian Society on the Kibbutz
Type: Videotape
Length: 58 minutes
Date: 1995
Source: Filmakers Library
124 East 40th Street
New York, NY 10016; Phone: (212) 808–4980
http://www.filmakers.com
Cost: $350

This film explores the attempt to create sexual equality between women and men on the Israeli kibbutz (communal farm). Historical footage and interviews illustrate the original goal of gender equality in the workplace and the abandonment of that goal as women and men began to embrace more traditional roles.

The Life and Times of Rosie the Riveter
Type: Videotape
Length: 65 minutes
Date: 1980
Source: Direct Cinema Ltd.
            P.O. Box 10003
            Santa Monica, CA 90410–1003
            Phone: (310) 636–8200
            http://www.directcinema.com
Cost: $350

This classic film was originally issued in 1980. The film interviews five women who worked during World War II, when ideas about the proper roles of women quickly broadened in response to the demand for workers in traditionally male jobs during the war.

The Maids: A Documentary
Type: Videotape
Length: 28 minutes
Date: 1995
Source: Women Make Movies
            462 Broadway, Room 500
            New York, NY 10013
            Phone: (212) 925–0606
            http://www.wmm.com
Cost: $225

This documentary focuses on the history of domestic work, especially by black women, in the United States. It provides an analysis of the racial and sexual divisions of labor that have occurred in the United States.

New Directions: Women of Zimbabwe;
Made in Thailand; Women of Guatemala
Type: Videotape
Length: 90 minutes
Date: 2000
Source: Women Make Movies
            462 Broadway, Room 500
            New York, NY 10013

Phone: (212) 925–0606
http://www.wmm.com
Cost: $295

This is a series of three individual videos packaged together that examine roles women have taken in three developing countries. "Women of Zimbabwe" explores the lives of five women who work in the traditionally male field of carpentry. "Women of Thailand" explores larger issues relating to women's status, educational opportunity, and health education. "Women of Guatemala" provides a portrait of female organizers who are working toward economic justice for Mayan women.

No Time to Stop: Women Immigrants
Type: Videotape
Length: 29 minutes
Date: 1990
Source: Women Make Movies
          462 Broadway, Room 500
          New York, NY 10013
          Phone: (212) 925–0606
          http://www.wmm.com
Cost: $250

This film explores the barriers three women of color face as new immigrants to Canada. The filmmakers investigate racial and sexual discrimination on the job and in the experiences these women have in seeking social services. Though the focus is on the concerns of women who have recently immigrated, the battles they face are those that many women and men of color must cope with in seeking and retaining employment.

Pain, Passion, and Profit
Type: Videotape
Length: 49 minutes
Date: 1992
Source: Women Make Movies
          462 Broadway, Room 500
          New York, NY 10013
          Phone: (212) 925–0606
          http://www.wmm.com
Cost: $275

This film investigates what women entrepreneurs in both developed and developing countries bring to their work. Anita Roddick, founder of the Body Shop, shows examples from Africa of women who are committed to the idea of "profits with principles."

There's No Such Thing as Women's Work
Type: Videotape
Length: 30 minutes
Date: 1987
Source: National Women's History Project
           7738 Bell Road
           Windsor, CA 95492
           Phone: (707) 838–6000
           http://www.nwhp.org/
Cost: $39.95

This video shows historical newsreels, photographs, and cartoons demonstrating the changing influence of women on the work force in the United States.

Sexual Harassment

Love in the Law Firm: When Does It
Become Illegal Sexual Harassment?
Type: Videotape
Length: 170 minutes
Date: 2000
Source: American Bar Association Continuing Legal Education
           541 N. Fairbanks Court
           Chicago, IL 60611
           Phone: (312) 988–6191
           http://www.abanet.org
Cost: $195

This program consists of mock oral arguments, mediation, and arbitration to address sexual harassment in the law firm. British and American legal systems and the preferences for different types of dispute resolutions are compared.

No Excuses: Sexual Harassment
Type: Videotape
Length: 26 minutes

Date: 1999
Source: Insight Media
          2162 Broadway
          New York, NY 10024–0621
          Phone: (800) 233–9910
          http://www.insight-media.com
Cost: $219

This video uses a series of vignettes to demonstrate the different types of sexual harassment that can occur, and some ways of dealing with harassment.

A Policy Is Not Enough: Leading a Respectful Workplace
Type: Videotape
Length: 19 minutes
Date: 2000
Source: Edge Training Systems
          9710 Farrar Court, Suite P
          Richmond, VA 23236
          Phone: (800) 476–1405
          http://www.edgetraining.com
Cost: $595

This video covers harassment in the workplace and suggests ways that managers can create a respectful work environment by modeling appropriate behavior and coaching employees to avoid behavior that could become a problem. Emphasis is placed on the responsibility of the supervisor and the potential liability to the company if supervisors fail to take preventive measures.

Prevent Sexual Harassment in the Workplace
Type: Videotape
Length: 30 minutes
Date: 2000
Source: Insight Media
          2162 Broadway
          New York, NY 10024–0621
          Phone: (800) 233–9910
          http://www.insight-media.com
Cost: $149

This is a practical video on ways to recognize and address acts of sexual harassment at work and how to eradicate sexual harassment from the culture of the workplace.

Sexual Harassment and the Law
Type: Web broadcast
Length: 29 minutes
Date: 2000
Source: Lawline.com Corporation/
            PBS Adult Learning Satellite Service
            63 Wall Street, 27th Floor
            New York, NY 10005
            Phone: (800) 529–5463
            http://www.lawline.com
Cost: Free on the web

In this cable television show, Lynn Schafran, an attorney from the National Organization for Women's Legal Defense and Education Fund, and Janice Goodman, an attorney for victims of sexual harassment, discuss what people can do if they have been victims of sexual harassment. They also examine the laws that protect victims of sexual abuse or harassment.

Sexual Harassment in the Twenty-First Century
Type: Videotape
Length: 22 minutes
Date: 2000
Source: Insight Media
            2162 Broadway
            New York, NY 10024–0621
            Phone: (800) 233–9910
            http://www.insight-media.com
Cost: $499

This video defines sexual harassment, provides examples, gives an overview of recent Supreme Court rulings, and discusses the consequences for individuals engaging in sexual harassment.

Sexual Harassment, Is It or Isn't It? Situations for Discussion
Type: Videotape
Length: 21 minutes
Date: 1998
Source: Provant Media
            4601 121st Street
            Urbandale, IA 50323–2311
            Phone: (888) 776–8268
            http://www.ammedia.com
Cost: $795

This video provides a legal definition of sexual harassment and gives employers and employees information about how to file, and respond to, a complaint. The video includes a number of short dramas that can be used for group discussion.

Sexual Harassment: New Roles/New Rules
Type: Videotape
Length: 20 minutes
Date: 1995
Source: Edge Training Systems
           9710 Farrar Court, Suite P
           Richmond, VA 23236
           Phone: (800) 476–1405
           http://www.edgetraining.com
Cost: $495

This video focuses on practical approaches to handling difficult situations relating to the issue of sexual harassment. The video also provides an explanation of current laws and guidelines to encourage people to avoid behaving in ways that could be perceived as harassment.

Taking on the Boy's Club: Women in the Workplace
Type: Videotape
Length: 36 minutes
Date: 1992, 1998
Source: Films for the Humanities and Sciences
           P.O. Box 2053
           Princeton, NJ 08543–2053
           Phone: (800) 257–5126
           http://www.films.com
Cost: $89.95

This video is part one in a segment about sexism in the workplace from the television program *20/20*. It was originally broadcast in 1992. Part two (also included in this segment) is filmed by ABC News in 1998 and covers sexual harassment in the U.S. military and other organizations.

Web Resources

The following is a selected list of web sites that contain substantive information about gender equity and employment, including full-text resources, databases, specialized libraries and collections, and extensive bibliographies and related links on this topic. The web sites are divided into two categories: sites that focus on the United States and sites that focus on international issues relating to gender and employment.

United States Web Sites

Bureau of Labor Statistics
United States Department of Labor
http://www.bls.gov

The Bureau of Labor Statistics is an agency of the Department of Labor. Included on its site are statistics on pay differentials between men and women, employment of women in different industries and occupations, rates of unemployment, and other employment-related statistics. In addition, this site contains publications and research papers on labor force trends, and a career guide to industries.

Catherwood Library Web Site
School of Industrial and Labor Relations
Cornell University
http://www.ilr.cornell.edu/library

The Catherwood Library at the School of Industrial and Labor Relations at Cornell University contains one of the most comprehensive collections in the United States of resources on nearly every aspect of the workplace. The library includes the Kheel Center for Labor-Management Documentation and Archives and Catherwood's virtual EArchives collections. The EArchives pages include government documents, statistics, and policy papers. Included in the U.S. government documents collection are indexed full-text reports produced by the Glass Ceiling Commission, the Commission on Family and Medical Leave, and the findings of other work-related symposia, task forces, and commissions. The Catherwood site also includes links to work-related search engines and a database of audiovisual materials related to work. Extensive research guides to primary sources on women and work and annotated bibliographies on labor history and related subjects are available through the Kheel Center's web pages, connected to Catherwood. An online exhibit of the Triangle Shirtwaist Factory fire that includes primary documents, photographs, a bibliography, and related links is also available from the Kheel site.

The Center for Women and Work
Rutgers University
http://www.rci.rutgers.edu/~cww

The center's web site includes extensive statistical data on the gender gap in pay. The site also contains dozens of bibliographies on different aspects of gender and employment. In addition, links to web resources on advocacy, research and data, legal issues and discrimination, and work-life balance are provided. Plans are currently underway to compile a larger collection of data on women and employment.

National Council for Research on Women
http://www.ncrw.org

The NCRW seeks to facilitate collaborative research and communication among its member centers and affiliates and to build stronger links between research, policy, action, and the media. Toward those ends, this web site contains a directory of member centers, an index of areas of expertise at these centers, a directory of affiliates, a directory of international centers, and a database of links to a variety of subjects relating to women, including employment and equity.

United States Equal Employment Opportunity Commission
http://www.eeoc.gov

The EEOC web site includes the text of Title VII of the Civil Rights Act of 1964, recent court cases involving the EEOC, press releases, information about filing a discrimination charge with the EEOC, and detailed frequently asked questions regarding federal laws prohibiting job discrimination. The site also includes statistics about EEOC activities and patterns of job discrimination, publications available for downloading, and links to U.S. government sites relating to job discrimination.

Virtual Library at the Center for Women and Work
University of Massachusetts at Lowell
http://www.uml.edu/centers/women-work/vlibrary/
vlindex.html

The Virtual Library is a collection of annotated links hosted at the Center for Women and Work at the University of Massachusetts at Lowell. The collection includes links to resources on equal pay, work and family, women and work in other countries, and the history of women and work.

Women and Work
Feminist Majority Foundation/Feminist Internet Gateway
http://www.feminist.org/gateway/sd_exec2.html

The Women and Work section of this gateway provides information on women in the work force provided by the foundation as well as reviewed links to resources and information provided by other organizations. The site includes an extensive annotated list of organizations involved in gender and employment issues.

Women's Studies Database/Gender Issues Section
University of Maryland
http://www.mith2.umd.edu/WomensStudies/GenderIssues

The "Gender Issues" section of the Women's Studies Database at the University of Maryland contains a comprehensive list of links to rich collections of resources on topics such as women in the work force, sexual harassment, sex discrimination, glass ceiling/sticky floor, and employment information and statistics.

Women, Work, and Gender Issues
http://www.wsu.edu/~mnofsing

Mary Nofsinger, a librarian at Washington State University, compiled this web page. The site contains links to resources about women and work organized under eleven different categories, including careers and occupations, sexual harassment, sciences and women, and legal issues.

International Web Sites

ELDIS: Gateway to Gender and Development Information
The Institute of Development Studies
http://www.ids.ac.uk/eldis/gender/Gender.htm

Electronic Development Information Source (ELDIS) is a gateway to information on development issues. ELDIS provides summaries and links to online documents. The Institute of Development Studies in Sussex, U.K., hosts the site. Included is a Gender Gateway section that contains a list of key web sites, collections of statistics, research centers, web directories, and discussion lists related to gender and development. The site also includes a database of full-text intergovernmental organization documents and reports.

Gender Equality Section, Europa
http://Europa.eu.int/comm/employment_social/
equ_opp/index_en.htm

Europa is the portal site of the European Union. It provides up-to-date coverage of European Union affairs. The Gender Equality Section of the site provides access to gender equality policies and documentation from the EU, and information on committees and groups working on the issue of gender equality. The site also includes an extensive list of links to organizations within the EU, international governmental organizations, nongovernmental organizations, and other institutions and groups involved in gender equity issues.

Gender Virtual Library
United Nations Development Program
http://www.undp.sk/

The Gender Virtual Library at the UNDP includes tools for gender work, including the full text of the "Handbook on Gender Mainstreaming." The site also contains links to organizations and institutions, web resources, and full-text documents and journals. Country and subject searching facilitates the use of this site.

International Labour Organization
http://www.ilo.org/public/english/index.htm

The International Labour Organization web site has a wide-ranging collection, from databases and virtual libraries to collections of materials, relating to employment from an international perspective. Their database page includes access to Labordoc, a collection of more than 250,000 labor resources, and Laborsta, a large collection of international statistics. In addition, their web site includes a section called "World of Work," which includes e.quality@work, a compilation of information on gender equality laws and policies, and Workgate, a virtual library connecting users to more than 350 relevant web sites.

Women and Employment
Social Science Information Gateway (SOSIG)
http://www.sosig.ac.uk/roads/subject-listing/World-cat/womenemp.html

The "Women and Employment" section of the Social Science Information Gateway provides a broad list of links to relevant fulltext reports, government documents, articles, bibliographies, educational materials, organizations, journals, and research centers. SOSIG is a database that is part of the United Kingdom Discovery Resource Network and is aimed at educators and researchers. The database is reviewed and edited by librarians, and its focus is on international resources.

**WomenWatch: The UN Internet Gateway
on the Advancement and Empowerment of Women**
http://www.un.org/womenwatch

WomenWatch is a joint U.N. project designed to share information and resources on global women's issues. The Division for the Advancement of Women (DAW), the United Nations Development Fund for Women (UNIFEM), and the International Research and Training Institute for the Advancement of Women (INSTRAW) created WomenWatch in 1997. Originally designed to monitor and update progress from the Beijing Women's Conference, the site provides a gateway to United Nations agencies, commissions, intergovernmental and treaty bodies, and instruments that relate to women's issues. It includes access to the Inter-Agency Meeting on Women and Gender Equality (IAMWGE) and the Women Ambassador's Network, which includes a list of female ambassadors from around the world. The site also provides access to conferences, events, news, documents, and databases on issues concerning gender and the United Nations. In addition, the site contains a comprehensive list of country- and region-specific commissions and other organizations, plans of action for women's advancement, and statistical and geographical information relating to important activities and key people working on women's issues around the world.

Glossary

The vocabulary associated with women's equality and gender equity in employment comes from history, jurisprudence, economics, and other behavioral sciences. It developed over the past forty years, beginning with the civil rights movement in the United States in the 1960s. The field of history has documented the rise of feminism and the women's movement and the changes in men's and women's jobs, education, and family obligations. Jurisprudence and legal cases have contributed terms related to discrimination prohibited by the law. The field of economics has furnished concepts and a vocabulary for understanding labor markets and the differences in pay between men and women. Sociology, anthropology, and comparative studies help to explain differences in cultural expectations of women and men in different societies and time periods and changes in the structure of the family.

affirmative action   In employment, a hiring strategy, and in higher education, an admissions strategy, that increases acceptance of underrepresented minorities in an occupation or an educational program. Affirmative action should not be confused with quotas, which set a specific number of hires or admissions as a target or as an upper limit on the number of persons of a given race, ethnic group, or religion who are either to be admitted or kept out. Affirmative action is based on the philosophy that people from minority backgrounds bring diverse talents and therefore should be included because they make a positive contribution on certain dimensions that are likely to be absent in the majority population.

breadwinner-homemaker families Families in which one spouse (usually the husband) earns the income and the other spouse (usually the wife) is a full-time homemaker. Such families are thought of as more "traditional." They were the norm until the coming of the modern women's movement and the entry of most married women and mothers into the labor force.

care drain A recent phenomenon in which foreign workers are imported from Third World countries to provide child care and domestic service in the more developed countries. The "drain" in care takes place both in the sending countries (where women leave their own families and children to work abroad) and in the receiving countries (where parents are not providing care to their own children and frail elders but are relying on paid labor to do so).

casual workers and casualization of the labor force A trend toward fewer permanent and regular jobs with a standard thirty-five to forty-hour week. Casual workers tend to be part-time and temporary; they come and go. As a result, they have fewer benefits associated with the job, and employers have fewer obligations and costs associated with their employment.

chilly classroom An educational climate in which school girls or college women are not encouraged to succeed. The teachers and the student peers communicate their devaluation of the female students' abilities and achievements in a variety of ways, ranging from overt negative behaviors to subtle discouragement that takes the form of giving the male students more attention or being more permissive toward their misbehavior and their mistakes.

comparable worth A term that refers to efforts to raise the pay of female-labeled jobs that typically pay less than male-labeled jobs but require an equivalent or even higher level of skill. The method of determining comparable worth is to evaluate all jobs in a given firm on the basis of job content. Job evaluation plans rate jobs in terms of skill, required effort, responsibility, and working conditions. Jobs with similar scores are then compared in terms of their salaries, and in those cases when there is a noticeable discrepancy in pay between jobs with similar ratings, discrimination is suspected and there is a case for raising the pay.

compensating differentials One popular explanation for the pay gap between women and men is "compensating differentials," whereby men are paid more for dirty and more dangerous work and women are paid less because they are said to work in pleasant, safe, and less demanding jobs.

consumer maintenance A concept put forward by economist Carolyn Shaw Bell to sum up the unpaid and unseen contribution that families (especially women) make every day to feeding, clothing, protecting, and nurturing (or "maintaining") the population of workers and consumers. The distinctive feature of Bell's statement was her focus, not on children, which is quite familiar, but on the private family needs of adult workers that must be met if they are to be productive workers and consumers in the national economy.

contingent work A type of employment that is likely to be temporary, or on call at the discretion of the employer. See also **casual workers** and **nonstandard work schedules**.

crossover pattern See **gender crossovers**.

crowding One of the explanations for the lower wages in female-labeled occupations. Because women are crowded into a few "feminine" occupations, they can easily become an oversupply and inadvertently lower their own wages. Employers may exploit this tendency by substituting labor-intensive production for investment in capital that would use fewer workers and promote efficiency.

discrimination See **sex discrimination**.

domestic feminism See **feminism, domestic or maternal**.

double burden The heavier work load of working women with families compared with that of working men. The reason for the inequity is that women are usually expected, in addition to their paid outside work, to do much more of the housework and child care than employed men who also have families.

dual-career families and dual-earner families Both of these types of family have a husband and a wife in the workplace. The term *dual-career family* implies that each member of the couple has a career (meaning a high-level and demanding job). In dual-earner couples, each member is employed, but in jobs that may not require the full-time commitment and demanding and autonomous work that is implied by *career*.

dual labor market A labor market in which there is a distinction between permanent full-time jobs in the primary sector with opportunities for promotion and benefits and temporary, nonstandard, and part-time jobs in the secondary sector that are often considered to be "dead-end" jobs and that carry low pay, little chance for promotion, and few, if any, health or other benefits.

earnings differential See **wage gap**.

equal work When the Equal Pay Act came into being in 1963, there was ambiguity in what was meant by *equal work*. In a series of legal cases, the courts made clear that mere difference in name did not make jobs different enough to avoid a charge of sex discrimination if the work was substantially similar.

Executive Order   The principal mode of administrative action on the part of the president of the United States.

face-time   Time spent in person at work. Efforts to make the workplace family-friendly frequently encounter resistance to the institution of flexible hours or working at home, because the worker is not visible, the employer and fellow workers cannot see his or her face, and therefore they are not sure that the worker is really working. Thus, workers sometimes decline leaves and flexible working arrangements in order to put in face-time, for which they expect higher rewards.

female earnings differential   See **wage gap**.

female-labeled occupations   When more than 50 to 60 percent of workers in an occupation are female, the job itself is more likely to be seen as "women's work," with the consequence that it is generally less well paid in comparison to jobs requiring similar skills that are held by men. Examples are the occupations of preschool teacher, secretary, and nurse.

feminism, domestic or maternal   Advocacy for the rights of women, especially as related to their private roles as mothers and caregivers. Domestic or maternal feminist movements are concerned with such issues as mobilizing resources to improve child, family, neighborhood, and community well being.

feminism, equal rights   Advocacy of equal rights for women, especially in relation to their public roles as workers and citizens. The woman suffrage movement and efforts to open equal educational and employment opportunities to women are examples of equal rights feminism.

flextime   A provision making it possible for employees to work full-time but at hours that depart from the typical 9-to-5 schedule on Monday through Friday. The variation may involve only the starting or ending times of the day, or it may take the form of bunching work into several very long days and being off work the rest of the week.

gender   Psychological, social, and cultural differences between males and females that are understood to be less permanent and more malleable than biological differences. *Gender* refers to the masculine or feminine identity of a person and to qualities of personality, occupation, or social roles that are typically associated with each sex. Implicitly, gender refers to behavior that is learned and is therefore open to changing definitions of what is masculine and feminine. See also **sex**.

gender crossovers   The process by which a woman takes on some tasks or responsibilities that were once accessible only to males, and similarly, a man takes on work or obligations that were once thought to be the province of women. This phenomenon is rare until male and female roles are broken into smaller, more easily replicated tasks that do not require craft knowledge or long socialization available only to one sex or the other. Positive examples can be seen in women's entry into formerly "male" occupations such as law, medicine, and engineering and in men's greater involvement in housework and child care.

gender gap in pay See **wage gap**.

gender stereotypes Overly simple ideas of what constitutes masculine or feminine mental, emotional, and social behavior that fail to take into account the wide variations within both the male and female populations. Examples of such beliefs are expectations that men will be strong and courageous and women dependent and weak, or that women are better at cooking and child care and men at home repairs.

glass ceiling The invisible barrier to higher pay and top executive positions that highly educated and achieving women encounter even when they are at the top of their fields.

globalization The change in the world economy and the economy of individual countries that has made nations more dependent on each other for their resources, labor supply, and consumer markets. Globalization has created a world economy in which the various regions are more interdependent and economically intertwined.

hostile climate This term particularly grew out of women's experience of sexual harassment in the workplace and the classroom and out of their legal arguments to define such behavior as not being casual erotic interaction or courtship but hostile and discriminatory behavior that was prohibited by equal rights laws. See also **sexual harassment**.

human capital theory An economic theory that explains workers' employment status and earnings as the result of their levels of education, training, motivation, attitudes, and such other personal characteristics as make them competent, efficient, and productive. Human capital theory would expect to find that women are paid less than men because they have less training, less on-the-job experience, and less single-minded commitment to the job because of their family responsibilities. See **crowding, dual labor market,** and **taste for discrimination** for alternative explanations for the wage gap.

index of dissimilarity between occupations A descriptive measure of the degree of sex-typing of jobs in the entire occupational distribution. This measure ranges from 0 (representing no sex-typing) to 100 (representing no overlap whatsoever between male and female occupations). The index is equal to the minimum proportion of women plus the minimum proportion of men who would need to change occupation so that the proportion female is the same in all occupations.

index of sex segregation A constructed measure that calculates sex labeling and degree of separation between male and female occupations by focusing on the total size of different occupations and the degree to which males and females are clumped in some occupations more than others. This measure sums the absolute differences between percentages of all employed females and all employed males in a given occupation that creates a total for all occupations and divides by two. The index of sex segregation is never higher than 50 and indicates the percentage of male workers and the percentage of female workers who would have to change jobs in order for there to be the same percentage of employed females in a given occupation as the percentage of employed males.

informal economy, informal labor market   Economic activities and jobs that are either unpaid or are not formally recognized by employers and government as a basis of taxation or entitlement to social benefits. Examples are street vendors, traders, home workers, and those in the underground or black market economy, as well as various other workers and caregivers who are paid in cash or in kind without being subject to formal regulation.

internal labor market   Another name for the dual labor market that operates within the firm and creates distinctions between workers in the primary sector who have better prospects for on-the-job training, higher pay, and promotion, and those in the secondary sector who are not given the same opportunities.

merit resolutions   A decision by the Equal Employment Opportunity Commission that finds in favor of a complaintant who has brought a charge of discrimination.

mommy track   A term that has taken on somewhat pejorative connotations as referring to a less demanding and more flexible work schedule that permits female managers opportunities for combining work, childbearing, and care of young children. Feminists worry that this concept may unwittingly contribute to the slowing of women's achievements, but a number of women in very responsible professional and managerial positions do, in fact, cut back their schedules and follow a less demanding work life, at least for some period of time, in order to meet the needs of their families.

nonmarket work   Economists refer to unpaid labor as "nonmarket" or "informal" work (meaning that it takes place outside the boundaries of the money economy). See also **informal economy, informal labor market**.

nonstandard work schedules   A variety of work routines whereby working hours fall outside the regular 9-to-5 weekday pattern and require work on nights and weekends, swing shifts, or work on call at the behest of the employer. The term is also sometimes used to include part-time and temporary work.

occupational overcrowding   See **crowding.**

occupational segregation   See **index of sex segregation.**

part-time work   Any work for fewer hours or in a different pattern than what is considered a full-time schedule. For example, part-time can mean working less than a full day, fewer than five days per week, or less than a full year.

patriarchy   A system of beliefs, attitudes, and institutions that regularly gives greater privilege and higher status to men. Feminist researchers suggest that patriarchy or "antimatriarchy" is the chief engine of sex segregation. Signs of patriarchal attitudes are seen in efforts to prevent women's entry into an occupation, to push women out who do gain entry, to flee from occupations when women have entered them, to ghettoize women, to devaluate them, and to deprive them of authority.

pay gap   See **wage gap.**

percent female   A widely used descriptive statistic that identifies the extent to which an occupation is feminized. See also **female-labeled occupations.**

preference theory   An explanation for sex-typing of occupations and women's lower pay that points to women's choices or preferences. The theory holds that to the extent that women give priority to family responsibilities over career commitment and make adjustments in their labor force participation to accommodate their families' needs, they are making choices that contribute to shorter working time and less commitment to their jobs. Their lower pay and lower chances of promotion are thus seen to be the result of their own volition rather than of discrimination.

primary workers   See **dual labor market.**

protective labor laws   The protectionist philosophy was first clearly stated in 1908 in *Muller v. Oregon* and argued that women should be protected from overly long working hours because of their perceived physical vulnerability and their maternal roles. Protective legislation was later extended to limit women's exposure to dangerous chemicals and other hazardous conditions. Many so-called protective laws were later seen by feminists as a ruse for discrimination and were overturned by the civil rights legislation of the 1960s and 1970s.

secondary workers   See **dual labor market.**

sex   The term used to refer to males and females as biologically differentiated variants of the same species. The sex of a person is implicitly treated as a given that only in rare instances is ambiguous or can be changed.

sex discrimination Ways that employers and others treat men and women differently and inequitably. Several kinds of behavior may be interpreted as discriminatory. Examples include hiring and promotion practices that exclude women from male-labeled occupations or that discourage men from taking parental leave; or pay scales that compensate women less than men for similar work.

sex-role crossover See **gender crossovers**.

sex-typed occupation See **female-labeled occupations**.

sexual harassment The imposition of an atmosphere and working conditions by supervisors, other authorities, or peers such that a worker (whether man or woman) is unable to do his or her job without the annoyance or threat of being treated as a sexual object. Sexual harassment is now broadly recognized as a form of sex discrimination in the workplace to be dealt with under the provisions of Title VII of the 1964 Civil Rights Act. See also **hostile climate**.

socialization The different kinds of upbringing and cultural expectations to which the sexes are exposed throughout their lives that cause them to prefer different kinds of work and make different choices in the occupations they pursue.

statistical discrimination Statistical discrimination occurs when the average profile of a group is applied to an individual member.

taste for discrimination A factor that economists posit to explain that portion of sex discrimination that makes employers less willing to hire female workers, makes fellow employees less willing to work with them, or makes customers less satisfied to be served by them. When these discriminating groups have no other choice, they expect compensation or a discount for the nonpecuniary cost of having to interact with female workers in a way that is distasteful to them. The "tastes" that economists refer to are the noneconomic values, preferences, or beliefs linked to culture and normative expectations. Tastes apparently alter as an occupation begins to admit more women.

telecommuting The use of computers, e-mail, faxes, and phones to conduct work without having to be physically present in an office or other public place of work. The advantages of telecommuting are an increased ability to balance work and family life, greater productivity, and lower stress.

wage gap The difference in earnings between men and women who are similar in education, occupation, and experience. It is usually the women who are being paid less.

woman-friendly occupations Fields such as nursing or elementary school teaching are classic examples of professions that are thought to be woman-friendly for such reasons as their flexibility of scheduling and the stability of knowledge required that can be maintained with little or no continuing training. These expectations presumably result in lower penalties for leaving and reentering during a woman's childbearing and child rearing years.

Index

Abernathy, James D., 144
Abortion. *See* Reproductive freedom;
   Roe v. Wade
Adams, Annette Abbott, 112
Adams, Fae Margaret, 126
Adam's Rib (film), 124
Adaptive women, 274–275
Adarand Constructors v. Pena, 150, 201
Adkins v. Children's Hospital, 116, 196–197
Advertising, sex-segregated
   employment, 130, 199
AFDC. *See* Aid to Families with
   Dependent Children (AFDC)
Affiliated Schools for Women
   Workers, 117
Affirmative action
   American Stock Exchange policy on,
     135
   court cases on, 201–202, 205
   defined, 303
   in education, 72–74
   effect on wage gap, 42
   in employment, 62–63
   history of, 260
   and quotas, 201
   and reverse discrimination, 272–273
   success of, 183, 187, 189
Afghanistan and women's
   employment, 142
AFL-CIO
   activism in, 58
   first female executive, 166
   merger, 127
   See also Labor unions
Africa
   women's educational attainment in,
     216
   women's literacy in, 216
   women's roles in, 11
African Americans and labor force
   participation. *See* Labor force
   participation by race

African Bushmen. *See* Hunting and
   gathering economies and gender
   equity
AFSCME, 63, 166–167
AFSCME v. Washington, 64, 189
   description of, 203
After-school care. *See* Child care
Agro-business and dependent labor
   class, 5. *See also* Globalization
Aid to Dependent Children,
   80
Aid to Families with Dependent
   Children (AFDC), 20, 93. *See also*
   Family Support Act of 1988;
   Personal Responsibility and Work
   Opportunity Reconciliation Act
   (PRWORA)
Albright, Madeleine, 151, 157–159
Allen, Florence, 116, 120
Alliance for Displaced Homemakers,
   136
Alternative work arrangements,
   87–90. *See also* Work and family,
   policies supporting
AM Chicago, 143
A.M. Kidder and Company, 127
Amalgamated Clothing Workers of
   America, 112
American Association for the
   Advancement of Sciences
   (AAAS), 153
American Association of University
   Professors (AAUP), 69
American Association of University
   Women (AAUW), 77–78,
   234
American Broadcasting Corporation
   (ABC), 130, 144
American Chemical Society, 138
American Express, 153
American Federation of Labor. *See*
   AFL-CIO

313

Equal pay laws in
  Argentina, 124
  Australia, 110, 135
  Austria, 140
  Cuba, 120
  France, 143
  Germany, 116
  Guatemala, 131
  Ireland, 137
  Israel, 125
  Italy, 124
  Mexico, 130
  Sweden, 140
Equal Protection Clause. *See*
  Fourteenth Amendment Equal
  Protection Clause
Equal Rights Advocates, 238–239
Equal Rights Amendment (ERA),
  57–59, 116, 125, 170, 172–173
Equal rights feminism. *See* Feminism,
  equal rights
Equal treatment, 203
Equal work, defined, 60, 198, 305
Equality, promotion of
  and attainment of citizenship, 7
  and suffrage, 7
  United Nations promotion of, 8
  and women's protest movements,
  8–13
Estate executors, court cases on, 60,
  199
Ethnicity. *See* Race and ethnicity
Europa Gender Equality Section (web
  site), 301
Europe
  part-time work in, 208, 223
  preschools in, 79, 224
  wage gap in, 23
  women's labor force participation
  in, 11, 21
  See also specific countries in
  Europe
Europe, central and eastern
  and public policies supporting
  gender equity, 5, 11
  and women's double burden, 8
European Women's Lobby, 252
European Women's Management
  Development, 252
Executive Order, defined, 306
Executive Order 10980 (1961), 129, 205
Executive Order 11126 (1963), 205–206
Executive Order 11246 (1965), 59, 171,
  188, 206
Executive Order 11375 (1968), 59, 62,
  69, 72, 132, 171, 206
Executive Order 11478 (1969), 62, 206

Exercise Your Options (video), 287–288
Expressive activities. *See* Gendered
  associations

Face-time, 88, 92
  defined, 306
Fair Employment Practices
  Commission, 122
Fair Labor Standards Act of 1938, 59,
  121
  description of, 190
Family and Medical Leave Act
  (FMLA), 89, 148–149
  description of, 194
  history of, 144, 188
  use of unemployment insurance, 90
Family demographics
  changes in, 218–221, 277
  and labor force participation, 270
  by race and ethnicity, 220
  in the United States, 19–20
Family formation. *See* Life patterns
Family friendly benefits, 78–91, 275
Family life and economic change,
  84–85
Family Support Act of 1988, 81, 93
  description of, 193
Faragher v. City of Boca Raton, 152
Farm work
  and globalization, 13
  in the United States, 15
Faulkner, Shannon, 149–150
Fauset, Crystal Bird, 120
Federal contractors and sex
  discrimination, 171
Federal Economy Act, 119
Federally Employed Women, 132
Felton, Rebecca Latimer, 116
Female earnings differential. *See* Wage
  gap
Female-headed families. *See* Single-
  parent families
Female-labeled occupations
  characteristics of, 37
  defined, 306
  internationally, 1–2
  and overcrowding, 175
  and wage gap, 25, 264
  See also Occupational segregation
Feminine Mystique, The (Friedan),
  84–85, 130, 168
Feminism
  defined, 175
  domestic, 12
  domestic, defined, 306
  equal rights, 12

About the Authors

Janet Zollinger Giele is professor of Sociology and Women's Studies at Brandeis University and founding director of the Family and Children's Policy Center at the Heller School for Social Policy and Management. She conducts research on the changing roles of women and their new life patterns. Her books include *Women and the Future; Two Paths to Women's Equality: Temperance, Suffrage, and the Origins of Modern Feminism;* and *Women's Work and Women's Lives: The Continuing Struggle Worldwide.* She has just completed editing a book on changing life patterns in Western industrial societies that reveals growing equality in employment of women both in Western Europe and North America.

Leslie F. Stebbins is a reference librarian at the Brandeis University Libraries where she serves as liaison to the Brandeis University Sociology Department, Women's Studies Program, and the Heller School for Social Policy and Management. Ms. Stebbins's previous works include *Work and Family in America: A Reference Handbook.* She is currently writing *Undergraduate Research and Critical Thinking in the Digital Age,* which will be published in 2004.